Reformer in
the Marketplace

Edward W. Bok

REFORMER IN THE MARKETPLACE

❧ Edward W. Bok
and *The Ladies' Home Journal*

SALME HARJU STEINBERG

Louisiana State University Press
Baton Rouge and London

Copyright © 1979 by Louisiana State University Press
All rights reserved
Manufactured in the United States of America
Designer: Albert Crochet
Type face: VIP Goudy Oldstyle
Typesetter: The Composing Room of Michigan
Printer: Thomson-Shore, Inc.
Binder: John Dekker & Sons, Inc.

LIBRARY OF CONGRESS CATALOGING IN PUBLICATION DATA

Steinberg, Salme Harju, 1940–
    Reformer in the marketplace.

    Bibliography: p.
    Includes index.
    1. Bok, Edward William, 1863–1930. 2. The
Ladies' home journal. I. Title.
PN4874.B62S7   070.4'092'4 [B]   78–23846
ISBN 0–8071–0398–5

In memory of my father,
Johan Edward Harju

Contents

Preface and Acknowledgments   ix

Introduction   xi

I   Groundwork for Reform   1

II   Living the "Six-Day" Virtues   34

III   The Editor's Aims, Strategies, and Risks   50

IV   Passageways to Beautiful America   75

V   Two Blows Against Ignorance   98

VI   Minerva in Battle   113

Conclusion   143

Notes   151

Bibliography   179

Index   191

Preface and Acknowledgments

Historians of United States business still have many stories to tell and histories to reconstruct about American business activities in the progressive era and after. This examination of an editor, a mass magazine, and a major publishing house—a round robin of a success story—is one of them.

A special problem for the researcher in business history is that all too often ahistorical values affect the decisions made by corporation administrators. In the case of the Curtis Publishing Company, a thorough house-cleaning was performed before each of the company's several moves to new buildings during and after the period of Edward Bok's editorship. As a result, the editor's and the publisher's descendants believed that no company documents and sources from that golden era were extant. Chance, not design, in the last half-century preserved some of the Edward Bok editorial letterbooks and some of the Cyrus Curtis letter files. These items were all but buried in a company vault in Philadelphia that guarded office party decorations. They came to light only because some observant Curtis employees interested in memorabilia remembered their existence.

Without the help and support of many people this study would never have been completed. I especially want to thank

Charles Ficke, retired vice-president of the Curtis Publishing Company, and Helen Comly, his assistant, who so graciously helped me to find company materials and who managed to fit my research needs into their busy schedules. I am also grateful to Mrs. Curtis Bok, Edward Bok's daughter-in-law and president of the American Foundation, who generously contributed her time and energy in the search for source material.

I am indebted to the staffs of many libraries, especially those at the Johns Hopkins University Library, the Enoch Pratt Free Library of Baltimore, the University of Pennsylvania Library, the library of the Historical Society of Pennsylvania, the Williams College Library, the Library of Congress, and the National Archives. In particular, I heartily thank Paul G. Sifton of the Library of Congress Manuscripts Division, Helen Finneran Ulibarri of the National Archives, and Neda Westlake, curator of the University of Pennsylvania Rare Book Collection, for their many courtesies and attentions.

To Alfred D. Chandler, Jr., of Harvard University, I am deeply grateful for his critical acumen no less than for his patience and goodwill while this project was underway at the Johns Hopkins University. I also thank Harold Williamson, professor emeritus of economics at Northwestern University, for his careful and helpful reading of an earlier draft of the manuscript, and my colleagues at Northeastern Illinois University, especially June Sochen, Gregory H. Singleton, and C. David Tompkins, who gave parts of the manuscript the benefits of their attention. Also, I thank the Danforth Foundation for the award of a Danforth Teacher Grant.

My debt to my husband, Michael Stephen Steinberg, is incalculable. His faith, his love, and his wise and perceptive scholarship helped me to bring this story of Bok and his *Journal* to an end.

Introduction

The golden age of the mass general-interest magazine began in the 1890s. These magazines fulfilled the demands of a large and growing urban middle class for news, comment, and entertainment, and they were, in effect, the first national newspapers. Their success also stimulated the development of a national middlebrow culture and served to promote general awareness of national needs and reform issues.

The *Ladies' Home Journal* was the most successful pioneer in the mass magazine field and a pacesetter for the industry. Its editor, Edward William Bok, and its publisher, Cyrus Curtis, president of the Curtis Publishing Company, provided the combination of good business sense, innovation, and an understanding of their readers that made the *Journal* the first magazine in the United States to have one million subscribers. The size of its circulation and advertising volume shaped the character of the magazine. At the same time, Bok's *Journal* spoke for reforms both characteristic and atypical of its period. While the *Journal*'s publisher exerted business leadership in the publishing and advertising communities, its editor tried to shape the reform conscience of his middle-class audience.

The mass magazines as we know them were inconceivable outside of an urban industrializing society. Their growth was closely linked to developments in big business. The magazines themselves were products that had to be marketed. Dependent on advertising, they revolutionized the advertising industry and provided a medium for hawking consumer products in the national market. In the 1890s one characteristic of this national market was what Edward Kirkland called the "feminization" of American purchasing.[1] The male-oriented general store declined in retailing importance when women began to purchase family needs in the dry-goods shops. As a result manufacturers addressed their advertising to women. Their chief medium was the woman's magazine.

Technological changes had prepared the way for mass advertising in magazines. Cheaper pulp that was more available and advances in photographic reproduction such as the half-tone process reduced the costs of publishing production. These factors helped to make the ten-cent magazine a publishing reality. Industrialists saw the advertising possibilities in mass journalism. In fact, businessmen were willing to invest heavily in this area of communications, because expansion in publishing was technically feasible and they were very likely to find a national audience of consumers.

Since the magazines were a product, their survival depended on their ability to conform to the needs of two sets of customers: readers and advertisers. Advertisers demanded large circulation figures and respectable editorial content that would provide "good company" for their advertisements. The readers, who were generally middle class, wanted to be entertained, kept abreast of contemporary issues, and given information they could put to practical use. They were also receptive to suggestions for those political and social reforms that could soothe their consciences and effect piecemeal changes but would not fundamentally disrupt the pattern of their lives.

The successful middle-class magazine effectively gauged the limits of the two audiences.

The coming of the cheap mass magazine coincided with the progressive era. From 1902 through 1912, certain magazines raked, in Theodore Roosevelt's phrase, more "muck" than others. These muckraking magazines were short-lived publishing enterprises that became known to historians and to contemporary publishers and critics as special-interest crusading periodicals. They depended exclusively on an audience attracted by exposure of society's ills, such as political scandal and corruption. But the wider middle-class audience of magazines like the *Journal* was also receptive to the exposures and remedies of the reformers. Reform journalism in the *Ladies Home Journal* was no less intense for coinciding with other services that the *Journal* provided. In fact, the strength of its reformism can be attributed to its multiple overall objectives. Each objective was responsible for attracting more readers, who became the audience for Bok's reform suggestions. Although the scope of its reforms did not equal that of *McClure's Magazine*, its long-range impact was greater because the *Journal* survived and *McClure's* did not.

As Theodore Peterson has suggested, the coming of large-scale advertising forced the publisher to think less about the material he offered his reader and more about the reader as a target for advertisers.[2] But Curtis and Bok resisted the pressures to comply easily with the wishes of advertisers. They succeeded in convincing the advertisers that their products would sell best if the medium was read and trusted.

What was good for the consumer often turned out to be profitable for the producer. Many of the singular *Journal* achievements in consumer help and education were of long-range value to the manufacturer. The trademarking of items, for example, encouraged not only standardization and reliability but also brand preference, which was a step toward the growth of product loyalty by consumers. The *Journal* also kept anxious surveillance over those other areas that were good for the producer but held risks for the consumer. After all, the *Journal*'s profit margin increased to the degree that its readers continued to be positively influenced by its advertising copy. The means used by the Curtis Company (as it was called after 1900) to maintain a close relationship with advertisers and to assert the magazine's service objectives is an important theme of this study.

The Curtis Company retained Bok as the *Journal*'s editor from 1889 to 1919. Bok endorsed and developed company policies and pioneered new ways to reach the reader. He interpreted advertising's role to his audience and taught it to discriminate among advertisements. At the same time, he liked to insist that he published what his audience, not he, wanted. In great measure, Bok's strong personal traits molded the characteristic goals and achievements identified with the *Ladies' Home Journal*.

In Bok's day, gossip columnists, or "paragraphers," as they were called, often made sport of Bok and a good many of his opinions. Mark Sullivan has written that Bok and his magazine were "made the target of stories and witticisms almost as frequently as Henry Ford was made the butt of jests about his automobile."[3] More recently, students of the progressive era who have read Bok's contemporaries too closely have been responsible for cavalier dismissals of his part in reform. Bok's contributions to American society are difficult to measure but nonetheless are central to understanding American society during that era.

Those historians who remember Edward Bok at all stress what they consider to be his role in creating the cheap excesses of mass culture while he resisted serious reform. A close reading of the *Ladies' Home Journal*, however, reveals that its most important reform campaigns were in the areas of health, public education, the raising of cultural standards, and sex education. In fact, Bok enjoys a not-too-distant kinship with Christopher Lasch's "new radicals," who were eager to plan "reform of education, culture, and sexual relations."[4] Like them, Bok was engaged in reform as cultural uplift, but he was more active in providing practical applications for change than in formulating theories.

Edward Bok regarded his editorship as a calling in the Calvinist sense. He strove for success at the same time that he conceived his position as a trust and stewardship. His mission was not only to fulfill the needs of his audience but to mold and shape it in a moral and forward-looking direction. His audience responded because they recognized him as one of them and because he impressed them with his sincerity.

Bok was the prototype of the personal editor. He nurtured the trust that his readers placed in him. In fact, he counted on that trust to win his readers to his views on important issues. One word, Bok affirmed, summed up the *Journal*'s goals and objectives: service. The *Journal* was more than a monthly entertainment; it was a handbook designed to guide the lives of middle-class Americans by answering their questions and by inspiring and instructing them—all under the leadership of a man who was fundamentally confident in the virtues of the middle-class ethos.

An inescapable theme of this study is the character of United States middle-class society from the 1890s through World War I. People like Bok and Curtis, whose careers depended on the needs and hopes of a large number of this group, used the *Journal* to create an ideal representation of the middle-class woman who was subject to the strains of a changing society. From this image, the achievements and shortcomings of the real women and men of the era can be measured. The Curtis-Bok team successfully outlined the economic profile of the *Journal* reader—where she lived and in what circumstances. But the more shadowy features of the reader were her attitudes and values and what would prompt her to remain a loyal reader of the *Journal*. The team tried to determine these features by heeding the dictates of their readers as revealed through letters to the editor and subscriptions to the magazine.

In a country with a viable national market connected by transportation systems, the wives and daughters of the burgeoning middle classes faced new problems and opportunities. While they bemoaned the scarcity of adequate domestic help, they eagerly bought packaged foods and commodities identified by brand names. They moved from country to city or suburb, they learned to consult physicians instead of relying on drugs and charlatans, and they had to confront the problems of urban water and sewage treatment as well as the chicanery of unscrupulous businessmen selling contaminated and adulterated foods. The *Journal* provided a service model these middle- and working-class women needed to cope effectively with urban problems, and it offered some predictable and reassuring answers to thorny problems at a time when uncertainty threatened the security of familiar customs.

The ideal woman in the *Journal* was eternally busy. If she was not baking, she was sewing "fancy work," or studying the Bible, managing a household bulging with children, or contending with a fussy husband. Especially before the turn of the century, middle-class women with more than adequate domestic help had long workdays arranging teas, calling on neighbors, and performing other duties. An extraordinary admission of the emptiness of this ideal life came in a post–World War I

Journal article that neglected the demanding aspects of the old life-style and instead referred to the earlier days as a time of "bridge and boredom." [5]

The *Journal* reader was also usually represented as a woman of comfortable means with an enormous awareness of her own self-worth and her place in society. She wore no cosmetics because she stressed her natural and inward beauty. She was ageless, at least in the pages of the *Journal*, since age was not mentioned except in references to the very young or very old. She respected self-control and derided pessimistic or gloomy attitudes. Basically she lived in a predictable society wherein manners guided actions. These social codes were all, in fact, that certain poorer women with that "gentle pride of birth and breeding" possessed. [6]

These characteristics of the ideal *Journal* reader, however false, were conceivably at odds with those of a reform-minded spirit. Bok learned regretfully that women with these ideas about themselves and their neighbors were often unconcerned about people in straitened circumstances or the inequities of an industrializing society. Their religious convictions, as Bok's investigations showed, certainly had little impact on the quality of their lives. Nevertheless, the rhetoric of the day demanded middle-class support for good works, and reform-mindedness was more easily aroused when problems impinged directly on *Journal* readers. Those issues that have continued to play a central role in middle-class reformism in this century, such as the environment, consumer protection, educational innovation, and sexual enlightenment—all self-serving reforms—can be traced in their early stages to *Journal* commitments.

Bok always believed that, in practice, reform depended on community pressure or a demonstration by experts that problems could be solved by useful reforms. The companion efforts of publicists and organized citizens groups were necessary to effect change; the political process in itself did not suffice. Bok maintained that if the middle-class man were given a reasonable explanation, he would perform on cue; the working-class man needed a bribe as inducement. Thus the editor was convinced that his middle-class audience could be aroused to assert meaningful reform leadership. How people and events betrayed these hopes is another facet of the editor's career.

The development of the *Ladies' Home Journal* in this period is a case history of modern magazine journalism. Beginning in the 1880s Bok and Curtis created the model for the mass general-interest magazine. In household service, public information, and entertainment, the Curtis Publishing Company explored diverse ways to appeal to a wide essentially middle-class audience. Their successful strategies were quickly copied by other entrepreneurs.

This publishing enterprise securely established the financial success of the *Journal* on the base of advertising revenue. The company took the initiative in setting standards and procedures for the advertising industry as a whole. From this secure base, Bok was able, after the turn of the century, to use the magazine as a springboard for reform. Beginning modestly with the Beautiful America campaign, the magazine took a measure of business risk and entered controversial areas such as patent medicines and sex education.

The advent of World War I presented new opportunities for public service and new dilemmas for the editor. Bok's own role and confidence in conventional routes of reform disintegrated, and his assessment of the politically changing world and new roles for women demanded more radical change than the editor's middle-class audience was willing to accept. Moreover, Bok's didactic moralism was out of step with popular currents in postwar America.

In his role as editor, Bok had to steer a course that could satisfy his readers, his advertisers, and his conscience. As a Progressive, he saw no conflict between these goals for most of his career. The triumph of his reform objectives would depend in fact on his business success; the larger the *Journal*'s circulation, the more readers Bok could persuade.

The uneasy coexistence of reform journalism and an increasingly powerful advertising industry is a central theme of this study, for the *Journal* had to confront this problem throughout the progressive era. The Curtis Publishing Company was a big business. For Cyrus Curtis the main goal was profit; for Edward Bok the primary job was effective service to readers. Together they proved that limited reforms and advertising success were compatible.

Reformer in
the Marketplace

I ❧ Groundwork for Reform

No evaluation of Edward Bok's editorial career with the *Ladies' Home Journal* is possible without an analysis of the publishing house that enabled him to pursue his goals largely free from the financial and ideological pressures of advertising. In much the same way that the editor persuaded his readers to trust him and the *Journal*, the publisher, Cyrus Curtis, persuaded the advertisers to have confidence in the Curtis methods for successful advertising.

Cyrus Hermann Kotzschmar Curtis was a self-made man. In 1869, before he was twenty, he left home in Portland, Maine, to go to work as a salesman in a Boston dry-goods store. He solicited advertisements for an advertising agency as a sideline. In 1872, he joined with a partner who promised the capital to publish a newspaper, the *People's Ledger*. Four years later he left Boston and went to Philadelphia because he could print his paper there at less cost. He sold the *People's Ledger* two years later and joined another newspaper, the *Philadelphia Press*, as its advertising manager.

In 1879, Curtis left the *Press* and again teamed with another man to start a weekly journal, the *Tribune and Farmer*, intended for a rural audience. He included a column for women, with items clipped from various press exchanges.

His wife, Louisa Knapp Curtis, derided his efforts and agreed to try her hand. Because Mrs. Curtis' column was well liked, it was expanded, first to one page, and by 1883, to a monthly eight-page supplement. In that same year Curtis sold his interest in the *Tribune and Farmer* and decided to concentrate his energies on the fast-growing monthly supplement. The first issue of the *Ladies' Home Journal and Practical Housekeeper* was published in December, 1883.

Under the editorship of Louisa Knapp Curtis and the business management of Cyrus Curtis, the *Journal and Practical Housekeeper* rapidly grew. By 1889, after several campaigns for subscriptions, it had 440,000 subscribers, and Curtis planned to raise the yearly subscription price from fifty cents to one dollar. Because it was doubtful whether his current readers would pay that sum, he decided to seek out a new class of readers. Since Mrs. Curtis was heavily burdened by her editorial obligations and her responsibilities to her daughter, Curtis hired Edward Bok, advertising director for the New York publisher Charles Scribner, to take charge of the editorial and art departments.

The *Journal* was, by 1889, a mass magazine, but Curtis wanted it to become what he called a "high class magazine." He decided to cast his lot with quality advertisers and a middle-class audience in the rapidly growing urban market. Because women were the leading purchasers of consumer goods by the 1890s, it was clear that a magazine ostensibly edited for them would affect the whole family's purchasing power. Both Curtis and Bok, though, viewed the *Journal* as more than merely a woman's magazine. They hoped it would appeal to every family member; consequently, it was the first American magazine to publish a political advertisement, for the National Republican Committee in 1892. Assuredly the *Journal*'s name was a handicap because it claimed exclusive appeal to women. The name *American Home Journal*, Curtis said, was more revealing of the *Journal's* purpose.[1]

The name was an accident anyway. When Curtis decided to title the women's supplement to the *Tribune and Farmer*, he chose the *Ladies' Journal*. The masthead carried a small picture of a house between the words *Ladies'* and *Journal* with HOME written underneath. Subsequently, the *Ladies' Journal* was inaccurately referred to as the *Ladies' Home Journal*, a title that Curtis finally accepted.[2]

To understand how Curtis achieved his goal of building a middle-class magazine, we must examine the ways in which, first, he built circulation in quality and number, second, he established his reliability both as publisher and advertiser, third, the policies and business organization of the Curtis Company helped to maintain the publisher's independence, and, fourth, the *Journal's* service objectives set the standards for advertising in the magazine. Because Curtis had a clear idea of the kind of magazine he wanted to publish, he was free to demand adherence to his standards for advertising in the magazine. This was the key to the general success of the company, because unlike many others, it could then maintain a certain discretion in its choice of advertising; and by 1890 advertising was the lifeline of mass periodicals.

Curtis' first strategy for building a big quality circulation was to capture the "good" social classes for his audience by combining excellent editorial copy and advertisements of expensive goods in an attractively designed format. Curtis and Bok frequently studied the neighborhoods where the *Journal* was widely read. A *Journal* prospectus describing editorial content for 1891 was sent to all names listed in the social registers of San Francisco, Boston, and Milwaukee. To persuade carriage-trade distributors and manufacturers to advertise in the *Ladies' Home Journal*, he had to shape and build the magazine's circulation. He wanted to show advertisers that the upper middle classes read the *Journal*, and he often solicited advertising by enumerating the socially prominent among *Journal* subscribers.[3]

In the 1890s, when Curtis tried to impress certain advertisers, he claimed that many readers in the *Journal* audience lived in "villadom." More realistically, he estimated that by 1891, 75 percent of *Journal* circulation was in towns over 10,000 in population. Two years later, he stated more precisely that the majority of *Journal* readers lived in the suburbs of large cities and were the respectable, church-attending people; also, he was convinced that his small-town readers belonged to the professional ranks in their communities.[4]

Curtis asked the Bon Marché store in Paris to consider an advertisement in a *Journal* issue for February, the time, he said, when most of the richer families planned their European trips. Not only did the *Journal* audience have "the means to gratify luxurious tastes" but they were "accustomed to buying largely through the mails." If his urban-situated audience did indeed buy expensive goods by mail, they did it, not from necessity, but for the wider selection of goods. So confident was Curtis of the gentility of *Journal* subscribers, he claimed that not one reader was tuberculous or epileptic. Nor, for that matter, were any of them "poor" people.[5]

Curtis found it humiliating when *Century* and *Harper's* carried advertising business his agents were unable to sign for the *Journal*; he claimed, after all, to reach the same people covered by those two magazines, only more of them. He encouraged his Chicago office to show advertisers the names of the "big bug" families, as he called them, who read the *Journal*. Generally, he disapproved of revealing his readers' names, but in these circumstances he permitted the lapse only for trustworthy clients.[6] For the sake of his pride, he said, he wanted "high-toned" advertisers to sell in the *Journal.* Curtis had a favorite anecdote to prove his convictions about the *Journal* audience. In a letter to the advertising agent, J. Walter Thompson, he wrote about his experience with the New York store, Lord & Taylor:

> They advertised something cheap to be sent through the mail which did not pay them at all. They could not be persuaded that fifteen hundred dollar India shawls could be advertised with profit in the *Journal*; but I instructed my representative to get that advertisement at our own risk: and much to their surprise, women from the surrounding cities walked into their store and asked for these goods advertised in the *Ladies' Home Journal*. It convinced them that the *Ladies' Home Journal* reached a moneyed class of people.

Consequently, Curtis often advised his advertising agents to emphasize the quality of the *Journal*'s circulation instead of its circulation statistics.[7]

Printers' Ink, a leading magazine for advertisers, caused Curtis much more anxiety than either *Harper's* or the *Century*. It published an article in 1891 that classed *Journal* readers with the audience reached by the *Farm Journal*. Curtis energetically denied the rural stigma, which he probably still carried from his association with the *Tribune and Farmer*. He often wrote to the editors of *Printers' Ink*, bitterly complaining of the way it treated the *Journal*, which it called a "paper," and a cheap one at that, for advertisers.[8]

A testament to Curtis' success in identifying the *Journal* audience with the readers of *Scribner*'s and the *Atlantic* appeared in an early advertising textbook. Two 1914 advertising displays for writing paper were contrasted. Crane's letter paper for women of "taste and refinement" was advertised in a cluster of magazines like *Scribner*'s, *Atlantic*, and the *Ladies' Home*

Journal, and Eaton's "self-respecting paper" display was in *Good Housekeeping* and the *Women's Home Companion*, the *Journal*'s arch rival.[9] To Curtis' satisfaction no doubt, the *Journal* was grouped at last with the quality magazines.

Notwithstanding this small success, the *Journal*'s position in the best homes was ambiguous. Ellery Sedgwick, one of Bok's friends and editor of the *Atlantic*, told about a conversation he had had with Bok. After Sedgwick had divulged the number of *Atlantic* subscribers on Beacon Street, Bok telephoned the Curtis offices "and found that the *Ladies' Home Journal* had almost precisely the same number in that refined but limited locality. The coincidence amused us both. 'But there is a difference,' Bok remarked. 'You see, Sedgwick, you go in at the front door, and I at the back. I know my place.'"[10]

Stressing a quality audience was a temporary strategy, designed only to rid the *Journal* of its rural past. When the Curtis Publishing Company began publishing the *Saturday Evening Post* in 1897, Curtis claimed that the *Journal*'s aim now was to reach the masses of people, and he wanted no advertisements for the *Journal* placed in papers like the Chicago *Evening Post*, which represented a "high grade constituency." Fifteen years earlier, the *Journal* had been advertised in the *Evening Post*.[11] But Curtis was fundamentally more interested in a big circulation than a small elite one, and the *Journal*'s middle-class public more than satisfied him.

By 1915 the *Journal* had decidedly triumphed in its appeal to the masses. The magazine was clearly written for the middle classes, with an edge given to upper-middle-class tastes and interests. In 1915, at one of the advertising conferences that annually and sometimes semiannually brought together all the *Journal* advertising managers and leading agents placing advertising in the *Journal*, Edward Bok was asked about the incomes of his readers. He said that the magazine's main attention was directed toward families having incomes from $1,200 to $2,500. Also, he said, the "class with incomes of perhaps $3,000 to $5,000... had supplementary attention, but the other classes above were not large enough in number to warrant specific appeal to them."[12] The growing urban middle class, then, was the pool for a mass magazine's subscribers. Still, a significant minority of upper-class readers and high-quality advertisements helped to reinforce a certain tone that Curtis wanted. But most of the advertisements came from national firms, such as the soap and cereal manufacturers, that supplied standard brands for the urban market. For all his interest in a prestige audience, Curtis was unwilling to limit his advertising or his circulation to the upper middle classes.

Eager to see his audience grow in number, Curtis implemented his first strategy for circulation growth—wide and intensive use of advertising. Many advertisers at that time were interested only in circulation tallies, not in the careful analysis of markets reached. Long before marketing research was standardized, Curtis showed advertisers how he accumulated subscribers by selective advertising. However, Curtis became known for his reputation as an advertiser of his own magazine before it became a leader in publishing advertisements. By 1900, the Curtis periodicals were more advertised than any other magazines.[13]

Advertising the *Journal* was for Curtis an investment in the future. It took nerve, he said, "to face what appears to be at first sight, a loss." He scorned novelty methods; only standard publications collected his money. And unless all details that concerned him about a newspaper or periodical were amply clear, he refused to advertise in it. For example, not until the New York *Times* revealed its secret circulation figures did Curtis use it for advertising.[14]

One Curtis advertising program intensively used every

periodical published in a given state. The publisher read the periodicals and visited the areas in an effort to determine the kinds of magazines that reached the best people and how much he should spend. He then bought large, illustrated space—occasionally whole pages—in good-quality publications. Often his objective was twofold; he not only was soliciting subscriptions but also was telling potential advertisers about the *Journal*. This pioneering technique of indirectly reaching advertisers while trying to reach potential readers was noted in the trade publications.[15]

Carefully supervising *Journal* advertisements, Curtis often admonished his agency, N. W. Ayer, when his advertising did not enjoy right-hand-side page position. Sometimes he sent Bok to visit a newspaper's offices if an undesirable spot had been given to a *Journal* advertisement. In one instance, Bok had been told that the Ayer agency submitted its advertising business so that it could "take the run of the paper." Curtis wrote an irate letter to his agency, claiming that *Journal* advertisements were to have preferred positions even if extra charges had to be paid. He wanted no more *Journal* advertising on sports pages, in bottom-of-page position, or even on the second-cover page (the inside front cover).[16]

Curtis also complained when an advertisement for the *Journal* appeared in a position surrounded by a large quantity of medical advertising. He wrote: "The preponderance of medical advertising is not to my mind an evidence of a first class medium for reaching the best class of people. I presume that for reaching country people there is nothing better for medical advertisers and if I were manufacturing a pill, I certainly would use your medium largely; therefore, I do not blame medical people for using your space, but at the same time, I do not care to be in their company."[17] So, Curtis asked N. W. Ayer to remonstrate with other publishers, even when special position had not been expressly paid for. Twin complaints, from publisher and advertising agency, he said, would bring attention. But when he thought an issue of the *Journal* was weak, he would not advertise in weeklies; he always wanted to highlight strong points from *Journal* features in advertising copy.[18]

Curtis advertised the *Journal* and received advertisements for it primarily through the Ayer agency.[19] He did not want or expect a publication in which he advertised to reciprocate. That kind of exchange was not in the best interests of effective advertising for the *Journal*. Occasionally, some advertising agents threatened to withhold business from the *Journal* if Curtis did not yield some of his patronage, but he refused to be shaken from his position against reciprocity.[20]

Curtis' vast advertising expenditures were possible only with friendly credit help. Financial help came, not from banks, but from paper suppliers and chiefly from his advertising agent, F. Wayland Ayer, who underwrote Curtis' loans.[21] Because the Ayer agency placed so much of the *Journal*'s advertising, a rumor spread in the trade that Ayer held control of the magazine. The self-styled doctor of advertising, Nathaniel C. Fowler, explained this rumor to Curtis, confirming that everyone thought it was true, including himself:

> They [Ayer] placed your advertising when the Ladies' Home Journal was not the success it is today, and when it seemed to me that the paper could not have paid sufficiently to have met such tremendous advertising bills, therefore I naturally inferred, placing the unanimous rumors alongside of natural inference, that Ayer had the control.
>
> I am delighted, for your sake, that he has no interest; I am sorry for him; I am sorry for any man who doesn't have an interest in your paper; I wish I had anywhere from one to five thousand shares.[22]

Sometimes Curtis cautiously bought advertising space in periodicals from an agency other than Ayer; if there was a "special object" to be achieved, he felt justified in a disloyal action.[23]

Until 1889 he had relied on direct advertising to gather subscribers; in 1890, however, he began to use solicitors. He divided the nation into regions, each with a director to oversee several district agents, who, in turn, supervised the subscription agents. His aim was to make every responsible newsdealer an outlet for urban sales and an agency for the renewal of *Journal* subscriptions. By 1901, Curtis counted thirty thousand subscription agents. Of this total number, five thousand especially active agents received a house paper that served as a tie between the company and the agents.[24] A company guidebook written for these agents explained that they were not left to their own resources in getting *Journal* subscriptions. Instead, the company paid for its advertisements in local newspapers over the name of the agent representing that locality. In addition, the company occasionally advertised for subscription agents, who were usually young boys. Although Curtis offered no premiums to subscribers, he encouraged his canvassing agents with premiums for new business.[25]

Curtis was willing to advertise for young solicitors in the *Woman's Magazine* and the *American Woman*—magazines in which he never advertised the *Journal* itself. He said these two magazines were mean-looking and "must reach the cheapest class of people, as the mental pabulum is of the cheapest kind." But because they had a paid circulation, he maintained that their subscribers would read them.[26]

In the 1890s, Curtis also used newsstand sales insofar as they served his general advertising purpose. He tried to persuade his agents to give discounts to large newsdealers, members of the American News Company. The Curtis Company could not give them, he said, because it received a price less than the cost of magazine sales to a news company. The only value for Curtis was to have the *Journal* displayed on newsstands "as a sort of advertisement... but the larger the circulation, the more I am paying for my advertising."[27] In other words, the more copies that newsstands sold, the higher were distribution costs, because every copy sold counted as money lost from magazine production and sales.

More than twenty years later, Curtis found a way to make newsstand sales profitable. First, unsold newsstand copies were no longer returnable. Second, beginning in January, 1910, the company sold the bulk of its magazines to wholesalers, approximately 1,535 buyers who were under contract to Curtis and were independent of the American News Company.[28] Curtis forced these distributors to enter *tying contracts*, which prevented them from selling any other magazines without the Curtis Company's express approval. For example, key rival magazines like the *Women's Home Companion* and *Every Week* were usually barred altogether. In some instances, distributors could sell competing magazines if they did not permit boys to hawk them. The boy vendor was a favorite Curtis device and had trademark importance no less significant than Minerva's head on the *Journal* cover. In July, 1917, the Federal Trade Commission instituted proceedings against Curtis for using tying contracts in violation of provisions of the Clayton and Federal Trade Commission acts. The commission issued cease and desist orders two years later, and Curtis was forced to allow the wholesalers to promote and distribute competing magazines.[29]

Curtis' early advertising of the *Journal* in the 1890s was only too successful. During three months in 1891, the *Journal* received nearly 200,000 new subscriptions, bringing circulation to 600,000. The advertising campaigns brought new subscribers more quickly than magazines could be produced by the physical plant. Naturally, some unhappy subscribers complained about delays in receiving their copies. Space limitations in bindery and press rooms precluded expansion. Not before 1894 or 1895, Curtis said, could the company handle new subscriptions on a larger scale. The Curtis plant then under construction was being built to print one million copies. Until it was finished, circulation could not be encouraged. Perhaps in an effort to identify the magazine with their economic problems, Edward Bok told his readers that the resulting slowdown in circulation growth was part of the general depression following the panic of 1893.[30] But after the depression and the opening of Curtis' new plant, subscriptions boomed with the restored circulation campaigns.

The *Journal* reached the million mark in paid circulation with the February, 1903, number. The fact that every copy of the *Journal*'s one million edition was bought at full price was exceptional among American magazines at that time. In October, 1904, the company decided to raise the single-copy price of the magazine from ten to fifteen cents. The Curtis staff had studied the question for over a year. After some trial months at the new single-copy rate, they planned also to raise the annual subscription price from $1.00 to $1.50. The *Journal* cost fifteen cents in December, 1904, and the subscription price raise was effective on October 1, 1906.[31]

For any measure of lasting success, Curtis had to show his clients that his circulation figures were demonstrably reliable. At no time did the Curtis Company inflate circulation figures. In the last quarter of the nineteenth century, magazine circulation figures were usually padded by distribution of sample copies and by flagrant lies. No sample copies of the *Journal* were distributed. Curtis practiced the novel idea of an honest public record, even when it involved declining circulation statistics. He wrote to his Chicago agent, "I 'reserve the right to be eccentric.' *I* think it would be the *soundest* business policy and would establish my reputation for absolute reliability as to any statements eminating [*sic*] from this office regarding circulation."[32]

The publisher sent to advertisers sworn statements of his circulation figures together with open invitations to investigate his claims. When the Canfield Rubber Company wanted verification of *Journal* circulation in 1889, Curtis, whose reputation for reliability had already been established, was surprised at the lateness of the request, but he invited the advertiser to visit the Philadelphia offices.[33] The Audit Bureau of Circulation (ABC), formed in 1914 by the merger of the Association of American Advertisers and the Western Advertising Agents Association, provided the first outside, or independent, verification of claims. At first, Curtis was reluctant to join. He maintained that his published circulation report was recognized by everyone to be honest and reliable. Finally, the ABC staff convinced Curtis to endorse uniform standards for the trade, and the Curtis magazines joined the ABC shortly after it was organized.[34]

To guarantee the legitimacy of *Journal* circulation, Curtis avoided tying the subscription to a premium. Mass periodicals of that time usually offered premiums or other inducements to potential subscribers. The publisher had tested this policy with a premium department in his own company and found that it was cheaper in the long run to avoid any kind of subscription bargains. Curtis said that subscribers tended to demand greater premiums every year before renewing their subscriptions.[35] Most important, advertisers knew that readers wanted the *Journal* and were not seduced by the attractiveness of a special premium offer.

The only exception to this policy was a campaign suggested by Bok, which enlisted young women to compete for free college educations by selling subscriptions.[36] Even before this education plan was tested, Curtis had discontinued his short-lived premium department. The second-prize winner in the subscription contest was reluctant to have her portrait published in the *Journal*; but Curtis urged her to reconsider and revealed his purpose for the contest: "The expenses are more than we get out of it in profit; all that we can hope for is the advertising advantages, and in these you share."[37] Again, the long-range goal in Curtis' plan was evident. Associating the *Journal* with education was altruistic *and* profitable.

Besides assuring the reliability of *Journal* circulation figures, Curtis was eager to prove to advertisers just how dependable an advertising medium the *Journal* could be. He rejected advertisements when he suspected that his magazine was not the right medium to fill the needs of the potential advertiser, and he carefully followed the results gained by *Journal* advertisers who used the magazine.[38] Curtis also discouraged small short-term advertisements. Fully convinced that a large advertisement would bring best results, he occasionally offered to pay the difference between a small and large advertisement. He urged persistent, continued display of large-scale, well-designed advertisements. In later years he wrote three-year advertising contracts to stress cumulative benefits from using the *Journal*. Curtis said that if the product was a "public necessity," expert advertising invariably brought results. To demonstrate the success of his advertising strategy, the publisher often reminded advertisers of his own expensive and prolonged campaign to sell the *Journal*. He gave much advice to

Journal advertisers, who knew he understood their problems from the clear vantage of his reputation as one of the heaviest and most successful advertisers "in any class." [39]

By the mid 1890s Curtis achieved his goals, which were grounded upon his belief that business integrity joined with shrewdness guaranteed commercial success. If he could prove his reliability as a businessman, he would gain the trust of his clients. Consequently, he stressed the honest record of *Journal* circulation, he refused to allow advertisers to submit haphazard advertising plans for *Journal* publication, and he consistently emphasized the long-range effectiveness of his policies.

Another aspect of Curtis' interest in establishing a climate of reliability for his customers was his demonstration that the Curtis Company was obliged to no one. Moreover, the publisher wanted to show that he had strict control of the company's affairs and was indeed boss.

No one outside the company could hope to gain a foothold in Curtis management. The family firm was organized into the Curtis Publishing Company on June 25, 1891, with a stock capital of $500,000. Curtis kept nine-tenths of the stock; the remainder was held by company employees. By February, 1892, Bok was the second largest holder of Curtis stock and vice-president of the company. [40]

Anticipating heavy expenses from the construction of the new plant in 1900, Curtis decided to issue interest-bearing bonds worth $500,000 instead of increasing capital stock. In 1900, a new charter permitting this type of financing was obtained and the name was changed to the Curtis Company. As Curtis explained, "The business had grown too large for its own capital, and . . . a collateral trust bond is much better for us than to increase the capital in the old regular way." By this means, Curtis could still retain assured control of his company; and even though the company was incorporated under the inviting corporate laws of New Jersey, its nature as a family concern would be preserved.[41]

Curtis was careful to prevent outsiders from purchasing stock. Company practice demanded in 1900, as it had in 1892, that stockholders who left the company turn back their shares. And in 1901, when the company stock was increased to one million dollars, Curtis still did not place it on the open market.[42]

Despite low cash reserves, especially in the depression years of 1891–1893, Curtis upheld his basic convictions about company administration. Once, after being away from the office, he returned to find that company salaries and rent had not been paid. He wrote to his Chicago agent, "When the cat is away, the mice do just as they please, and sometimes they think they know more about the business than the old cat himself."[43] Curtis' own strategy was to squeeze savings by building an integrated firm capable of important cost reductions. To this end, the publisher first decided to stay in Philadelphia. In this period, American businessmen often made a scapegoat of Philadelphia businesses and called them slow, inefficient operations. Curtis worked hard to counter any charges of ill-managed business practices. Despite Bok's arguments (such as fondness for his home town) in favor of moving the plant to New York, Curtis refused because New York costs were too high to justify uprooting. When Curtis was planning the company's new home in 1891, he realized that building in New York would cost almost $100,000 more than in Philadelphia. He was hesitant, however, about staying in Philadelphia; New York provided paper supplies and most of the advertising. The problem, he said, was that "the capitalists of this town [Philadelphia] are not big enough for its proper development."[44]

Three years later, however, the new Curtis Company buildings were under construction, and Curtis was unmistakably resigned to being a Philadelphian. In fact, when he described his company's methods of operation as "straight-out business with no trimmings," he called it "the Philadelphia idea." Curtis became such an apologist for Philadelphia that when some New York newspapers belittled it, he refused to advertise in those papers until he exacted a promise from the publications that they would not attack Philadelphia again.[45]

Another step toward an integrated business resulted from Curtis' high standards in printing, which impelled the firm to print its own publications. In 1891, the publisher estimated that the company saved almost 25 percent in costs by printing the *Journal* in its plant. Writing about his company's infrequent use of the early two- and three-color process, Curtis said: "Our facilities are large and ample for such slight color work as we sometime attempt, and what we cannot do in our own establishment is left undone, as we do not think it at all necessary to go outside for any work needed, nor, should we care to attempt anything that we could not do ourselves."[46]

The move toward integration demanded a reevaluation of the company's attitude toward by-products. In the earliest years, company policy permitted reprints of published *Journal* items, provided credit was duly recorded upon publication. When the *Journal* began to publish its own reprints, the policy changed, giving reproduction rights exclusively to the original authors or artists. By 1905, the *Journal* was becoming less interested in handling its own by-products. Worrying about sales and distribution of an occasional *Journal* illustration or article was an unnecessary waste of energy. The *Journal* had more important concerns and objectives. For example, more money for a better magazine could be secured from printing press economies than from distributing a few pamphlets. Of course, the *Journal's* London office continued to make a remarkable profit through the resale of *Journal* articles and stories to English magazines.[47]

Curtis purchased the *Saturday Evening Post* in 1897 and applied his proven strategies with the *Journal* to make the *Post* a swift national success. There was much advertising sales potential in a magazine for men; but even more important, the *Post*, a weekly, could solicit companies that needed frequent or short-notice advertisements. Clearly, Curtis was anxious to reach a wider market. He paid one thousand dollars for the *Post*, getting with it the claim that the paper was a direct descendant of Benjamin Franklin's *Pennsylvania Gazette*. Before Curtis solicited advertisers, he said that he wanted 100,000 subscribers to the *Post*. In the first two weeks of advertising the *Post*, the subscription list grew to 10,000. Curtis wanted to publish the *Post* as a supplement to the *Journal*, not as a competitor. It was to be "simply an addition, an aid and a help to building up the *Journal*." In an unguarded moment, however, Curtis said that he wanted to publish the *Post* "for glory, to see just how good a thing I can make of it" and to help young American male readers "accomplish something."[48] But Curtis remained fully aware of the advertising income opportunities that came with the *Post*.

The development of the Curtis Company demonstrated that this was no traditional journalistic venture. For the first time, magazine publishing was clearly big business. The *Journal* was the base upon which a large integrated firm was constructed. Integration was not only profitable, but it also reinforced the company's independence; and Curtis recognized that his financial objectives could best be achieved by continued family control of the firm. The magazines remained the core of the company, and their success rested in part upon their independence from outside interests. The single most important component in the company's financial success was advertising. How Curtis managed to guard his independence from his advertisers was a vital part of his design for success.

The business side of a mass magazine was created by its advertising revenues. This was plain to readers in the 1890s who received their magazines with reading matter pages that were uncut and advertising pages that were cut and ready for perusal. In addition, experimental color printing was used for advertising, whereas the regular use of color in editorial copy appeared much later.[49] But whose interests would the mass magazine serve? For the *Journal* in the Curtis–Bok era the answer was clear: the readers'. Certainly, Curtis adjusted his views for the benefit of his listeners when he told a group of advertisers: "Do you know why we publish the *Ladies' Home Journal*? The editor thinks it is for the benefit of the American woman. That is an illusion, but a very proper one for him to have. But I will tell you; the real reason, the publisher's reason, is to give you people who manufacture things that American women want and buy a chance to tell them about your products."[50] Nevertheless, the Curtis policy was to control the advertisers very carefully so that the character of the advertising was influenced by the *Journal*'s service objectives to its readers.

The publisher followed the dictates of his readers in determining advertising policy. In 1890, readers were requested to submit their criticisms to the *Journal*. Of the thousands of readers who responded, nine-tenths criticized the inclusion of patent-medicine and cosmetics advertising. Curtis told one of his advertising managers, "The wishes of our subscribers are paramount to those of advertisers."[51] Because of the response, Curtis reached his decision in September, 1890, to refuse future contracts to the offending advertisers.[52] He was convinced that the *Journal* constituency had radically changed in two years and that advertised nostrums no longer belonged in the magazine. For minor ailments, readers now turned to their family physician instead of to patent medicines. His 1890 policy statement is the earliest evidence of his decision to abandon patent-medicine advertising when various contracts expired. In 1889, in fact, Curtis had already rejected some patent-medicine advertisements, but he was not then systematic in his exclusions.[53]

For Curtis the patent medicine posed no moral issue. Instead, it was his business conviction that advertising the nostrum in the *Journal* would be unsuccessful for its manufacturer and dangerous for the *Journal*. When fraud or danger were clearly evident in any product or advertisement, he always rejected the advertisement. He endorsed every product advertised in the magazine. In his view, fraud never was good business; nor was ignoring his readers' complaints. And the men he called his high-class advertisers did not want their advertisements to share a magazine page with those for cosmetics and nostrums.[54]

This decision to eliminate patent-medicine advertising was a significant one, because at that time the nostrum was the most important product group in the advertising business. In fact, patent-medicine proprietors were pioneers in national advertising. After the elimination of patent-medicine advertising between 1893 and 1897, the total number of *Journal* advertising lines declined, but revenue increased because of rises in advertising line rates.[55] In addition, Curtis was then free to solicit more desirable advertisers. His policy of gradually letting patent-medicine contracts expire enabled the magazine to keep its good business record concerning contract commitments.

One way for Cyrus Curtis to promote consumer confidence in the *Journal*'s editorial and advertising copy was to keep the editorial and advertising departments rigidly separated. He informed prospective and current *Journal* advertisers that the editors, not the publisher, decided the contents of their copy and were under no pressure to accommodate advertisers or to attract them by describing the advantages of their products. No "first-class publication," said Curtis, contained mention of goods in editorial copy.[56] Keeping firmly to this precept enabled Curtis to elude the advertising hordes who wanted special favors in *Journal* columns. On this point the editor and the publisher were in agreement. In very strong words, the usually mild-mannered managing editor, William V. Alexander, told an advertiser in 1899 that Bok believed "it would be a ruinous policy for him to make a practice of directing their [department editors'] attention to goods advertised in our columns, as a bare hint from him might be misinterpreted as an order. . . . [Bok] cannot go so far as to sacrifice his editorial principles merely for the sake of insuring satisfaction to advertisers." In addition, no editor was allowed to receive any gifts or samples, for there was no way to return a "favor" except in violation of company policy.[57]

In one exception to the policy, Bok's managing editor asked a department editor to prepare an article on cereal recipes, giving at least one recipe for each of twenty-five brand-name preparations. This policy exception was probably motivated by the company's wish to encourage competition among advertisers and thus avoid the dangers of advertising revenue losses from a single manufacturer dominating a field. In one instance, however, Bok found it necessary to deny that an entire *Journal* article was based on advertising by a single manufacturer.[58]

Despite Curtis' care in avoiding collusion between editorial and advertising matter published in the *Journal*, it was not until the November, 1894, issue that advertisements disguised as reading matter were explicitly barred. The announcement in that issue said: "The special rate of eight dollars per line for such advertising has been withdrawn. All advertising hereafter found in the *Journal* will be of the regular display nature, in the regular places assigned it, and no artifice will be allowed to deceive the reader that it is anything else. This rule has been made by the *Journal* entirely for the protection of its readers."[59] Eighteen years later the *Journal* practice became general law for United States periodicals. This advertising law, enacted by reformers, required all reading matter that was paid for to be "plainly marked" as advertisement.[60]

By 1891, the Curtis Publishing Company refused to show or sell their general list of subscribers. The *Journal* nevertheless had problems with various department editors who submitted to interested companies the names of readers who made inquiries on specific subjects. In 1901, with the approval of the publisher, the *Journal*'s editor made a central policy statement to every editor and contributor, and a copy was automatically sent to all new contributors for a few years. First, it stated, reader correspondence was inviolable and not to be given or sold for anyone's reading. Second, no advertising matter of any kind was permitted in a department editor's replies to readers. Forbidden, too, was any mention of an editor's own books or pamphlets.[61]

The amount of advertising in an issue partly determined the space allotted to reading material or editorial copy. The usual *Journal* ratio was two or three columns of reading matter for every column of advertising. Maintenance of this policy from the earliest years, Curtis wrote, would help the *Journal* to be the ideal publication he intended, and he did not wish to "spoil it by too much advertising matter." Some minor editorial columns varied in space allotments according to the amount of advertising in an issue. When advertising pressures were very great, advertising copy occasionally replaced editorial.[62]

Long before the company had consistently refused to permit any apparent *Journal* endorsement of a product, advertisers had used *Journal* articles for their own commercial purposes. After the new policy was established, Curtis did guarantee the advertised products to be reliable, although the company could not guarantee quality. He said, "Should the goods prove to be less valuable than others bought for the same price, that would be a question of price, which it would be impossible for us to regulate; should, however, the goods prove different from what has been advertised, showing clearly an intention to deceive, then we should feel responsible to our subscribers." In one instance, an advertisement for *Farm and Home* magazine offered *Journal* readers a trial subscription at low cost. One woman submitted her twenty-five cents and was harassed by *Farm and Home* to renew her subscription and pay for additional numbers of the magazine sent to her without her consent. When she complained to Curtis, he promptly and angrily wrote to the publishers of *Farm and Home* and to their collection agency. He warned them that he would publicize the incident unless the publisher of *Farm and Home* mended his business tactics.[63]

When Curtis knew a certain article was in preparation for *Journal* publication, he sought companies that would want to advertise in the issue featuring that article. For example, he wrote to his New York advertising agent, W. S. Niles: "In the

January [1892] number we have a discussion on 'Wine on Fashionable Tables.'. . . Such matter as this ought to appeal to the china and glassware people." If an issue featured a particular region, Curtis agents were encouraged to contact advertisers whose products would be most likely to interest inhabitants of that area.[64]

Bok's managing editor, however, frequently reminded advertisers that there could be "no direct connection between any editorial feature and an advertisement." But he was eager to place a silver company's advertisement next to an article on silver. In fact, *Profitable Advertising* pointed out that the International Silver Company really "secured a page for the price of a column" in the October, 1901, *Journal.* This was not an unusual episode. In 1898 the *Journal* had already been cited with a few other magazines for its careful placement of advertising copy close to related editorial content. If readers frequently inquired about an item, Curtis wrote to the appropriate advertisers to solicit advertisements.[65]

By 1910 the company was issuing an advertising code to its agents. To protect Curtis readers and advertisers, the code provided rules for "discouraging unfair, and even unmannerly, competition in our advertising columns." The *Journal* and *Post* accepted no mail-order advertising of general merchandise, no installment buying, no alcohol or patent-medicine advertising, and no immodest text or illustrations. In addition, the *Journal*'s special restrictions prohibited financial, tobacco, and playing card advertising, and, by 1910 (despite the popularity of fashionable tables), references to alcohol, "even illustration of wine glasses or steins."[66]

The digest of the code stated the central policy: "We cannot permit any appearance of collusion with the Editorial Department, and we cannot admit copy which indicates that any particular advertiser has been favored with advance information which is not available to everyone." In addition, express Curtis Company consent was required for any editorial quotation to be used in *Journal* advertisements.[67] These published rules helped advertising agents to convince advertisers of their general application.

The advertising code was also designed to aid the advertiser. For example, it cautioned that the use of undue superlatives and exaggeration in advertisements was unprofitable. Another company manual stressed the need for news value in advertising. And the decision to use color in advertisements was guided by the standard of sales returns and necessity, not aesthetics or shock impact.[68] Also, Curtis often advised advertisers to write a straightforward advertisement unencumbered by guessing games and prizes, because *Journal* readers were not impressed by advertising gimmicks. He encouraged honest displays with full name and address of the advertiser included.[69]

The *Journal*'s advertising rates were raised several times in two years. On July 1, 1890, rates climbed from $2.00 per printed line to $2.50, and on July 1, 1891, to $3.00. Rates were higher for preferred position, that is, for placement next to reading matter and for pages preceding editorial matter. When advertisers complained of the high rates, Curtis said that the *Journal*'s circulation warranted the rates and that many leading magazines actually cost more because of their limited circulation. The only cash discount was 5 percent, given if the bill was paid by the twenty-fifth of the month or if payment was made with order. By 1900, the back cover of the *Journal* was the most expensive advertising position in American magazines, and in 1914, the *Journal* still enjoyed the highest advertising rate per page of any leading magazine.[70]

Curtis forced advertisers to use the *Journal* on a cash-and-carry basis. The publisher adhered to his one-price policy for all advertisers. He was willing, however, to make one concession. If a particularly desirable advertiser was not yet satisfied that the *Journal* would be a successful advertising medium for his product, Curtis eagerly offered a sample of his wares by running an advertisement without fee to the advertiser.[71]

Rate cutting was a familiar burden carried by major publications in the 1890s. Because Curtis refused to cut *Journal* rates to any advertiser, he was unable to renew the contract of the Royal Baking Powder Company. It was, along with Ivory, Pears, and Sapolio, among the chief single advertisers of that time.[72] In late 1890, the Royal company wanted a special rate. Curtis explained his refusal: "We have absolutely but *one price*, and knowing that, you are secure in the supposition that no other house has any advantage whatever over you."[73] Nevertheless, the Royal Baking Powder Company continued to demand rather sharply Curtis' "lowest rates," and only after it received them would it consider the *Journal's* claims to "amount and character of circulation." In a letter published in *Printers' Ink*, Curtis publicized that he maintained his one price in spite of the Royal company's pressure. He wanted advertisers to know that the *Journal* would not change its rate to Royal even though many of the "high-toned" magazines had capitulated.[74]

At a time when 45 percent of *Journal* advertisements came directly from advertisers, Curtis was not eager to support commission agents who sold space for advertisements in the *Journal*. In late 1889, he discontinued the use of all commission accounts except the very largest, whose commissions he reduced from 20 percent to 10 percent. Why should he lose even 10 percent in commissions, he asked, when he could fill *Journal* columns twice over at the full rate? If, however, a desirable "line of business" was available only by commission, then he would use it.[75]

For that reason he employed J. Walter Thompson, a major advertising agency. Although Thompson himself placed a very large amount of *Journal* advertising, he was not known to recommend the *Journal* or to give it an available appropriation. Discussing the value of Thompson's service with his New York advertising manager, Curtis said that Thompson paid the bills on time. As to whether the company would lose Thompson's accounts if he were eliminated, Curtis asked, "How much of the business that he sends us do you suppose he actually controls?"[76]

Thomas Balmer, the *Journal*'s western advertising manager, was based in Chicago from 1892 to 1900. He was considered by many to have helped Curtis achieve some of his major business objectives. According to John Adams Thayer, Balmer originated the idea of contracts between publisher and advertising agent that barred the agent from giving rebates to his clients from the commission paid to him by the publisher. In these early years, however, only the N. W. Ayer Agency granted Curtis a fixed-price contract with no rate cutting allowed. Ayer refused similar requests from all other publishers.[77]

Curtis wrote to the Lord & Thomas advertising agency that, because "the advertising agent is the agent of the advertiser instead of the publisher, the advertiser should pay for his services instead of the publisher."[78] Although he protested, Curtis continued giving commissions to advertising agents.

As advertising copy grew in importance, Curtis made the *Journal*'s appearance one of his active concerns. At a time when only a handful of United States magazines paid any attention to typography and aesthetics, he wanted the advertising columns to be as carefully edited as the editorial copy. In 1892, he hired an advertising expert and an artist to create attractively designed advertisements that he could submit to advertisers for their approval. One strategy he developed was snipping out an advertisement in another periodical and sending it to the advertiser with proposed changes designed to make the display more attractive. In little more than a decade, the *Journal*'s art bureau was considered to be one of the best in the nation, and it innovated the introduction of a different cover design for every issue. Even before Thayer, the typographical expert, became the Curtis Company's general advertising manager in 1892, Curtis had eliminated advertisements with heavy black type and gothic type. He did this because the best artists refused to subject their work to heavily inked pages.[79]

Curtis favored large, well-illustrated advertisements with plenty of white space. In March, 1888, 42.67 percent of *Journal* advertisements were illustrated, and in March, 1899, 47.33 percent.[80] Because advertising-line costs rose in this period, these figures are significant.

Many advertisers resisted Curtis' encroachments upon what they said were their own territories. They were unhappy to see their electrotypes spurned in favor of Curtis' own type, particularly if trademark identity had been established with a repeated advertisement. But Curtis was certain that "they will come around to our way of thinking, as old fogies do to new and progressive ideas." Sears, Roebuck, and Company refused to relinquish its heavy, black-face display advertising and, consequently, never advertised in the *Journal*. But unlike his zealous advertising managers, Curtis insisted on receiving the advertiser's approval of any copy changes before publication.[81]

In a short time Curtis had more advertising business than he had space in the *Journal*. He wrote in 1893, "We have been obliged to leave out not only columns, but whole pages of the most desirable business, and it is creating a great deal of friction and ill feeling." In these circumstances Curtis could clearly afford to be selective. Occasionally, however, when the *Journal* went over the regular 32-page length to accommodate extra advertising, the additional columns did not pay for the greater costs of hand folding in the manufacturing and mailing departments.[82]

The large page size (11" × 16") of the *Journal* was at once a source of joy for advertisers and regret for readers. Complaints about the magazine's unwieldiness often came to the Curtis offices. The publisher explained that if the pages were folded in half, readers would lose about four pages of reading matter to allow for margins. A more basic reason was that machinery conversion costs would be very high. When the magazine was inching toward being a regular 48-page paper, Curtis said that the additional problem of buckling would be surmounted without any need to change the page size. After all, cutting the page size meant reducing the amount of available advertising space too. By 1899, larger advertisements often made effective use of the page size. In fact, magazines with small page sizes often made the change to a larger page after 1900. The *Journal* turned to a smaller (9¼" × 14¼") size in 1913, but slightly increased it in 1921.[83] Boxes for rural free delivery were manufactured big enough to accommodate the *Journal*'s size.

As advertising revenue increased, new worries came to the Curtis Company. It was not in the financial interest of a publishing house to secure advertising accounts only from the largest firms in a major business area. When smaller manufacturers were eliminated from the competitive field, there was theoretically no need for one large combine to advertise. However, at the 1915 Advertising Conference, Charles Coolidge Parlin said that advertising would "establish a good will for each [a group of six large manufacturers] . . . and each must advertise in order to prevent elimination." At the same conference, the Curtis advertising manager said that the company's growth areas were not in new accounts but in "big increases from a few advertisers"[84] Business mergers threatened to prevent the continued growth of the persuasion industry.

In fact, throughout the early history of the company, what Curtis most appreciated was "the capture of a *new* customer."[85] This attitude may explain the radical policy exception made in 1901 when specific mention of many brandname cereals was included in a *Journal* article in an effort to encourage advertising competition. Although the company supported its policy and feared business consolidation, "early friends" were excluded from its strictures. One year, two *Journal* issues had no advertisements for Ivory Soap. When Percy Proctor asked that the whole *Journal* page facing the first reading page in those two issues not be sold to another soap advertiser, Bok agreed.[86]

To help the advertiser make more effective use of *Journal* pages, the company pioneered in marketing research. It attempted to stretch the returns from the dollars invested in *Journal* advertising by establishing a division of marketing research whose findings were available to all advertisers. Marketing research was used to assess merchandising habits and industrial trends. For example, the Marketing Research Division did an estimate and analysis of the percentage of the buying population in all United States cities over 5,000 to find out who purchased the dress and blouse patterns sold in the *Journal*.[87] Stanley R. Latshaw, who showed Curtis the importance of systematic commercial research, recommended Charles Coolidge Parlin to head the Marketing Research Division in 1911. This division's study of industry by carefully canvassing a potential market was not being done by other agencies or publishers. Through travel and field work, the division's staff interviewed manufacturers, jobbers, and retailers across the nation. The office force prepared analytical reports that were given to the advertising director and to each of the advertising branch managers. From these reports the Curtis advertising team tried to evaluate "the advertising possibilities of an industry and to assist manufacturers and advertising agents with general merchandising suggestions. The aim is to formulate the general principles underlying the merchandising of an industry rather than to study the particular problem of an individual manufacturer. . . . to supplement rather than to replace agency service. . . . to develop industry along sound merchandising lines rather than to stimulate advertising."[88] At a testimonial dinner to Parlin many years later, Latshaw explained that the statistical surveys in the field were comparatively simple to undertake and that the real issue was the "necessity of convincing a manufacturer as to the desirability of advertising and extending his markets."[89]

Curtis placed his business faith in the rising fortunes of the middle-class market, which could be expected to buy more and more prepackaged brand-name commodities. Because he believed in this long-range process, he was willing to assume short-term risks, as he selected and shaped appropriate *Journal* advertisers. He established the reliability of his magazine's circulation at a time when misuse of statistical figures was rampant. He wanted to establish his honesty in business and prove that the highest ethical standards would yield the most profitable returns.

Journal advertisers initially had misgivings because Curtis did not simply place advertisements in his successful magazine. He shaped advertising copy to his requirements in design and content. He did so because he was certain that he was following the lead of the *Journal* audience in what they would and would not tolerate. And he was innovative in demanding adherence to his total concept of the kind of magazine the *Journal* had to be. The successful Curtis method consisted of careful analysis of his own and his advertisers' markets and systematic exploitation of the findings.

The publisher promoted general standards for all *Journal* advertisers. He insisted on one rate for all advertisers and refused to allow them to influence his editors; but he was willing to let potential advertisers know about relevant editorial copy in forthcoming issues of the *Journal*. Advertisers who agreed to the terms set by Curtis closed a good bargain. Big and small advertisers profited from the Curtis Company's innovations in art standards and marketing research. The company's resources were being used to provide what formerly had been an expense of the advertiser. Also beneficial to advertisers was the association of their products with a quality mass magazine having the lofty purpose of serving its readers with advice, entertainment, and instruction. Finally, *Journal* readers could be counted upon to be the chief consumers in the increasingly urban national market.

It is noteworthy that the publisher, not his advertisers, set these standards. Significantly, both Curtis and Bok had been employed as advertising managers before their *Journal* careers began. That experience helped them to understand the needs of advertisers, and they instructed advertisers on how to reach a measure of sophistication in design and content in the mass magazine. Without guidance, advertisers tended to seek short-term satisfaction. As long as the Curtis Company kept its advertisers subordinate to its own goal of service to its readers, the publisher could count on a satisfied audience and, ironically, a contented set of advertisers.

The influence of Cyrus Curtis upon his magazine was plain. His motivations were complex, for certainly he wanted to make a profit; and at the same time, his business philosophy led him to stress what he saw as the quality of his products. His choice of advertisers, his attention to the most effective means of advertising display, and his open and honest business policies were all basic aspects of the total product. He was determined to prove that quality paid handsomely. His success was assured by his shrewd assessment of the psychology of the new mass market. *Journal* advertisements paid because the middle-class housewife trusted the magazine. Businessmen were eager to advertise if it could be clearly demonstrated that their investments paid dividends. As a result, many Curtis innovations were quickly copied by other publishers and became lasting features of the advertising industry.

The Curtis Company promoted consistently reliable business methods and successfully protected the interests of its advertisers, its readers, and its own shareholders. With vigorous, direct, and successful business tactics the company convinced subscribers and advertisers alike of the *Journal*'s service objectives. Above all, the Curtis Company guarded its independence from creditors and advertisers.

The magazine had earned that rare freedom to enter programs of reform and uplift that other magazines did not have. The will to reform and the means to carry it through were abundantly present for the *Journal*. To what degree it achieved its own program of service-oriented reform remains to be seen. First, however, the character and interests of the man in the editor's chair and in whom Cyrus Curtis placed his confidence, Edward William Bok, will be explored.

II ❧ Living the
"Six-Day" Virtues

Cyrus Curtis was anxious to show advertisers that the *Journal* reached a middle-class audience, and he had to rely on the editor, Edward William Bok, to produce a magazine designed to be read, talked about, and trusted by that audience. Central to the Curtis Company's success, then, was Bok's energy, insight, and deft articulation of his readers' needs and ambitions.

Bok understood his audience because he shared many of its values. To be sure, his early life was different from the experience of most of his readers. He was an immigrant, and his childhood in Brooklyn had been poor. The Boks had been solid, sometimes prominent, Dutch burghers in the Netherlands, and his mother was careful to cultivate in the young boy the sturdy values of the old country, such as honesty, efficiency, frugality, and hard work—values he retained throughout his life. The Dutch side of Bok, the solidity and sense of tradition, appealed to his readers, who were usually only a generation or two from rural life and still imperfectly adjusted to the demands of an increasingly urban society.

The genteel poverty of Bok's immigrant boyhood was another bond with his readers. He grew up with the expectation of a better life. His own experiences made him a shade suspicious of the wantonly rich in society, and he was no less anxious about the character and life-style of the poor. For most of his *Journal* career, he affirmed his faith in the middle-class citizen as the best part of United States society. He could speak effectively to his readers because he was more perfectly middle-class in values and attitudes than they.

Although Bok was proud of his Dutch background, he wanted to become part of America. He outdid his readers in his faith in the myths and hopes of his adopted country—free enterprise, the possibilities of reform, and the need for civic responsibility. He also affirmed his hopes for American life and institutions with greater vigor. His sentiments were all the more compelling because they reflected not so much what his readers did believe as what they thought they should believe.

A survey of Bok's experiences before he went to work for the *Journal* will suggest the origin of some of his ideas on success and the good life, and of his emphasis on ethics rather than traditional religion; and an evaluation of his ideas about social class and minorities will help to suggest the impulse, the framework, and the limits of his reform program.

Bok edited his own life story with much of the fervor that he used the blue pencil as editor of the *Journal.* Even when he spoke with his sons, the two boys were never quite sure whether Father was "editorializing" to better demonstrate a truth. [1]

In the editor's own era Bok was a household name and frequently the subject of extensive press coverage. His origins, as recounted in the newspapers, undoubtedly stemmed mostly from interviews, because they coincide with his autobiography. His father, William J. H. Bok, was a rich man who held diplomatic posts at the royal court of the Netherlands. [2] His grandfather, William Bok, a lawyer at the Hague, became chief justice of the Supreme Court of the Netherlands, and his great-grandfather was an admiral-in-chief of the Dutch navy. When Edward was a small boy, his father made unwise investments, lost the family's riches, and migrated to the United States. As Bok frequently emphasized, his father had to begin a new life at forty-five, with two small children and a wife who had been accustomed to comfort and security. Whether in fact Edward Bok had a background of riches and comfort is moot.[3] He claimed his origins were upper class, and they were certainly upper middle class.[4]

Bok wrote the first of his two autobiographies, *The Americanization of Edward Bok,* in 1920. Written in the third person, this strongly didactic best-seller was awarded the Pulitzer Prize in 1921. Five years later, he wrote *Twice Thirty,* considered by his family to be more revealing of the man than the first autobiography, which was characterized by a certain smugness. The *Americanization* was a typical success story, in which Bok candidly narrated his pluck, his trials, and his cunning in achieving success.

In 1870, when the Bok family came to the United States, neither Edward, who was almost seven, nor his brother, William, who was eight, knew English; consequently, they suffered various humiliations in the Brooklyn schools. Bok said later that in school he learned nothing about how to become an American. The poor quality of his public education became the target for many of his editorials. As a small boy, Bok held many jobs, but he left school at thirteen to earn more money and ease the financial strain on his parents. In a 1915 interview Bok said, "I never went to school again. I have hustled from that time until now." He went to work as an office boy at Western Union at the same time that Frank Munsey was employed there. Both future journalists left the company in 1882.[5]

While working in his next job, as a stenographer, Bok

started the *Brooklyn Magazine* with limited capital resources. It was designed to be read by young parishioners attending the church of Henry Ward Beecher, the popular Brooklyn preacher. From that editorial position, he assiduously made literary contacts that later helped his publication to become a successful feature syndicate with 137 subscriber newspapers. Bok began this project when Beecher, his friend and mentor, agreed to supply a weekly article for reprint sales to American newspapers and magazines.[6] In 1886, Bok formally established the third American feature syndicate. Two years earlier both Irving Bacheller and S. S. McClure had founded newspaper syndicates. While editing *Brooklyn Magazine*, Bok went to work for Charles Scribner, then a young New York publisher, and in a few years became director of Scribner's advertising department.

Bok liked working for Scribner. When he received offers for other positions, he was quick to reject them. Then, in 1889, Cyrus H. K. Curtis dropped a few hints that he was looking for a "working editor" for his six-year-old magazine. Because Bok found his current position so agreeable, only salary could entice him to leave it. Curtis' offer was satisfactory, so the twenty-five-year-old Bok went to the *Ladies' Home Journal* in November, 1889, to take charge of the editorial and art departments. Less than four years after joining Curtis, Bok was engaged to marry the only child of Cyrus and Louisa Knapp Curtis, Mary Louise.[7] They were married in 1896.

For one year Bok continued to own and direct his syndicate. Material unsuitable for *Journal* publication could at least be considered for the syndicate. This was an attractive proposition for writers who touched upon subjects controversial in the 1890s, like dancing and skating. As the *Journal* began to occupy more of Bok's time, much of the syndicate responsibility was delegated to his brother, William.[8]

Bok's early career successes were not without their price.

The hard work of editing the *Journal* cost him his health. He and his associates referred to his illnesses as prostration from exhaustion, stomach ailments, and neuritis. One of his son's earliest memories of his father was seeing him bent over in pain but nonetheless busy with work.[9]

Because Bok held the *Journal*'s highly paid position of editor, he often seemed compelled to comment on the nature of poverty and success. Success, he said, was the sure reward of those men who were moderate in all things except perseverance and who were thorough and rigidly honest.[10] Luck had scarcely any part in the making of a success. "The only lucky young man," Bok declared, "is he who has a sound constitution, with good sense to preserve it; who knows some trade or profession thoroughly or is willing to learn it and sacrifice everything to its learning; who loves his work and has industry enough to persevere in it; who appreciates the necessity of self-restraint in all things, and who tempers his social life to those habits which refresh and not impair his constitution. That is luck—the luck of having common sense."[11] Bok's own practice of relying on common sense, that often elusive yet practical trait, led him more often to challenge convention than to accept it. After all, he said, although caution should temper the young man's rise in business, the "automaton," or the "plodder," would never reach any genuine success.

Most businessmen, Bok maintained, were usually not college-bred. Indeed, he suspected that a college education harmed a man's chances for business success. Successful businessmen were characterized by traits like practicality, which he asserted no college could teach. The best school for success was poverty. This seemingly luckless condition, he wrote, brought valuable experiences to a boy and nurtured the growth of compassion.[12] Of course, he said, a boy should work his way out of poverty. Quite unfairly, some of his contemporaries accused Bok of admonishing the poor to cherish their alleged blessing of poverty. But as one of them wrote, Bok's own poverty had been "accidental and amateur... grim but... not chronic."[13] Bok failed to acknowledge the difference between a life of unceasing poverty and one in which poverty was a temporary setback.

Bok counseled young men to avoid public discussion of religion, though he occasionally forayed into the camp of dogma to preach a more humanistic religion. "The Young Man and the Church," an essay Bok published in *Cosmopolitan Magazine,* was severely attacked by conventional-minded religious persons. When the article was republished in book form in 1896, Bok's preface acknowledged the vituperative criticisms heaped upon him; but he basked in the praises, or at least the "respectful dissension," accorded him by some leading clergymen and laity.[14] In this book and in much of his writings on Christianity, Bok called for the application of Christian faith to modern man's life. Regarding the average sermon's content, he asked, "What possible reason can there be in such a constant application of the parable of the prodigal son to the needs of the active and respectable young man of today." The young man who attended church obviously was not an adulterer or drunkard, and these preachings were not fulfilling his needs. For this reason, Bok suggested, young men often did not attend church. They could more profitably spend their time in meditation and reading. He believed, however, that they did need an affirmative creed, and he wanted the clergyman to consider his approach. The modern young man met so many social and ethical problems that Bok claimed he would obtain more appropriate guidance from the greatest success story of all, the Gospel according to Saint Matthew.[15]

Underlying Bok's criticism of the modern minister was his

realization that in the changing times the clergyman had lost his position as intellectual and moral leader. More pointedly, Bok said, "The average minister can say all he need say, or is capable of saying—with any hope of interesting—in twenty or twenty-five minutes."[16] That was why he commended the Episcopal Church for attracting members with the twenty-minute sermon.

His concern with the practical side of religious faith was often reiterated. In his second autobiography, *Twice Thirty*, he wrote: "I have always felt with Henry Drummond when he said that the tendency of religions has been to care more for religion than for humanity, whereas Christ cared more for humanity than for religion, or to put it in another way, His care for humanity was chief expression of His religion."[17]

Bok's ideas on religious faith influenced the pages of the *Journal*. In the earliest days of his editorship, he hired the Reverend Dr. T. De Witt Talmage, a former contributor to the *Brooklyn Magazine*, to "mould the religious sentiments of our readers." Less than one year later, he advised Margaret Bottome, the *Journal*'s ardent religious columnist, to write a "familiar talk" rather than a sermon.[18] He spoke more sternly in his "Problems of Young Men" column in May, 1895. A married man, twenty-six years old, wanted to leave a "good position" to begin studies for the ministry. Bok wrote: "A man's first duty is to his wife and to his children. I place that above everything. It is my gospel. I know it is not strictly a theological one, but if a man is true to those whom God has placed within his keeping, he is true to God, and his work will be acceptable to him." Similarly, he wrote two months later that "to amuse the baby and to romp with it is sometimes quite as much a religious duty as to pray for it."[19]

Harsh and superficial judgments of men and customs, Bok said, had no place in the Christian life. He eagerly reinforced one of the more charitable sermons of the crusading minister, Dr. Charles Parkhurst, by saying that "there is a good deal of current tenderheartedness bestowed to prodigals and Magdalens of a couple of thousand years ago, but precious little on prodigals and Magdalens living at date."[20]

The *Journal*'s contributors also frequently reinforced the humanistic approach to religion. Edward Bellamy wrote a startling piece, "Christmas in the Year 2000," thoroughly in keeping with his popular account of a fully socialized society, *Looking Backward*. About the celebration of Christmas, he wrote: "The devotion of the day to the purposes of the family reunion and a feast of kinship . . . was not the less a singularly complete perversion of the meaning of the occasion. . . . Christ came to preach not the love of kindred, but of humanity."[21] Bok approached Charles Sheldon, a popular clergyman-author of the 1890s, to contribute a department column based on Sheldon's best-seller, *In His Steps*. The editor wanted to provide reading for men comparable to Mrs. Bottome's column for women, "The King's Daughters." When Sheldon refused, Bok invited the Reverend Francis Clark to write on certain everyday questions, the "six-day questions" as Bok called them, that were concerned with the virtuous application of a moral philosophy to the daily decisions made in home, civic, and business affairs.[22]

The six-day virtues informed most of Bok's life work. Because aid to man was more important than ritual creeds or the conventional offering of praises to God, he was convinced that philanthropy supplied the test of a man's success. If a man spent years in the acquisition of wealth, so, too, he must spend time in its distribution. He wrote, "A man's life is like the soil of a farm: the time comes when he must put into the soil what he has taken out; else life becomes barren and unproductive."[23]

To insure successful philanthropy Bok insisted that sound business methods had to support altruistic projects. Business methods, then, were a positive force leaving no taint to diminish the value of altruism. With Dr. Samuel McClintock Hamill, an eminent physician of his day, Bok founded the Child Federation, whose aim was to "do good on a business basis."[24] If Bok had anxieties about the laws of the marketplace, they are not often apparent in his writings.

Although business efficiency could effectively manage altruism, Bok said that ethical standards came from men like Theodore Roosevelt, "who always put ethics above economics."[25] And Bok, too, clearly saw the difference. He willingly acknowledged that the businessman's motivation for reform was pragmatic as often as it was ethical because it *paid* to be honest. *The Ladies' Home Journal* occasionally chose the side of reform because it was in the long- or short-range best interests of business—either the magazine's own or its advertisers'. But *Journal* reform under his editorship was not limited to that. The *Journal* carried on serious reform programs such as the sex education campaign, which were independent of the impact on its business and even on many *Journal* readers.

Bok's early attitudes on reform were well defined. Like Ralph Waldo Emerson, he held that the members of a society must be changed, not the society's institutions. Organizations were valuable for requiring the cooperation of people. But the individual man would always provide the initiative for all sound endeavors, and he could succeed without the organization.[26] There were limits, however, to individualism; it could not reject all authority. The young editor feared the "spirit of free criticism" and accused the American newspaper of foisting that evil upon people. Bok wrote in 1894 that the depression developed "the spirit of intolerance on the part of the humbler class of our country toward those of wealth and position. Every respectable man and woman despises the spirit of anarchy and yet, in a small way, too many of us are nothing more or less than anarchists in an amateurish way. The spirit of discontent is rampant. And what, after all, is anarchy but the poisonous product of discontent."[27] Assuredly, the *Journal* was not ready to offer the more accurate definitions by such anarchist spokesmen of the 1890s as Emma Goldman or Voltairine LeCleyre.

Bok's attitude toward the temperance movement illustrates his views on the individual reformer. Because he endorsed temperance in his own life, he wished to see widespread acceptance of temperance principles. He rejected, however, the attempt to make temperance into a national crusade with compulsory legislation as an objective. In his judgment, if the consumer were informed about the dangers of alcohol, the "root of the evil" would be plucked out.[28] In the long debate over prohibition, the *Journal* continued to publish both supporting and opposing views of the temperance idea and committed itself to neither side until the coming of World War I.

Bok was flexible. As new kinds of problems emerged in an increasingly organized urban and industrial society, he was prepared to alter his attitudes on reform and try to change institutions rather than people in hopes of protecting human life and dignity. Certainly this approach was evident in his agitation for controls over patent medicines. In the *Journal*'s other major reform episode, on the need for sex education, Bok risked attacks from subscribers for his oblique references to social disease, an unmentionable subject. When his audience revealed shifting views on the position of women, he followed its lead. From its position as an opponent of women's suffrage, the *Journal* did not become an advocate but did open its pages to both sides of the controversy.

Bok had confidence in the United States of his day to the degree that he kept his faith in the American middle classes.

The middle-class American woman was the stabilizer between the "unrest among the lower classes and rottenness among the upper classes." To preserve the character of the middle classes, he solicited an article urging girls not to marry men "below their position in life."[29] Nevertheless, his commitment to the middle classes as a force for good was not uncritical. His job, as he conceived it, was to reinforce the good features of middle-class life while he exposed its weaknesses. His own views, however, reveal many of the limitations of the middle class.

Bok wanted to widen the sights of his audience by encouraging more charity and generosity between people of various social ranks. *Journal* readers were told that "great men eat with the wrong fork quite as often as do shy girls from the country." The correct forms, of course, were widely broadcast in *Journal* columns and advice sections.[30] But the spirit Bok hoped for was charity before convention. He also wanted people at least to hear what other groups and classes were saying. Social workers, for example, provided some challenging anecdotes about tenement life for *Journal* readers. Naturally, *Journal* writers approved of these good women carrying baskets of food and sundries to the impoverished. The social workers, however, were calling for more. Genuine help required sensitive, personal attention to the bodily and spiritual needs of the poor.[31]

Although Bok was occasionally interested in reporting the conditions of life outside middle-class America, he did not want sensational stories. Instead, he requested articles on the lives of mill and factory girls—with a dollop of sunshine, if possible. In 1898, he guided the completion of a manuscript on United States prisons, written by a social worker well acquainted with prison life. Bok wanted the manuscript to contain discussions of conditions requiring improvement as well as an outline of proposed reforms. Over a decade later, he was invited to write a message to prisoners. He declined and asked his managing editor, William V. Alexander, to explain that he could "think of nothing in particular to say to them."[32] There was a nice integrity in his refusal to preach the common-sense gospel of success and virtue to rebels and beaten-down members of his own society. Generally speaking, the cheerful side of life was most often presented to *Journal* readers, causing any *Journal* revelations about the seamy face of life to be all the more startling.

There was a homogeneity in outlook evident in the *Journal*'s attitude toward minority groups. In 1901 an author submitted an article on life near the Suwannee River. The manuscript was unacceptable because the writer discussed "several matters which are of really no value whatever to us, such as the Crackers and Negroes. If any references at all were to be made to these two classes, we should consider it worthwhile to have only the slightest references."[33] Scarcely any mention was made of the American Negro, except in advertisements, which carried such popular illustrations as the Gold Dust twins and other caricatures of blacks. A cereal advertisement, for example, offered "six extra funny darky cards" as a premium for the purchase of two packages of Korn-Kinks.[34] In thirty years the *Ladies' Home Journal* published only one essay about a black. And that article, in its emphasis on novelty, resembled a circus sideshow more than a piece of journalism. The story was about the blind pianist Thomas Wiggins, who had been a slave for twenty years. A child prodigy, he was still making concert tours at the time of the article. Many prejudicial stereotypes were present in the article, which stated that Tom had not shown "any vicious inclinations," although he was "weak-minded" and "childlike" because of his volatile temperament.[35] Most *Journal* readers were not exposed to blacks and poor white southerners in their daily lives, and the magazine did nothing to enlighten them.

Other minority groups fared somewhat better in the *Journal* than did blacks. Bok once commissioned several rabbis to explain the Jewish holy days of Hanukkah and their relationship to Christmas.[36] The *Journal* also published such articles as "Why Jewish Names Are Not There," a discussion of the low divorce rate among Jews. In some essays on material success Bok emphatically stressed the demonstrated philanthropy of American Jewry. He wrote that people erred in believing that successful Jews did not partake of the service ideals which inspired Christian success. To support his position, he listed some leading American Jews who were noteworthy in philanthropic enterprises.[37]

Bok frequently had to answer the anti-Semitic bigots in his audience who protested that the *Journal* published too many articles about Jews or written by Jews. On one occasion he quoted from his correspondent: "That's right; go on baiting the Jew, and get his subscription. But remember this: for every Jew you get you will lose two Gentiles." Bok continued, "How interesting! And written from a church parsonage too! So progresses true Christianity."[38] After realizing the enormity of ignorance on the part of some of his readers, he publicly answered one of his critics, saying: "Well, suppose some day when you have a little leisure from writing anonymous letters to editors, you go to some library, ask for a good work on Jewish history, and read it. And if you read that history aright, perhaps you will find in it somewhere something that will explain why we should have a soft spot for the Jew."[39]

Bok's ideal woman found her complete role in the home, and he was attracted to that precept in Judaism. His managing editor wrote to the Reverend Dr. Gustav Gottheil: "One thing I specially liked in your article was that of the Jewish woman's circle of influence being home. She is not a 'new woman'; she is not a 'club woman'; her home is her empire and in that she is supreme."[40] Another reason for Bok's enlightened view on Jews, in all probability, was his background in the Netherlands, where toleration was customary.

Bok said that certain nationalities had more admirable characteristics than others, and he occasionally encouraged his American readers to emulate foreign ways. He was convinced, for example, that the English and the French were particularly thrifty, a trait that wasteful Americans should acquire.[41]

Before the war, Bok sometimes lapsed into prejudicial comments about certain ethnic groups, especially if they lived among native Americans and were not cloistered in a ghetto. The *Journal* warned against placing children in the care of "illbred" Irish immigrant girls. In a strident tone, Bok warned parents about the allegedly predatory Greek male: "Mothers of working-girls know about the evil of dance halls and Chinese restaurants, and warn their daughters against them. But they do not know about the cruel rapacity of the average Greek vender [*sic*] who has no family ties in this country—it is said that there are only about sixty Greek women in all America— and who preys on the innocence of even the youngest child he can tempt with candy and pink soda-water."[42] Occasional references, good or ill, to several religious and ethnic groups were exceptional instances, in keeping with the usual *Journal* practice of carefully avoiding minority representation and expression. Not until World War I did the *Journal* and Bok revise their bigoted views on ethnic minorities and assert that cultural pluralism was desirable for the United States.

Of course there were singular exceptions as well as changes in this policy. In the 1890s, the Roman Catholic church was one of several taboo subjects. Only a decade later, however, the *Journal* published an exclusive feature article and photographs of Pope Pius X with a pilgrimage.[43] Because there seems to be no internal evidence in the Curtis Publishing Company to explain the policy change, it is likely that the new policy was a response to the climate of greater tolerance in the early years of the new century. As John Higham has pointed out, anti-Catholic feeling turned a sharp corner after 1900 and mysteriously abated for a decade.[44]

Bok was a registered Republican throughout his life. In his first autobiography he referred to Abraham Lincoln and Theodore Roosevelt as the nation's greatest Americans. His political friendships were not without significance for the *Journal.* He convinced both Benjamin Harrison and Theodore Roosevelt to become active *Journal* contributors. After cheering heartily for Roosevelt, Bok joined the admirers of Woodrow Wilson. Despite Bok's GOP allegiance, he respected Wilson, even more enthusiastically after the Paris Peace Conference. Obviously Bok was in the reform wing of the Republican party.

Although Bok encouraged middle-class participation in political affairs, he was reluctant to be identified with partisan politics or to publish serious political commentary in the *Journal.* The journalist Esther Everett Lape remembered that even as late as 1919 Bok refused to permit her to write deeply on political topics, even though he had accepted her immigration articles. Nevertheless, a few articles were published on foreign affairs.[45] One exception to company policy occurred during wartime, before the 1916 election. Bok's managing editor asked President Wilson's secretary if the president would agree to an authorized interview or to write an article explaining the Democratic platform. Some months later, the request was refused.[46]

Bok styled himself a reformer. He sought to lead his audience rather than to cater to its prejudices. Yet, in many areas he shared the shortsightedness of his readers. His framework remained fundamentally middle-class American, and his impulse was to ignore those aspects of American life that he found unpleasant. These were the blindspots, the America of poverty and ethnic and racial minorities, about which Bok and his readers little knew or cared. In this respect the *Journal* reflected the narrowness of the day, though it is to Bok's credit that he increasingly fostered a more tolerant attitude toward minorities.

Even so, Bok was in many areas several steps ahead of his readers. Politically, he was always a staunch backer of the Progressive men and forces of his day. Bok's detractors might have accused him of jumping on the reform bandwagon to sell magazines, but they would have been misled. His commitment to philanthropy and personal reform activities extended beyond his journalistic career into the years of his retirement. In his post-*Journal* career, Bok at last could practice active reform without any ties to business—an ideal he had always preferred.

III ❧ The Editor's Aims, Strategies, and Risks

Edward Bok's personal qualities, especially his dedication to the humanistic values of his generation, profoundly influenced his conduct as editor. Although he often preached from his own experiences, he liked to insist that he had to repress his own personality, which he called Edward William Bok, to allow his *persona*, Edward Bok, the middle-class model for his generation, to edit the *Journal*. [1] The pages of the *Journal* do not bear him out, however. The man underestimated the editor; indeed, he judged him too severely. The editor accomplished most of what the man endorsed. The man of sixty, conscious of his age, remembered the vain hours he had spent on the problems of knitting and embroidery when important ideas begged to be explored. In the 1890s Bok certainly had accepted the limitations of the *Journal*'s objectives. His was a woman's magazine, not a "free lance" eager to spar with the "combative questions." [2] The *Journal*'s record reveals, however, that Bok and his audience eventually outgrew these limited aims.

Bok's successful editorship was the result of his carefully attuning himself to his readers, sensing their fears, and giving them what they wanted to read and a little bit more. This combination, more than any other factor, assured the *Jour-*

nal's large circulation and its consequent choice by advertisers for spending their revenues. Just as Cyrus Curtis had gained the confidence of his advertisers, Edward Bok cultivated the trust and assurance of his readers.

Bok created this special quality between his audience and himself in several ways. First, his definition of his role as editor and his relationship with his staff contributed to the climate of trust and confidence. Second, he built up his readers' trust in products advertised in the *Journal.* And, third, he shrewdly measured the needs and wishes of his female audience and always tried, as far as his conscience permitted, to keep pace with their developing interests and expanding role.

The student of Edward Bok as editor can learn more about his achievements than his procedures. The records simply are too few to illuminate his methods of editorial negotiations with writers and contributors. He preferred to use personal interviews and was willing to travel to conduct business. Although Bok and his journalist contemporary, S. S. McClure, had many business connections, only occasional references and notes to McClure are extant in the Bok letterbooks. Peter Lyon, McClure's biographer, said he did not remember seeing a single Bok item or letter in the bulky McClure papers. As Bok told one of his contributors, "A half-hour's talk together would do more than all the letters we could write."[3]

To show the differences between the two Curtis publications—Bok's *Journal* and George Horace Lorimer's *Saturday Evening Post*—the contemporary business journal *Profitable Advertising* published a short essay. The editors of both magazines, the article said, were eager to satisfy the readers' interests; but Bok's magazine consistently mirrored his audience, while Lorimer's more often reflected Lorimer. In reality, Bok's influence was just as pervasive as Lorimer's, only more subtle.

He often said, however, that an editor could only be a good listener and give readers a magazine that they, in effect, wrote themselves. To achieve his ends Bok stayed at home one or two days out of every week reading the thousands of letters that inundated the Curtis Company offices. His ideas for articles, deletions of material, everything, he said, came from his readers. He did qualify this statement by admitting that his successful editorship came from being a "huckleberry or two" ahead of his readers.[4]

From the start Bok hoped to do more than merely reflect the audience. He wanted to raise the aspirations of his readers by giving them what they wanted but in a more profound way. Believing that the *Journal* was a tool for educating large numbers of American women, he tried to guide their interests to areas he thought would benefit them. He noticed, for example, that many people were concerned about raising the ethical standards of their communities, and he was convinced that sooner or later such people would look to the Bible for answers. Because no religious newspaper provided such guidance at that time, Bok and the *Ladies' Home Journal* decided to step into the breach by hiring the Reverend Lyman Abbott to counsel questioning readers with biblical wisdom.[5]

Bok enjoyed being a didactic editor. He once told Bernard Shaw that the *Journal*'s editorial pages were the world's "largest possible pulpit." One of his main techniques in education was to use his editorial page as his witness on topics that concerned him. Because an occasional article on an important issue had the greatest potential impact when published in editorial form, Bok sometimes asked contributors if they would permit editorial adaptations of manuscripts they had submitted to the *Journal.*[6]

Part of the editor's strategy was to create a forceful public personality, often remonstrative, always personal. He wanted to know his audience and his audience to know him. Although his photograph was not printed in the *Journal*, it was available for a small fee from the publishers. The Bok correspondence also reveals his initial eagerness to accept lecture engagements. But by 1906 Bok was willing to lecture only in his home state and its close neighbors—Pennsylvania, Delaware, New York, and New Jersey. In addition, he asked higher fees if he was unable to spend the night in his own house. When he decided that the public attended his lectures only to stare, he permanently discontinued his engagements on the lecture circuit.[7] Bok did not like public display or fanfare after he had become a public figure, and he realized that lecturing did not build the *Journal* audience.

Bok's ideas prevailed, too, in the type of fiction acceptable to the *Journal*. Any criticism of life had to be balanced by a suggestion of hope, an offer of remedy. Similarly, sadness had to be offset by humor, because Bok believed the stories should entertain, amuse but not sadden. When lessons were to be taught through fiction, Bok often advised writers to come only to the threshhold of disaster, sparing the reader from too great an emotional shock. Even if a manuscript was nearly in accord with Bok's ideas, he often requested changes in theme or handling before acceptance.[8] When too many changes were in order for a manuscript, it was rejected. Unhappily Bok returned Samuel Clemens' story "My Platonic Sweetheart" and wrote apologetically to the author, "It must be like bitter gall to a humorist to be told that the public always wants funny things from him, but it does from Mark Twain unquestionably."[9] The predictable, not the unusual, was standard for *Journal* fiction.

Although Bok solicited fiction from some first-rate writers, the authors could not transgress Bok's anti-realistic bent. As a result, Bok published Rudyard Kipling's *Just So* stories and the work of writers like the "smiling" realist, William Dean Howells. A typical *Journal* novel was Jean Webster's *Daddy Long-Legs*.

Journal fiction, from the editor's viewpoint, should not narrate the way life was but rather the way life *should* be. In 1890, one essayist was eager to write an article on the character of contemporary fiction. Bok told her to avoid discussing the popularity of certain leading realist and naturalist writers: "I almost fear that the statistics . . . on the sale of such writers as Zola and Tolstoi would be so large that it is best not to acquaint the public with it."[10] Another writer submitted a short story using the theater as background. Bok wrote to the author, "Nothing could be more directly against our policy than a story the scenes of which are laid on the stage; and to make matters worse you give me a suicide at the end."[11]

Bok saw no need to excite his readers by presenting them with a barrage of controversial and disturbing material. It was much shrewder to court them in unimportant matters so that he could preach his big concerns more effectively. Moreover, because his own literary taste was uncultivated, he willingly gratified his readers' preferences for happy, sentimental writing. And he was sure to hear from them if he violated this formula.

The dominance of Bok's personal philosophy at the *Journal* offices was maintained through his careful selection and control of the staff. Although the editorial staff was filled with highly professional and talented associates, Bok retained a commanding view over his chosen experts. By 1890 he had an editorial board made up of writers from whom he could request short articles on subjects of his choosing. Other editors read manuscripts and selected articles to submit to him. After he set a price on the manuscripts, they were given to his editorial assistants. Bok also placed other assistants on editorial salary to keep eyes and ears open for material of *Journal* interest in various cities. By 1898, he had a staff of twenty-two members, who formed an important element in developing the readers' trust in the magazine.[12]

Cyrus Curtis guaranteed editorial freedom to the *Journal* and *Post* editors, but members of Bok's staff were hardly free from their editor's influence.[13] He closely supervised his writers' contributions and often wrote samples of the kind of copy he wanted. Because his interests and capabilities were so extensive, he did not hesitate to write a column for a new series on social usage or advice to the lovelorn. Whatever the topic, he tried to be on the frontier of change. He pointed out the impracticality of a dwarf lemon tree for a table centerpiece as deftly as he reminded an associate art editor of new developments in printing technology.[14]

After advice columns on various subjects such as home nursing and child feeding had appeared in the *Journal* every month for a year or so, Bok discontinued the heading and placed it in the *Journal* service directory. Readers could then write to the staff editor in charge of the subject and receive personal answers. Bok admitted that, after twelve published columns, the basic questions on a topic were answered and the department only took space away from new topics.[15]

Despite the appearance of well-coordinated staff work, Bok's editorial assistants often failed to meet his exacting standards. The editor complained that he could entrust painstaking research problems to few American writers because Americans were not sufficiently thorough in their research methods. Not until 1911, when Karl Harriman became Bok's managing editor, were many trivial editorial problems removed from his anxious surveillance.[16] Bok had to supervise his staff very closely, since the *Journal*'s mainstay in serving its readers was the personal reply promised to every inquiry; and the volume of reader correspondence grew quickly. (The *Journal* offices received 59,000 letters in the last four months of 1911 and 97,000 letters in the last four months of 1912.) Every six months Bok wrote a letter under an assumed name to each of his department editors. He disliked the spying character of this method, but it enabled him to learn how attentive, accurate, and neat his editors' replies were. He praised good responses to his fake inquiries as strongly as he censured slipshod replies.* Bok and his staff tested their rival magazines' services in the same way and found them wanting in contrast to the *Journal's*.

Biographers of Bok's journalist contemporaries sometimes used him as the tranquil foil to highlight the distraught lives of their hyperanxious subjects. Bok was wholly uncomplicated to some observers and to others a jolly mover of men who worked without strain.[17] His associates knew better, however; he was not an indulgent editor. Perhaps this characteristic gained more victories for him than it lost contributors and staff members. His first managing editor advised office visitors to come prepared with definite ideas to discuss with the editor in chief; Bok had no time for a "rambling talk."[18]

Journal editorial copy had to be in the office at least three months before publication. Bok often made layout decisions several months before this deadline. He also made last-minute changes in the magazine's makeup. When he left the office for business trips or vacations, the magazine was made up far enough in advance to cover the issues he would not be present to supervise.[19]

---

*To one editor, Bok wrote, "Your letters to me have shown rather careless typewriting and two of them have gone unsigned. These are points which I do not like." (Bok to Emma Hooper, July 5, 1901, in Edward Bok Letterbooks, Historical Society of Pennsylvania.)

Although Karl Harriman's predecessor, William V. Alexander, enjoyed a long tenure as managing editor from 1899 to 1911, he had walked uneasily on a thin line between his own responsibilities and Bok's wishes. He was authorized to open all Bok's mail, including that marked personal, and knew the ins and outs of all office issues; but he avoided making independent managerial decisions, preferring instead to wait for Bok's judgment. His caution annoyed Bok.[20]

Alexander certainly did not believe that Bok was uncomplicated, and occasionally he complained about his chief's capricious editorial decisions. He did not, for example, understand the seemingly inconsistent criteria used by Bok in selecting illustrations for publication.[21] On one occasion, Alexander received an irate letter from a writer who complained that her manuscript had been unwisely edited. Apparently Bok had made inaccurate "corrections" in the manuscript, which was about Holland. Alexander admitted to her that *Journal* staff members would not dare to question any textual changes made by a Hollander about his native Netherlands.[22]

Perhaps Bok wanted Alexander's main job to be to instill fear of the editor's wrath into bothersome or delinquent *Journal* contributors. Alexander did write to contributors about his harrowing sessions with the editor after Bok had been informed that a writer might be unable to meet a scheduled deadline. Alexander also tried to squeeze concessions from contributors by threatening to direct Bok's attention to the matter at hand.[23]

Only the rare writer, like the rare managing editor, met Bok's standards. Esther Everett Lape remembered that once, close to the end of Bok's editorship, he complimented her: "I feel very stimulated. At last I have found a real writer."[24] Bok complained that, in addition to their generally poor quality of writing, too many writers wanted to break office rules. They fought unsuccessfully against his requirement that all manuscripts submitted to the *Journal* were on approval; that is, nothing was guaranteed publication before Bok himself read and accepted it.[25]

Bok's editorial standards were high but so were the fees paid to writers published in the *Journal*—one advantage of the magazine's large circulation.[26] Bok had no fixed scale of payment; he judged each manuscript on its merits alone. He argued that payment by word weakened literary craftsmanship, and thus he paid in lump sums only. Despite an occasional reference in his letters to a *Journal* policy of not soliciting manuscripts, Bok did solicit most articles and some fiction. Many of his editorial practices, such as lump sum payment and manuscripts on approval, were still regarded as novelties by other publishers before World War I.[27]

Bok carefully nurtured contributors' trust in the *Journal* and its editors. He enjoyed Benjamin Harrison's confidence, for example, and he made all the book publishing arrangements for the collections of Harrison's articles on the presidency that had been originally published in the *Journal.*[28] In another instance, Finley Peter Dunne, the creator of "Mr. Dooley," could not finish a serial for the *Journal* because he was in poor health. Bok wrote to Dunne telling him to keep the advance the *Journal* had already paid him and, upon his recovery, repay in token by giving the *Journal* the first chance to examine any new work he finished.[29]

One indication of the editor's interest in maintaining confidence in his magazine was his care to avoid abetting plagiarism. The *Journal* staff had to guard constantly against the dishonesty and unreliability of some contributors. Problems of real and suspected literary piracy haunted the editorial offices throughout Bok's thirty years as editor. In most cases

Bok demanded acknowledgment of error and confession by the guilty plagiarist, whereupon he dismissed the case. One literary thief begged the young editor for his mother's sake not to publish news of his wrongdoing. Bok agreed.[30] In cases of copyright infringement the *Journal* tried to settle out of court. One magazine reprinted an article published in a British magazine, which had bought the article from the *Journal.* William Alexander wrote many times to the offender and demanded restitution. When the culprit sent fifty dollars, Alexander returned the check with a letter stating, "From the beginning our stand in the matter has been one for principle alone, and as you have given us all the satisfaction that we felt it is our duty to demand we wish now to prove to you that we have nothing but the kindest and most neighborly regard for you."[31]

Bok's idea of the editor as steward demanded that he personally supervise the myriad details affecting the publication of his mass magazine. He complained about his editorial burdens but did little to lighten them. Everyone from reader to staff member knew it was Bok who stood behind the *Journal;* he would guard their trust and confidence in him. His job was his vocation, in the religious sense. He knew what middle-class Americans wanted and expected to hear, but he also gave them a pinch of what they should hear if they were to grow in compassion and understanding of themselves and others.

The personal approach Bok used in his editorship extended to the purely business side of the *Journal,* the province of advertising. Indeed, advertising had an integral place in his vision of the magazine's purpose. He wanted everything published in the *Journal* to be trustworthy and useful. At a time when suspicion of business was manifest among the middle classes, Bok tried to show that society accrued countless benefits from commercial and business undertakings. Because he also criticized some features of advertising, he contributed to the credibility of the Curtis Publishing Company.

Bok often said that he believed in the businessman's power for performing good works. Businessmen were not the sordid people so often pictured, he said, and they were the great patrons of the arts and medical research in the United States. In addition, just and efficient business methods could be successfully applied to all sectors of life, including home and the Church.[32] Although he lauded business, he knew that far more important values transcended the marketplace.

In the reorganized Curtis Company the president defined the jurisdiction of the business manager. In the president's absence, the manager would be responsible for general business, only if the vice-president was *not* an editor of one of the magazines. If the vice-president was an editor, he would manage business affairs in the president's absence. The manager would not, however, have jurisdiction over either *Journal* or *Post* editor.[33]

By 1892 Edward Bok was the vice-president of the company. Curtis therefore regarded him as his chief lieutenant in business matters. Bok filled this post somewhat reluctantly. Part of his responsibility involved occasionally soliciting advertising for the Curtis magazines or checking advertisements sent out by the *Journal* or *Post*. Usually, he wanted nothing to do with conducting the *Journal*'s business affairs.[34]

Although Bok had to solicit advertising in Curtis' absence, he quietly attempted to withdraw on Curtis' return. But agents and customers continued calling on him to finish their particular negotiations. Apparently he was reluctant to tell these clients to work with Curtis and stop taking his time. The publisher wrote to his western advertising agent: "I would prefer that Mr. Bok would fight his own battles and if his tact prevents him from expressing himself clearly, I have made up my mind to do so for him so as to prevent as much as possible his ruffling up my nervous system with complaints." Thus Curtis, in an effort to steer clients away from discussions with Bok, often advised them that Bok knew no more about advertising than an office boy.[35]

After he retired, Bok fondly remembered writing advertising copy about *Journal* articles. Certainly he might have written some advertisements, but it is unlikely that he wrote many. Curtis said, probably a bit more accurately, that *he* wrote the advertising copy. Company records reveal Curtis' references to writing some advertisements but no evidence to support Bok's statement.[36] In fact, records only testify to Bok's annoyance when he was in any way associated with the business of *Journal* advertising.

Bok was, however, consistently interested in the quality and craftsmanship of advertising. In 1923, four years after he had retired from the *Journal,* Bok endowed an advertising award to be administered by the Harvard University Graduate School of Business Administration.* In announcing the endowment, Bok said that he wanted advertising to improve through the correct use of English, more economy in language, higher standards in art and typography, and a meaningful relationship between the advertisement and a company's plan for production and distribution. The billion-dollar-plus industry practiced "so little originality and advancement of standards" that something had to be done to fight the annihilation of quality by the sheer weight of quantity. Displays in the competition were judged on design and tastefulness. Because sales results from the publication of winning advertisements were not counted, advertising men criticized the award

---

*The award was discontinued in 1930 when its endowment was exhausted.

program for being irrelevant and not in the best interests of the advertising industry.[37]

Bok's most important innovation for advertising in mass journalism was the profitable practice of mixing advertisements among editorial pages. Formerly the advertising was relegated to pages in the front and back of the magazine, and feature articles and editorials were self-contained in the middle. With the new format, however, articles were continued in the back pages, where the reader could not avoid noticing the advertisements. Bok said that he invented the practice in 1896. His correspondence, however, shows the accidental nature of this invention and indicates that he was initially reluctant, on aesthetic grounds, to use this method.* All misgivings aside, Bok quickly became aware of the commercial value of this practice.[38]

The editor's chief contribution to the *Journal's* advertising fortunes was his frequent justification of the slick advertisements that the *Journal* carried in ever greater numbers. Not only did the advertisements make the magazine attractive, he wrote, they also enabled literary and artistic excellence to thrive by supplying funds otherwise unavailable.[39] And he urged *Journal* readers to patronize the advertised products. In 1898, Bok reinforced his views on the benefits of advertising to readers by assuring them that the *Journal* carefully maintained the proportion of advertising linage to the amount of reading matter in any issue. "The more advertising there is," he said, "the more reading matter there is, and twice over."[40]

---

*President Harrison's article exceeded his word limit and Bok decided "to carry some of the latter portion of the article to the back of the magazine. This," he wrote, "is not a good way of 'making up' a magazine, but I would rather do it than lose anything you have said in the paper" (Bok to Benjamin Harrison, September 11, 1895, in Benjamin Harrison Papers, Manuscripts Division, Library of Congress, and *LHJ*, XXVI (November, 1909), 1).

In 1901 Bok bluntly told his readers that "a magazine is purely a business proposition. It is published to earn money for its owners. . . . As he [the editor] succeeds or fails in this [getting subscriptions], the magazine secures or fails of an advertising patronage." Ten years later he told readers that without advertisements no magazine could exist. He also undoubtedly helped the advertising income of the *Journal* by quoting letters from readers who reported how useful and reliable they had found the *Journal* advertising pages to be.[41]

The editor did, however, discriminate. Advertising was not always suitable, especially if it seemed to be at odds with important values. Bok always carefully avoided collusion between advertising and editorial copy in the *Journal.* He said at the 1915 Advertising Conference that it was inadvisable for the editorial department to supply readers with names of dealers carrying advertised products because "it would harness the Editorial Department too closely to the advertising." Bok refused to permit any advertising in a series of pamphlets published by the *Journal* because he feared that advertising might be inappropriate to the subject.[42]

Cyrus Curtis inadvertently summed up Bok's ideas on advertising when he visited Bok's public bird sanctuary in Lake Wales, Florida, in the 1920s. Curtis noticed two parking lots, one large and one small. He said to his companion, "How typical of Bok to provide one lot for the subscribers and one for the advertisers."[43] But Curtis certainly understood that Bok, though he carefully guarded his readers, acknowledged the importance of advertising and in many ways assisted the advertisers. Bok found no reasons to jumble the interests of subscriber and advertiser; each enjoyed his own niche, and each was forced to respect the foothold of the other.

Bok's muckraking contemporaries and their spiritual heirs have categorically agreed that the "masters of the magazines," were the influential advertisers as well as the "money power," or investment bankers.[44] Upton Sinclair, in his indictment of American journalism, *The Brass Check,* called the Curtis publications a "colossal advertisement-distributing machine." Money, Sinclair wrote, came from the advertisements, and reading matter was only necessary to fill the empty spaces between advertisements. The Curtis editors, he said, forced a contributing author to sacrifice "pretty nearly all his ideals of truth, humanity and progress."[45] No doubt this overall diatribe was stimulated by Sinclair's outrage at the *Saturday Evening Post*'s antilabor position at that time.

Surely, however, Sinclair had not read the *Journal.* If he had, he would have found the following reference to the cunning techniques used by many advertisers. The monthly "Country Contributor" wrote, "I often look at the advertising pictures of modern family circles. There is a smug suggestion of the imitative and conventional about them that makes me sick." It was better, the offended staff member wrote, to remember the old hymn-singing family group than to see the "sophisticated families bearing the hall-marks of fraternities and wearing the badges of 'first-class' society in poor money-mad America." An earlier article by the president of the American Home Economics Association, Ellen H. Richards, urged women to resist the "influence of hypnotic suggestion" in advertising, "the science of creating wants." She asked, was it necessary "to spend so much on eating and drinking, clothes and bric-a-brac? Will not a better investment be made in the line of real social progress, better education, better appreciation of art and music, of Nature and travel?"[46]

Because the *Journal* was the most important single magazine for advertisers of consumer products in the progressive era, it is startling to find within its pages criticism of the industry. A cynic might ask whether the critical appraisals were yet another seduction of the middle-class consumer, making him believe all the more fervently in the claims of legitimate advertising. Nevertheless, as J. R. T. Hughes suggests in his discussion of the multiple motivations guiding Victorian entrepreneurs, other factors besides greed surely must be included in any analysis of an earlier era's businessmen.[47] Certainly it would be hard to find Bok's attitudes about advertising evident in more recent mass magazines.

To be sure, Bok did not regard advertising as the primary purpose of his magazine. Nor did he view it as a necessary evil. His attitude was founded in his unquestioning faith in the American business system. For Bok, advertising made an inexpensive mass magazine possible, and, subject to well-defined controls, advertising could provide an important additional service to his readers.

Underlying Bok's sense of mission and service to his readers and the protection he gave them from the dangers of advertising was his knowledge that most of them were women. And women, in Bok's view, represented the nobler part of the human race, though they were also decidedly limited creatures who needed protection. Ambiguity obscured much of his attitude toward women. His eagerness to idealize women diminished through the long years of his editorship and tended to be replaced by a deep sense of frustration and disappointment in the actions of the women of his generation.

Once, Bok intended to ask Finley Peter Dunne to bring a Mrs. Dooley "into life and fame" as the wife of Dunne's serialized character; she could "hit at some of the girlish foibles of the day." The topics, Bok said, would be "almost endless"— "society, women's clubs, the woman suffrage movement, the Browning and similar social fads."* That series was never

---

*The Browning clubs were societies formed to read and extol the poetry of Robert Browning.

published, but Bok's interest in it revealed some of his characteristic amusement when studying so-called women's interests. Ellery Sedgwick, editor of the *Atlantic*, defended his friend, saying that if Bok "laughed at his readers, it was in a friendly and understanding spirit."[48]

Edward Bok professed to understand the home as an institution, and he assumed that a woman's worth was measured by the quality of her home and homemaking. Her sphere included her husband and children, her books and music. Her very integrity and fulfillment, therefore, had to stem from the home. The ideal American woman lived a simple life and enjoyed quiet delights; otherwise, she was likely to be judged a failure by society or even possibly to become very sick.[49] In a period when much talk centered on women's widening horizons, Bok wrote to one of his contributors, "My idea, you know, is rather to keep women in the home especially as there are enough writers who are trying to take her out of it." His concern was particularly acute because of his belief that the middle-class woman was the hope of the nation and the "steadying influence" in American life.[50]

During Bok's thirty years as editor, the reach of the American home and its mistress expanded to include civic problems. The *Journal* reader from 1889 to 1919 progressed from learning about the art of fine bread baking to agitating for clean prepared baked goods, from reading "literary leaves of gossip" to participating in responsible citizenship programs for immigrant and native alike.*

Bok's views about women were exposed to the erosion of time and change. As he grew older he shed the inflexibility and, perhaps, insecurity of youth and learned to listen to the

---

*Instruction on food preparation was an important part of the *Journal* throughout Bok's editorship, but the magazine's role in household management changed.

needs of a new generation. After a decade of editing, he less often romanticized woman and her all-but-divine mission and began to give broader types of answers to the key questions raised about women in the period from 1900 to 1920: What is woman's role? How can she best fulfill it? How should she be educated? What is her relationship to the community and to the nation?

Woman's chief aim in life, the young Bok had said, was to improve man by the force of her moral power, because she was "better, purer, conscientious and morally stronger." What Bok wanted to see was a "woman of heart," not of theories. Woman's very *progress*, he claimed, depended on the degree to which she remained constant to the old traditional beliefs about her proper role. This contradiction implied that those women who wanted to vote, for instance, threatened their own progress.[51]

By 1894, however, Bok was convinced that women wanted civic education. Readers kept requesting information about the government and its institutions. Bok, therefore, hired Benjamin Harrison to write a series of articles on the national government. Harrison focused on the national and state constitutions. Some months later, Bok urged him to write another series that would provide an "intelligent knowledge of the real basis upon which all government reforms rest." Six years after becoming editor, Bok announced that "one of the healthiest signs of the times" was woman's interest in learning about the United States government. This did not necessarily mean participation in the democratic process, only an eagerness to learn about it.[52]

In the same spirit, Bok condemned the women's clubs if they neglected civic affairs and directed a woman's efforts away from her central tasks in the home. He declared that clubs wasted her time and energy with vapid "cultural" lectures by unknowledgeable members. The clubs would earn their right to exist when they began to examine town problems and tried to accomplish some reforms. He expressed this idea throughout his career, but his emphasis changed from a general criticism and distrust of the club principle to an endorsement of clubs with meaningful aims.[53] The February, 1913, issue of the *Journal* included the opening of "the first official department of the Federation of Women's Clubs." An essay on club organization in the October, 1914, issue stressed that a club's central obligation was to study civic needs.[54]

Despite Bok's apparent speed in accommodating his notions about women to the freer spirit of the times, his magazine stayed for many years on the same plateau addressing civic education for women. Not until 1910 did a major article endorsing women's suffrage appear in the magazine. Before that article by Jane Addams was published, scores of anti-suffrage essays had crowded the *Journal's* pages. Publically proclaiming the *Journal's* neutral position on suffrage until 1912, Bok changed the *Journal's* stand to outright opposition in the March, 1912, issue. He said that much research and study on the question revealed to him that women were not ready for the vote.[55]

Bok's arguments against suffrage were familiar to his readers because they had read them in the *Journal* all along. Some opponents of suffrage argued in the *Journal* that the issue ought to be additional limits to suffrage for men, based on property and intelligence. Others, including Bok, examined the effects of women's votes in the western states and decided that women and society gained nothing from women's suffrage. Despite the western women's votes, the areas that Bok said belonged to women's instinctive concerns showed no appreciable reform. Those areas, which focused on the protection of life (in contrast to man's instinctive protection of property), included such problems as venereal disease and the saloon and marriage laws. Holding another view, Ida Tarbell wrote in a *Journal* article that she feared women's energies would be misdirected if they voted; they would forsake civic affairs for political activities. [56]

By 1912 Bok had slowly accepted the arguments about woman's expanding role, as publicized by many Progressives, notably Jane Addams. For, as Aileen Kraditor pointed out in her study, there was in this period a basic change in the arguments for suffrage. No longer did suffrage promoters argue from the vantage of justice, but expediency. They maintained that women were in a better position than men to evaluate some political issues. The new approach stressed a woman's responsibility to her household. The main reason for a woman to engage in her community's civic life was to protect that very household. [57]

Kraditor considered Jane Addams' *Journal* article, "Why Women Should Vote," to be the "ideal expression of the new philosophy." Three years later, at the Curtis Company's 1913 Advertising Conference, Bok spoke about his new view of woman's role and fully reinforced the progressive idea of government as "enlarged housekeeping." He said, "Those questions which hitherto we have considered as outside of the home, have, by this evolution of public interest become really attached to the home." He then explained that he had recently hired Jane Addams to join the *Journal* staff and to enlighten his readers about social service. In a laconic aside, Bok said that the editors endorsed much of her work; however, "the probability is that now that she sees the chance [to discuss social issues], she will not touch women suffrage." [58] By 1913, of course, the *Journal*'s official stand was against women's suffrage, and the debate was temporarily closed.

Within a few years, women's suffrage was being taken for

granted by some *Journal* contributors. Also, the new burdens that the world war had placed on women contributed in great measure to their courage in speaking up for their political rights.[59] Even Bok admitted in an editorial that women should enjoy a rightful voice in any parliamentary body, if men knew little about a subject. Well in advance of the 1916 election, Karl Harriman, Bok's managing editor, tried to enlist President Wilson to write an article explaining the Democratic party's platform to women. Harriman said that the *Journal* "could do nothing better in the way of serving the vast number of those women [the four million women voters in 1916]" than to publish such an article.[60] Wilson, however, refused the request.

In the next few years, frequent articles in the *Journal* described women's expanding horizons in employment and education.[61] Bok's own ideas about women's work outside the home had significantly changed three times in a period of fifteen years. In 1901, he had argued that married women were mistaken to work outside their homes. Only "superlatively clever" women, he said, could successfully perform both jobs. He also said that the number of businesswomen had decreased because "you can't make a nightingale do the work of a horse." In 1907 he said that nervous conditions afflicted women who tried to do more than they should in suffrage and reform work. Little more than three years later, however, in 1911, Bok began to write editorials describing employment opportunities for which women were eminently suited.[62] Of course, articles on vocations for women were hardly unusual in the *Journal,* but Bok began to add special emphasis to this favorite topic by referring in a positive tone to women employed as ministers' assistants and trained social workers. In 1912, he enthusiastically described another job, the visiting housekeeper, as appropriate for women. Bok's third change was evident three years later when he called editorially for a "community mother" to give some freedom to women with children.[63] In the same year he announced that he was considering a special *Journal* department devoted to the needs of businesswomen, because their ranks were so rapidly growing.

By 1915, then, Bok gave guarded support to an enlarged role for women, but faint echoes of his earlier ideas could occasionally be heard in his editorials. In April, 1916, he asked his readers just how many of them would exercise their privilege to vote; some months after that, he explained the success of one woman by writing that she had no interests outside her home to consume her energy or time. Basically, however, Bok's new view about women did not change. He wrote in a 1915 editorial, "There has been too much in the mind of the American man, in connection with his woman-kind, of the doll idea instead of the live-woman idea—a being full of latent possibilities, which, as he did not help to develop, is now trying to develop according to her own ideas."[64]

Bok's ideas about women and their place in American society may have handicapped the results of his own reform campaigns. These notions helped to mold a *Journal* audience that may have excluded potential leaders and activists and instead closed ranks with the more conventional-minded women. In one instance, woman's club supporters, annoyed by his position against the clubs, tried to wage economic warfare against Bok and the *Journal* by organizing a boycott of *Journal* sales. Bok prevented this action by threatening to bring suit under the provisions of the Sherman Act of 1890.[65]

Bok's very caution may have influenced the conservative women in his audience to listen attentively to his reform counsel. Because he was sensitive to this kind of audience, he had to be more cautious about how he presented his reform programs. His audience was not likely to have built-in readiness to accept new and sometimes startling ideas. Just at the prelude to the *Journal*'s agitation against patent medicines, which began in 1903, Bok published three articles, all of which reinforced a limited role for women. First, an unidentified author wrote in the April, 1900, issue about the involvement of women in reform efforts since the Civil War. The writer urged women to stop busy work and social climbing in their reform activities and, instead, return to their homes. About one year later, the same author wrote another article decrying the lack of large families among woman reformers and professionals. As an added fillip, the reader was referred to census statistics on the decreasing numbers born "in the Northern States of white children of American birth." And there could be little respectful argument with James Cardinal Gibbons' article published in the January, 1902, *Journal*, in which the prelate told all American women to model themselves on Mary, the mother of Christ. In their zeal for "prerogatives," he said, women's rights supporters omitted mentioning women's duties and obligations.[66]

Throughout these years, the *Journal*'s anonymous "Country Contributor" included such pronouncements in her crackerbarrel commentary as the fact that reading was "dissipation." In fact, Bok's major interest in women's education centered on the need for studying the domestic sciences. A few years later, however, in 1908, Bok described the typical *Journal* reader in a letter as the woman who *does* things.[67] Perhaps his ideas changed in response to the efforts of his readers in the patent-medicine agitation and the saving of Niagara Falls from power exploiters.

By fighting the current of women's rights, the editor placed into jeopardy not only his reform activities but his magazine's circulation. As he said at the 1913 Advertising Conference, "I can turn the Journal to-morrow in favor of woman's suffrage and probably gain 100,000 subscribers by doing it." But that kind of tactic, he said, was "the line of least resistance," which other magazines, not the *Journal,* could practice. Bok said, "We find the line that we think is absolutely honest, and then go ahead on it." [68] Because that honest policy was often profitable for the *Journal,* there was no reason to undermine its integrity of purpose.

In the early years of his *Journal* career, Bok had been a cautious editor. He immediately rejected any manuscript that might cause controversy. With advancing years his courage grew so that his convictions became ever more inseparable from the contents of the *Journal.* Young Bok once refused to publish an article on superstitions because he did not want to increase the burden on his conscience by "adding the discomforts and unhappiness of a few hundred of our readers." [69] But in social issues that mattered, such as sex education and the dangers in patent medicines, he defied hostile public opinion for the sake of truth as he saw it.

Bok's editorial career demonstrated his wisdom in knowing when to make unimportant concessions to advertiser and reader to gain their support on important issues. He obviously could take few gambles with his readers' wishes, because advertising income was dependent on circulation growth. Through his exceptional editorial talent, Bok was able to marry the interests of readers and advertisers. To fulfill the social and commercial objectives of his magazine, he could not afford to misunderstand the needs of either group.* His attempts to understand the changing position of women,

---

*It should be noted that not only women read the *Journal.* The magazine was "third in the official War Department list of the most desired American periodicals" by servicemen in World War I (Edward Bok, *The Americanization of Edward Bok* (New York: Pocket Books, 1965), 283).

however, were much more troublesome for him than his acute evaluation of the direction and character of periodical advertising.

All the while, Bok upheld high standards for both editorial and advertising copy in the *Journal.* His innovative leadership helped advertising to become an accepted feature of the mass magazine. He used honest, efficient editorial procedures that were as characteristic of his values as they were consistent with the demands of a successful mass magazine.

Bok succeeded in convincing his readers that everything published in the *Ladies' Home Journal* was trustworthy. He then used the opportunities created by his relationship with his readers to help raise the standard and quality of life in the United States through limited reform efforts.

IV ❦ Passageways to Beautiful America

One of Bok's favorite family sayings was the advice his grandmother gave to her sons: "Make you the world a bit more beautiful and better because you have been in it."[1] An heir to this charge, Bok used his *Journal* editorship to work toward a better American society. But his contribution clearly centered on helping middle-class Americans enjoy a more attractive life in the United States. According to the journalist Mark Sullivan, Bok claimed that "the way to lead women to appreciation of beauty was not to print an essay by Ruskin but to tell them how many packages of flower-seeds you can buy for fifteen cents, and print a diagram of how to plant them."[2] This suggests the inherent superficiality of Bok's objectives.

The weight of his chosen responsibility as steward became even heavier with each of his insights into the needs and limitations of his audience. Essentially, his editorial actions seemed to stem from the premise that he best served his readers by offering them a vision. In fact, he had to give them an image of a better society before he could expect them, especially his more passive readers, to make any active and positive response to change. The editor once said that the average American lacked the "imaginative quality: our age is too commercial: our conditions too material: we accept things as either real or unreal."[3] He considered it his job to inspire his all too unimaginative audience.

Bok reinforced the idea of the *Journal* as a pulpit throughout his editorial career. In fact, Cyrus Curtis apologetically defended the *Journal*'s inclusion of etiquette advice by saying that not only should women know "these little things" but "we feel the necessity of something besides preaching all the time."[4] Preaching was, however, a characteristic voice for the magazine. The *Journal*'s first editor, Louisa Knapp Curtis, told Bok a month before her death in 1910 that he had "kept the faith" of the service objectives she created for the *Journal*—"to make work easier, to make outlooks broader, lives more complete or hearts lighter." The publisher, too, underscored the fact that everything printed in the *Journal* had to fulfill these objectives. This reassurance, of course, pleased Bok very much. At the end of his editorship he could claim that even the entertaining features in the *Journal* might properly be construed as part of its services.[5]

Bok explained to his readers that the main job of the magazine was not so much to attack the "evils of the day" as to awaken readers to the "tremendous influence of personal power" in correcting these evils. Although Bok tried to elicit a personal response to his campaigns by soliciting letters from his readers to their congressmen and senators and, of course, by urging intelligent buying in the consumer market, most advertisers did not regard the *Journal* as a crusader but as a "friend of the family," welcomed into American homes every month.[6]

Because so many different subjects came under the heading of service to readers, the main reform focus of the *Journal* was clouded. The impact of Bok's major campaigns—patent medicine and sex education, for example—was often dissipated by his equal attention to many lesser reforms. More

radical contemporaries often ridiculed him for editorially pur-
suing such innocuous threats as the public drinking cup and
the plush draperies in Pullmans. And though Bok had no
desire to upset the general order of American society, he did
acknowledge the impelling necessity for change. In one editorial before World War I, he wrote, "The causes for which men
and women have to fight today are not as spectacular as those
in times of war, but they are none the less important. They
have to do with immigration and housing problems, with high
prices, with the social evil, with fairness to the employed as
well as to the employer."[7]

Although the magazine was edited for the middle classes,
Bok increasingly instructed his audience to be more sensitive
to the needs and trials of less privileged Americans. He counseled against charities that avoided responding to basic needs
of the unfortunate. In other words, he advised women not to
teach fancy embroidery to farm girls, who needed instruction
in more fundamental crafts. Throughout his career, Bok urged
his readers to avoid either sympathy or criticism when working
with the poor; tact was imperative. Moreover, his idea of
charity meant helping a man to help himself.[8]

Bok wrote several editorials on the need to consider the
feelings and health of working-class girls. He suggested that
the true character of a woman was revealed in her manner
toward a waitress. Bok was alarmed at reports that women
demanded standing shop clerks to serve them while they com-
fortably sat examining wares, even though they knew this
practice was physically exhausting to the clerks. He publicly
deplored the thoughtlessness of travelers who mislaid items in
hotels and immediately cried thief to the management. Did
they not realize, a contributor asked, that a chambermaid
speedily lost her job upon being accused, whether she was
guilty or not.[9]

Bok was most outspoken about the hasty, severe judgments made by the middle class on the habits and values of the poorer classes; yet he offered few alternatives to working-class behavior patterns. One of his editorials sympathized with the girl who loitered in amusement parks and on street corners:

> Have we given her a place where she can sing and dance and have a good time under safe and good conditions? "Is that exactly for us to do?" we ask. Perhaps, or perhaps not: It depends on how we look at our fellow kind. But one thing is certain: So long as we who can do not provide for those who cannot provide for themselves, have we a right to criticise [*sic*] a girl if she uses the only places she has: the street corners, the park seats, the railroad stations, the amusement parks, to meet her kind and try to have a good time? If we do not choose to help this girl let us, at least, desist from criticising her.[10]

Clearly this editorial suggested no social meeting between various classes or a desire to lift the working-class girl into the middle class. It was simply a call for a pinch of understanding. Bok's interest in the working girl had grown from curiosity about her to a sensitivity toward her feelings. In 1898 and 1899, for instance, he planned some articles on mill and factory girls. He was searching for an impartial account, not sensational stories, wrote his managing editor. Bok urged the writers to describe the daily life of a typical working girl, and Alexander told them, "If there is more brightness than darkness, so much the better."[11] A decade later, Bok was no longer reluctant to discuss the gloomier sides of working-class life.

In 1913 Bok urged a rethinking of the entire "servant question." Editorially he advocated standardization of wages, non-live-in help, and regulation of hours. Here, he was certainly offering a hand to domestic servants that would help lift them at least into the substratum of middle-class life, where they would be able to enjoy a private life apart from their work. In addition, Bok advocated better living conditions for live-in domestic help.[12] To that end, he ordered architects to include changes such as cross-ventilation in servants' quarters in blueprints for *Journal* houses.* The barriers between many groups of Americans were formidable. The *Journal* was not trying to break them down; it merely hoped to inspire more tolerance between people of different backgrounds.

Two groups of Americans had special roles to play in serving as carriers of Bok's vision and his hopes for a beautiful America—churchmen and farm people. He hoped that the Church could serve as the cutting edge for many social issues, but it too was ridden with old prejudices. Before the Church could fulfill her mission of meaningful salvation to everyman, a fresh wind had to clear away some cobwebs of trivia, waste, and pride.

Bok was dismayed at the vast amount of social exclusiveness in churches, the very places where presumably the Gospel triumphed over all artificial barriers. "Respectability," he said, had replaced religion.[13] To demonstrate the extent of parishioners' coldness to newcomers, particularly those strangers wearing "very plain clothes" and having no social introductions, Bok hired a writer to visit churches throughout the United States and to note the treatment she received. The most common finding of the researcher was that she was ignored by ushers and members of the congregation. Occasionally she was seated in obscure parts of the church where she could neither see nor be seen.

Bok, however, continued to endorse the idea that the Church should be bringing all classes of men together in significant ways.[14] After he had examined the thoughtlessness of church members and their frequent lack of concern for any

---

*The plans for *Journal* houses were sold at nominal sums to readers.

society outside their own corner, the *Journal* increasingly emphasized the Church's responsibilities both in goals and methods. Bok included several articles by ministers who affirmed the social gospel. Regarding his concept of the minister's job, a clergyman wrote that the cleric was one with the prophet who had to push his disciples into confronting the social issues of their day. In a wartime editorial, Bok called for the elimination of fairs and bazaars from the parish church calendars. During that tragic time, secular pastimes certainly were out of place in the Church. One minister reinforced Bok's editorial little more than one year. later by urging the Church to be relevant in a war-clouded world.[15]

Besides emphasizing the mission of the Church, which he said had to save bodies and minds as well as souls, Bok urged the Church to apply new developments in business and communications for the sake of its meaningful survival. He envisioned the pastor of the future as "a businessman, familiar with business temptations and equipped for fighting the devil on his own ground." This wartime thought was many times removed from a *Journal* contributor's emphatic statement in 1899 that church and business interests did not jibe. In that same article, Charles Sheldon stressed that the successful businessman often was not Christian in his actions.[16]

In less than two decades, however, confidence in the businessman's positive contributions to American life was evident in *Journal* commentary and reflected the popular rhetoric of the day. Various churchmen wrote about the need for bringing successful business techniques into the service of the Church. A few writers argued that because advertising was so essential to successful business practice, the Church too should advertise. Generally, Bok believed that a little more pep, punch, and efficiency in the life of the Church would only do good. One writer used the words "a businessman for God" to explain his feeling that it was the minister's actions that counted, not his preaching.[17]

Since the Church's prestige was at stake, Bok was anxious to revive the formerly important position of the minister in the community. He wrote several editorials urging realistic salaries for ministers and pointing out that business firms were much more generous with their employees.[18]

The Church's job was to render its service in the most efficient way possible and to become a socially useful institution. For this reason there was no justification for two half-filled churches to exist side by side. Often, old arguments had split a congregation into two or more seceding factions, but Bok said that devout women ought not to have such "long memories."[19] Therefore, he urged that one half-empty church be turned into a community library or used for some other good purpose. He had little patience with the roots of any purported theological controversy.

The other carrier of the editor's vision of a beautiful America was the farmer, who expressed Bok's hopes through the life he lived in the rural reaches of the United States. Bok, like all Progressives, looked nostalgically to the past, which represented the farm and the rural values that in many respects matched his own traditional values. Yet he had a tendency to deprecate the waste and hardships of the farm at the same time that he idealized rural life. This attitude was reconciled in an idealization of suburban living as the best and happiest hope for every American.

In all of Bok's commentaries on places where the good life could be lived most successfully, there emerged three viable options: the small city, the suburban community, and the efficient farm. The farm was still the hope of America and promised to continue providing the "great brain power of the country." The farm voice would save the nation from "so-

cialistic anarchistic revolution." One *Journal* article explained
that a child raised on a farm received untold benefits because
he was tended by his own mother, unlike the middle-class city
child, who was often cared for by a nurse. The article further
suggested that this advantage might give credence to the belief
that "some of our best and noblest public men have been
country born and bred." The farm could also offer solace to
urban man. Bok suggested that the best vacation was spent on
a farm rather than at a resort hotel. Although the *Journal*
bewailed the abandoned New England farm, it also encouraged its readers to buy those country sites and use them to
enjoy healthful holidays.[20]

Journal fiction reinforced the positive values of farm life.
Since Bok was eager to publish views of the way life should be,
not the way life was, he wrote to one author that he wished
she "had made the country girl come out victorious in the
story, instead of the young lady from the city; but perhaps, as
you say, it will do no harm to reverse things for once." At
another time, he requested a story "depicting that type of the
farmer's woman, who is everlastingly baking herself to death,
whereas she could easily afford to have outside help, and her
family might do with much less on the table."

Certainly the farmer's wife needed advice on how to make
her work more manageable. But the tone used for counseling
farmers was gentler than that used for town readers. On the
magazine's puzzle-of-errors page, designed to entertain and in-
struct, Bok strongly objected to a drawing submitted by the
artist Grant E. Hamilton. It showed a man with a napkin bib,
and Bok thought this would antagonize his rural readers.[21]

Bok was concerned about easing those rural conditions that
imposed hardships, especially on farm women. Beginning in
1894 the *Journal* frequently advised farm women on all aspects
of more efficient rural life. One series aimed to lighten the

farm woman's burdens by outlining basic health care in diet and ventilation, advising on how to avoid the malady of "early aging," and stressing the need for mental stimulation. [22]

Certainly this service to farm women was in keeping with overall *Journal* objectives. But, because the farmer was buying more in the growing American consumer market, the *Journal* had further reason to bring him actively into the purview of advertisers. In 1905, *Printers' Ink* quoted Frank Long, the president of an advertising agency for agricultural publicity, who said, "One of the best mediums for certain kinds of agricultural advertising is not a farm paper at all, but a general magazine—the *Saturday Evening Post.*" He noted that the *Journal* had "an extensive small town circulation and also goes to the farms." [23]

The number and character of the *Journal*'s rural readership was, however, debatable. In 1910, one farm paper editor surveyed his audience and found that of 3,456 readers who replied, only 54 said they read the *Journal.* [24] Two years later, however, Bok announced his plans for adding a full-fledged farm department to the *Journal*. He said that the action was warranted because the *Journal* offices had "had a great many letters due to the change of conditions on the farm." [25] In the Curtis Company's studies of the farm market, analysts identified some 5 to 10 percent of all farm families as "leadership" farmers. Their families belonged to the county farm bureaus and read not only the farm journals but also "all those periodicals in which they have confidence." Just before the First World War more than half of all Americans lived either in small towns or on farms. Consequently, the *Journal*'s rather wide distribution in urban and rural communities is indicative of its general appeal, unshared by the *Post*, which drew its greatest number of readers from cities, or the *Country Gentleman*, which attracted a more rural audience. [26]

Along with the *Journal*'s success in attracting a broadly based audience was the growing acceptance by the rural population of urban middle-class values. Rural buyers no longer accepted any out-of-fashion styles rejected by city shoppers. By 1918 it was clear to market analysts that farmers "have automobiles and want the same kind of merchandise as the city people."[27] However, the farmer could not be influenced as easily as the city man by the barrage of advertising media. The analysts claimed that the farmer remained more of an individualist than his urban brother because he did not read the newspapers three times a day. But rural isolation and individualism was disappearing as the telephone, automobile, and newspaper became more a part of the farmer's life.[28]

Bok maintained that the suburban community promised to meet most effectively the future needs of many urban Americans, because it combined the virtues of town and country. Next to the suburb, Bok said, the small city promised "the surest chances for business success and for domestic happiness." Bok wrote to Benjamin Harrison, who was interested in the ideal city, that he wanted "young men to seek cities like Indianapolis, Detroit, Minneapolis, Buffalo &c and keep them away from such hotbeds of strife as New York, Chicago, &c."[29] Bok's idealization of farm life was characteristic of urban people at the turn of the century and certainly formed the basis of many of his ideas about church and farm in a potentially beautiful America.

Bok had misgivings about the general quality of rural life, but he consistently maintained, along with many of his progressive contemporaries, that the last, best hope of democratic America would be found on her farms. Although Bok argued that the future happiness of the farmer depended on the degree to which he enjoyed a middle-class, urban standard of living, he was quick to criticize city people's snobbishness and foolish misconceptions about the quality of small-town life. He liked to say that if he had a chance to give people the opportunity to travel, he would select citizens from big cities.[30]

Just as modernizing influences were revitalizing the character of church and farm and leading to greater efficiency and productiveness, Bok was convinced that formal education had to weigh the power of the present as much as the past in its curriculum. Most of his hopes for a beautiful America rested on major reforms in education. Many salutary practices such as temperance and healthful diets would be inevitable end products of a successful educational experience for Americans.

Bok's first public interest in education was mainly evident in his magazine's editorials and articles on the need for curriculum changes in the schools. For several years the *Journal* advocated a child-centered school in which children would be allowed to learn at their own pace without any "pushing" from parent or teacher. Not only would better learning result, but fainting from nervous exhaustion—a common malady of the day, it seems—would be eliminated for teacher and pupil. Bok included an essay on the Batavia, New York, experiment, which illustrated the good results of no home study and a classroom situation in which two teachers, one of whom assisted the slow learners, were in constant attendance. Theodore Roosevelt also endorsed the *Journal*'s ideas on elementary education. In his *Journal* column the president urged giving schoolchildren a chance to play as earnestly as they studied.[31]

Another of Bok's interests was publishing essays on new techniques in education and information about some pioneers in the profession. Articles occasionally appeared on the value of field trips, kindergartens, the Montessori method, and various experimental attempts to improve the quality of education.[32] The *Journal*'s writers endorsed such innovations in education as small classes, language studies in early school years, no homework, no grades, and "fresh-air" programs.

In addition to presenting these ideas of education reform, Bok engaged his magazine for a little over a year in an intensive campaign challenging the very basis of American public education. A spirited series of articles in the *Journal*, provocatively entitled "Is Our Public-School System a Failure?," left Bok with few friends in professional education circles. The editor was convinced that the public school was not giving its best to American children; rote learning outweighed critical thinking. At that time few pupils continued their studies into preparatory or high school levels, and fewer still attended colleges or universities. For this reason, Bok held that it was wasteful and unkind to educate all children in the same way, that is, with studies leading to the traditional academic disciplines. He called for a specialized education relevant to the needs of a particular child in a specific place and time. He was alarmed that many high school students could identify the heroes of antiquity, while few had any knowledge of newsmaking contemporary figures. In one example, candidates for admission to San Francisco State Normal School in 1912, when asked to identify Gifford Pinchot, Charles Darwin, Booker T. Washington, Robert La Follette, Jane Addams, and Samuel Gompers, failed markedly, though they recognized the names of Cassius, Queen Elizabeth, and Hamlet. Bok's general ideas on education echoed his view on the desirability of a special education for women, to teach them what would be most useful. Of course this meant the study of household economics in addition to studies in language, history, the arts, and mathematics.[33]

The *Journal* offered its readers little help, however, toward ways to achieve these ends in education. How politics affected the character of public education was hardly examined at all.

An early article only mentioned the unwiseness of depending on school boards to choose teachers. Men on the boards, Bok reported, occasionally were such blackguards that honest men refused to enter business contracts with them.[34]

Bok was prepared for attacks from those who he said had an interest in maintaining the American public school system without any changes, and during the early months of his criticisms, the *Journal of the National Education Association* accused him of misusing statistical evidence. After publishing several articles disputing Bok's statistics, it finally attacked him on ideological grounds, warning against overemphasis on vocational education.[35]

Bok told Curtis advertisers in 1913 that some educators charged him with having biased educational reform interests because he was a Roman Catholic and, therefore, presumably opposed to public education. He was not a Roman Catholic, and certainly all Roman Catholics were not opposed to public education. Bok did have faith in the potential of public schools, but he said that public education was not "educating the boys and girls in practical living." He explained that the *Journal's* year-long series analyzed defects but also contained a constructive group of articles describing successful public school experiences. The series was not published "just for the fun of attacking the public schools," for that would pointlessly offend people.[36]

Another program for a beautiful America was the *Journal's* participation in the temperance movement. To many Progressives the hope of a temperance victory promised great rewards in national health and productivity. Bok led the *Journal* on an uneven temperance course; he did, however, consistently endorse two ideas. First, to be successful, temperance had to be a personal decision based on education; it should not have to be legislated. Second, abstinence from alcohol held no inherent evil and there could be no arguments against that. [37] Bok went on record rather cautiously as a supporter of total abstinence, if the alternative was drinking to excess. Bok urged young men to ask, "Is it wise rather than is it wrong?", before they imbibed alcohol. In the same way, he deliberately avoided commenting on any moral aspects of the question when he suggested to his *Journal* readers that good taste limited the number of wines served at women's luncheons. He also said that little wine was actually drunk at these luncheons, and what remained ("the show of glasses") was pretentious. [38]

Over a twenty-year span, Bok's editorials reinforced his ideas about temperance. He enjoyed explaining that alcohol consumption was declining and that many businesses closed their career doors to imbibers. Prohibition, from the *Journal's* view, promised significant gains for the American business community. [39] Merchants would find more business because workingmen would not squander their wages on drink, and gainful employment would be found by everyone who formerly worked in the liquor trade.

Implicit in Bok's argument was the notion that when the middle classes understood the value of temperance, they would adjust their lives accordingly. After all, he said, moderation in all things marked the sensible man. For the lower classes, something more in the way of inducement was necessary. One point repeated by Bok many times was that the workingman had no social gathering place except the local tavern. If enacted, prohibition would destroy the one congenial spot the laborer enjoyed at the end of his workday. Before prohibition could be successful, a community had to provide a substitute for the tavern. In one editorial Bok offered an additional reason why men frequented saloons—too many of their wives were incompetent cooks! [40]

Bok's later editorials and his contributors' articles on temperance usually omitted some of the key issues raised by the opponents of prohibition. Only once did Bok mention that some intelligent people were opposed to prohibition because they feared a loss in personal liberty. Soon after that article was published, he included an article by William Howard Taft in which the chief justice attempted to prove that prohibition was not a violation of personal liberty. [41] By the time of the Volstead Act, the *Journal* was ready to help legislate a new morality, in spite of Bok's earlier misgivings.

The health of Americans was a favorite subject for Bok to explore in the *Journal*. Whether it was interest in physical fitness, fresh air, proper diet, germ-free travel, clean milk and bread, or poisons in medicines and foods, he led a vigorous campaign. Bok struggled against the common drinking cup in public places and wanted to suppress the common Communion cup in Protestant churches. Before long, many denominations had changed to the practice of individual miniature cups for communicants. Bok's publicity against the use of germ-ridden feather dusters and the plush in Pullman car draperies became well known. He even wanted a germ counter to be invented and placed in each room of every house. The editor's language was more moderate ten years later, when he simply called for a gadget that would tell when the air in a room needed changing. [42]

One of Bok's long-standing concerns about the health of the nation was his interest in banning the sale of fireworks. The foolishness of explosive Fourth of July celebrations too often led to lockjaw and the maiming of children. Consequently, he tried to outline the multiple dangers of fireworks in children's hands and to show citizens how they could prevent the tragedies of mutilation and death. He urged the enactment of town ordinances forbidding the sale of private fireworks. [43]

After town and countryside had been enlightened about the

need for change and better education, and after temperance and good health had become commonplace, the nation was ready for the specific targets of a "Beautiful America" campaign. The job of obliterating urban ugliness, said Bok, was not to be left to politicians but given to the craftsmen, the technically able. Here the editor was in accord with dominant progressive thought, which favored technology over politics for achieving improvements. *Journal* emphasis, however, was mainly on aesthetic technology.

The *Journal's* chief proponent of a beautiful America, J. Horace McFarland, contributed a monthly column that emphasized aesthetics and, therefore, was decidedly outside the mainstream of progressive thought on conservation.[44] Key conservation concerns of the *Journal* reflected the dominance of McFarland's viewpoint. Most Progressives wanted to run roughshod over the preservation of natural beauty whenever resources could be efficiently used to harness power. The *Journal's* aesthetic-minded conservationists successfully rallied reader support to preserve the wild natural beauty of Niagara Falls, and they championed a bill in Congress that prevented further use of the falls by private power companies.* Theodore Roosevelt had asked Bok to prove the seriousness of *Journal* readers' opinions on Niagara Falls by asking them to write their representatives in Congress. Because the readers so roundly responded, Roosevelt ultimately gave *Journal* readers credit for saving the falls.[45]

J. Horace McFarland, a native of Harrisburg, Pennsylvania, an accomplished photographer, and an owner of printing and publicity establishments, had long been active in civic reform. When the American League for Civic Improvement merged

---

*The Beautiful America campaign also prevented advertisers from stretching the world's largest billboard along the rim of the Grand Canyon.

with the American Park and Outdoor Art Association to become in June, 1904, the American Civic Association, McFarland was president. He was a "good fighter," as even his adversary, the conservationist Gifford Pinchot, acknowledged.[46]

In the December, 1903, *Journal,* McFarland started his monthly department, "Beautiful America: Devoted to Beautifying Our Homes and Towns." His first column suggested to "progressive women" that they form Beautiful America clubs and affiliate with the American Civic Association. The aims for the clubs were stated as follows: "Together we will clean up our home grounds; we will move for sightly streets and towns; with one accord we will attack, and I hope demolish, unnecessary advertising signs, and reduce the number of hideous electric poles; we will raise our voices for grass and flowers, instead of ashes and garbage, and insist on play grounds and parks."[47]

Among the campaigns for an aesthetic environment, the *Journal's* attempts to wipe out billboard advertising met some opposition. Bok later wrote that *Journal* advertisers who profitably used billboards protested angrily. Some threatened to withdraw their accounts from the *Journal* if it did not stop the campaign, but no accounts were actually withdrawn.[48]

The first *Journal* editorial on outdoor advertising appeared in July, 1903. In "How Women Can Be Good Americans," Bok said that noisy patriots were of little value to anyone; what the nation needed were women who would put their patriotic sentiments to work and stop the destruction of national beauty by opposing outdoor advertising, particularly that form of it which defaced farm buildings.[49]

In the "Beautiful America" column, elimination of the billboard continued to be one of McFarland's key interests. After a few years, however, Bok urged a new emphasis. In his autobiography Bok claimed that he "had started the first serious agitation" against outdoor advertising that threatened the beauty of the landscape. Notwithstanding his claim, enough antibillboard agitators had won local victories to draw coun-teractions from billposter associations and attacks from adver-tising trade papers like *Printers' Ink*. [50]

Although experts at *Printers' Ink* ranked outdoor advertis-ing last in importance for the general advertiser, they called it one of the trunk lines of advertising media. Consequently, trade journals continued to promote the value of billboard advertising. *Profitable Advertising* admitted that billboards oc-casionally were mishandled aesthetically but that this factor did not warrant legal restrictions in size or location. [51]

Although local civic groups often endorsed limitations on billboards in placement and size and by taxation, McFarland continued to demand the annihilation of billboards. Bok and McFarland's assaults on the billboard were published in the *Journal* from 1903 to 1905. Their tactics varied little in this period. McFarland urged citizens to use either persuasion or compulsion to rid the nation of the billboard. His slogan was "Organize, educate, act!" *Journal*-sponsored contests encour-aged readers to search their towns for an ugly billboard, photograph it, work locally to secure the bill's removal, and then photograph the billboard-free spot. The reader was to submit the photographs to the *Journal* along with a signed guarantee from the billboard's owner that he would not re-place the billboard. This document was to be countersigned by a "pastor of a church" in the same town. The guarantees were necessary because Bok found some cases of fraud wherein a reader put up a sign, photographed it, took it down, and submitted the photographs to the contest. McFarland suggested to his readers that they look behind the billboards for debris and "thus gain an additional argument for their removal." The *Journal* published the Beautiful America campaign results and in this way gave witness to the dream of a nation without billboards.[52]

At its beginning the *Journal's* antibillboard campaign confronted the problem with contests and frequent references to the subject. In May, 1905, the managing editor wrote McFarland a curious letter about the August "Beautiful America" column. He urged McFarland to "hammer away once more, for the last time, at the bill-board question, repeating the offer of prizes made in July. As this will be the last time the subject will be taken up by us at all, it is important to present the situation as clearly and forcibly as possible."[53] The intensity of the campaign tapered off in the summer of 1905, but the subject was by no means forgotten.* That July, Bok wrote a strongly worded editorial ("What a Country Might be Ours!"), urging each reader to work toward the removal of one billboard. Thereafter, "Beautiful America" stressed other topics and mentioned the ugly billboard only in larger contexts. But the editor occasionally came back to his plea for the abolition of the advertising sign. In his final mention of it, he took a new approach; he tried to shame the farmers who used barn advertising. Such advertisements, he said, only revealed a farmer's low finances and lack of credit.[54] In his first autobiography Bok acknowledged without bitterness that his campaign against billboard advertising had achieved little. But in small ways perhaps it had succeeded, if only to draw attention to the issue.

Scattered among the articles against billboards in the "Beautiful America" columns were instructions to readers on how to make their homes and communities more attractive and healthy. For beautifying streets and roads McFarland of-

---

*The abrupt closing of the official campaign suggests that advertisers might have persuaded Curtis to ask Bok to stop, but there is no evidence to prove this contention.

fered the sound advice to clean them and then plant and properly care for trees. McFarland's columns included a range of subjects: public and private gardens, the protection of wild plants and flowers, the correct care of trees, the elimination of flies and mosquitoes.[55] In subsequent years these topics were analyzed as part of the backdrop of larger problems such as urban ugliness and the hazards of big cities. In one instance, McFarland tried to include too much in a single article. He had planned to rail against telegraph poles in an article on billboards. Through a letter from the managing editor, Bok advised him to omit the pole issue because better results could be obtained if less were attempted at one time.[56]

Despite the apparently genuine concern of Bok and his contributors for almost two decades, their exhortations for civic reform generally lacked the spirit of risk and adventure that marked the *Journal*'s more exciting ventures in patent-medicine and sex education reform. The *Journal*'s "dirty cities" campaign began as an extension of the billboard contest; photographs of before and after scenes, this time of small towns and villages, were solicited. In the beginning no prizes were offered because Bok did not want to follow the billboard contest too closely in design. The same spirit of aesthetic priorities was, however, present.[57]

The *Journal* publicized, and sometimes threatened to publicize, the need to clean up the dirty spots in American towns and cities. This method of *Journal* reform campaigning closely resembled a technique of the muckrakers because it cited the problem areas by name and clearly identified as many miscreants as possible. In the exposé on Wilkes-Barre, Pennsylvania, McFarland wrote: "Those who read these words will probably have no trouble in remembering, close by, worse conditions than those here shown. Other cities will have a place on this page in 1906—unless the nasty spots are cleaned up before we get a camera trained on them. There are smaller cities and villages, too, that ought to be cleaner and neater and better to live in. Must we show their unpleasantness?"[58] *Journal* photographers reached Lynn, Massachusetts, and Atlanta, Memphis, Philadelphia, and Pittsburgh before the citizens got busy and cleaned their dirty urban wounds. The *Journal* also reported the work done by the people of Memphis to clean their city, much to the mayor's delight. Regardless of the thrust-and-parry character of the exposés, many *Journal* readers objected to the campaign, particularly if their local pride was assaulted. Bok answered his critics by saying that the publicity given to urban eyesores was clearly within the province of the *Journal* because it touched the health of the nation.[59]

Essentially the campaign aimed to improve the quality of middle-class life. During this time Bok was reinforcing the Beautiful America theme throughout his editorials on civic improvement and the role women should have in that job, especially women of leisure.[60] The debris of carelessness was unsightly and had to be swept away before it could offend middle-class sensibilities. As Bok said in his first autobiography, the dirty spots were often near business districts, key municipal buildings, or the best residential areas. The problems of slums were beyond the limit that Bok was willing to broach at that time and were not mentioned.

The *Journal*'s Beautiful America theme continued right through Bok's editorship. Articles included essays on conservation, scenic improvement, local and national parks, good roads, private back yards, and sanitation, and even occasional paragraphs on public welfare programs for children.[61] At the very time when the nation was experiencing rapid growth and was subject to the stresses of industrialization and urbanization, Bok was trying to give his readers a vision of an American style of life that was supported mainly by preindustrial values. He did not explain to his readers why America was changing, nor did he ever fashion a consistent program for environmental reform. Conserving the nation's beauty, health, and peaceful countryside, preserving the strengths of community life and democratic society, Bok's Beautiful America program was often more visionary than practical.

There was an ambiguity about Bok's stress on traditional standards and virtues as provided by the Church and farm. Progress, the editor insisted, would have to characterize both the rural life and the Church's functions. The Church had to be infused with new operating methods designed to revitalize the preaching of the good news. This change would attract and keep members by making the Church into a useful and relevant social institution. But could the Church's mission sustain secularization? Bok avoided the question.

Like many of his readers, Bok was a city boy to whom the farm realities meant very little. The farm had to be transformed into a business institution to meet the demands of progress and efficiency. The *Journal*'s advice to farm women was geared, in fact, to help them become more middle class in standards of comfort and material values. To Bok and his urban readers the farm represented an ideal of tradition, hard work, thrift, and wholesome air. In reality, it was a good place to have been born and a fine spot to spend summer holidays.

During the Beautiful America campaign, Bok's talent for attuning himself to his audience was evident in his emphasis on the pragmatic interests of middle-class citizens. First, the issues that were raised directly touched the middle-class. Dirty cities were unhealthy and unattractive places for visitors and workers; billboards ruined the face of the countryside and often concealed germ-ridden garbage heaps. To keep up appearances, to take pride in community and nation, and to avoid sickness—these reasons sustained the *Journal* drive for clean cities and unsightly billboards.

Some hint of the burgeoning new era and a citizen's need to be adequately prepared for it was evident in Bok's interest in education reform. He asked for education to be more concerned with the present and to train young people in critical and analytical thinking, which would enable them to live more effective lives. The *Journal*'s education analysts stressed the fact that the costs of the traditional public school system far exceeded the poor educational value received.

Up to this point Bok's readers assuredly agreed with him. When he chanced to go beyond middle-class self-help and pocketbook objectives in reform and began to focus on the class consciousness of Christians, he was walking on an uncertain path. The editor's own motives for reform were considerably more informed and high-minded than his readers'. But as he told a group of *Journal* advertisers, it was "desirable in effecting reforms that your public be unconscious of the reform purpose"; in fact, he added, "we publish nothing merely for journalistic purpose."[62] As long as Bok's Beautiful America reforms respected his readers' interests and did not push hard against narrow-mindedness, they simply guarded the outward face of middle-class respectability. The *Journal* sex education and patent-medicine campaigns, however, aimed to protect middle-class life and limb.

V ❧ Two Blows Against Ignorance

If the *Journal*'s Beautiful America campaign was ineffective because of its haphazard method and self-defined limitations, the magazine's work in patent medicines and sex education represented a more systematic approach and provided a measurable success. In the Beautiful America campaign, the *Journal* tackled many public issues that its readers were eager to discuss. With patent medicines and sex education, Bok had to combat his readers' deep-seated fears and ignorance; nevertheless, he remained convinced that enlightenment was the key to social reform.

Legacies of the Victorian age, patent medicines and sexual prudery flourished in an atmosphere that repressed physical nature and gave exaggerated emphasis to personal privacy. In Bok's day, sex was a subject not discussed by well-bred women, especially with their children. The undesirable intimacy of consulting a physician often drove women to seek help from mailbox cures, pills, and potions.

The success of the *Journal*'s incursion into its readers' intimate lives revealed that changes were taking place in American society, especially in an urban environment where more doctors were available. Moreover, unwanted pregnancies and venereal diseases were more conspicuous in urban society.

Still, the *Journal* faced great risks in these two campaigns because the magazine confronted not only attitudes about personal privacy but also a major industry.

In nineteenth-century America, the patent-medicine business enjoyed many commercial advantages, even though it lacked a reputation for integrity. A big profit margin came to the nostrum manufacturer because costs of materials and transportation were so low. Brand loyalty was quickly achieved because the taste and effects of an elixir of honey and alcohol were far more dramatic than those of rosewater. Advertising the little bottle, of course, demanded sizable expenditures, and periodicals and billboards were the preferred mediums. *Profitable Advertising,* a respected trade journal, placed the profit motive above every other consideration when it discussed the often-unattractive character of patent-medicine advertising, which used horror techniques to persuade customers.[1] Then, as now, the nostrum manufacturer relied on the willingness of the average person to prescribe a cure for himself. Once that person learned to consult a physician, he relied less often on the promises of patent medicines.

The manufacturers of patent medicines were among the first large-scale users of national advertising, and their advertisements were commonplace in popular magazines of the 1880s and 1890s.[2] It was the *Journal* reader who actually called for an end to the patent-medicine advertisement in her magazine. When Cyrus Curtis discovered that *Journal* readers rejected the health quackery represented by patent medicines, he speedily put an end to their advertising in his magazine. Too, the big-name advertisers did not want the company of patent-medicine advertising.

Why, then, almost fifteen years later, did Bok decide to reopen the subject of dangerous nostrums? Did he want his readers to be the crusaders in their communities and protect women who were not likely to read the *Journal*? Perhaps the most satisfactory resolution of this question rests in the difference between ideal and reality during the period after 1900. Although the *Journal* reader often could afford the advice of a physician, she sometimes bought patent medicines to relieve small ailments such as headaches; furthermore, she was reluctant to seek medical help for her "female troubles."

Bok's methods for effecting change were threefold. First, educating his audience was paramount, as most of his editorials and feature articles illustrate. A couple of years before the *Journal*'s campaign against the nostrum began, Bok told his readers that the *Journal* was unique in not publishing patent-medicine advertisements, "one of the largest sources of income to all the other magazines."[3] Second, the readers received advice on how to eliminate the menace. Third, Bok indicated what governments had to do. In 1907, he published a letter from a *Journal* reader asking why the magazine did not "attack some of the great evils of today like cigarette smoking, drinking, Mormonism, tight-lacing, theatre-going, card-playing" in the same way it had attacked patent medicines. Bok replied that the *Journal*'s real purpose in the patent-medicine episode was not to "attack" nostrums but to counsel against self-prescribed cures. "One lifetime is too short," he said, "to 'attack' the 'evils' here cited: any one of them would call for years of study, investigation and research."[4]

Bok occasionally tried to shock *Journal* readers out of ignorance and naïveté. In one of the first editorials devoted to patent medicines, which also hinted at the Beautiful America campaign, he wrote: "It is a curious fact that... an earnest W.C.T.U. woman had refused to allow an advertisement of a certain beer to be painted on her husband's barns, and then gave her consent to the exploitation of a patent medicine which contained thirty-eight percent more alcohol than did

the beer." He continued: "As one painter of these advertisements remarked to me not many weeks ago: 'It always makes
me smile when I am painting one of our advertisements on the
side of a temperance woman's house. If she only knew what
was in the stuff!'" [5]

Because the *Journal* zealously listed the percentages of alcohol contained in various patent medicines and contrasted
them by the ounce with the percentages in distilled spirits,
wines, and beer, many readers were surprised to learn that
beer had less alcoholic content than some nostrums. This fact
enticed some brewers to claim publicly that the *Journal* approved of beer as a beverage. In asking that the copyright line
be used in reprints of *Journal* material, Bok's managing editor
said, "We intend never to be caught in that way again, and if
any brewers were to use copyrighted matter we should have
good legal ground for proceeding against them." [6]

Bok was anxious to protect the farm women, who often
found it impossible to visit a doctor. [7] After all, he said, those
women were the most loyal *Journal* readers. He also suggested
that women in general were too frequently duped by bogus
cures. The editor once quoted a patent-medicine manufacturer as saying, "Men are 'on' to our game; we don't care a
damn about them. It is the women we are after. . . . We can
make them feel more female troubles in a year than they
would really have if they lived to be a hundred." [8] The *Journal*
also warned that the names of women who wrote to the quack
doctors and described their ailments were often made available to other nostrum purveyors and that the letters were sold
to whoever wanted the contact name. [9] This form of exploitation had always been despised by the *Journal* and the Curtis
Company.

Bok sometimes ferreted out the lies of nostrum manufacturers. In one instance he printed a photograph of the tombstone

of a woman who, according to a manufacturer, was still advising her correspondents about female troubles. In addition, his editorials emphasized that the ingredients in patent medicines were dangerous and often addictive; blindness and other infirmities, even death, occasionally resulted from prolonged use. He publicized the tragedy of infant deaths resulting from "soothing syrups" that unthinking mothers and nurses gave to babies to quiet their crying. The patent medicine was a trap well baited with disguised alcohol, morphine, and opium.[10]

When the *Journal* began its active crusade against the patent medicine, it, like the muckraking magazines, tried to give its readers factual information and thus avoid lawsuits. To this end, the editorial staff was anxious to check out the validity of anything they planned to publish. After a year of writing editorials, Bok decided that his reporters would write the inside stories they had discovered. He hired the young journalist Mark Sullivan to make some investigations, report to him, and publish an article under his own name.[11] Up to that point, Bok had used contributions solicited from other writers, but he recast them into the voice of his editorial persona so that an article appeared to be the *Journal*'s own idea. The hope was that this enabled an article to "carry more weight than it otherwise would."[12]

Undoubtedly the $200,000 lawsuit brought against the Curtis Publishing Company by Dr. V. Mott Pierce had something to do with the decision to diffuse responsibility for the crusading articles. Pierce brought suit against the company because the table of ingredients purportedly analyzing the contents of the Pierce remedy was in error. The *Journal* had carefully checked the analysis through impartial boards of inquiry, but apparently an older compound of Pierce's nostrum had been used and the new formula was different. The managing editor's task was to try to secure other analyses that corresponded with the *Journal*'s. He requested a copy of any analysis that the Illinois State Board of Pharmacy might have performed on "Doctor Pierce's Favorite Prescription." Although the *Journal* lost its case in the courts, the company had to pay only $16,000 in damages. The unfavorable outcome for the *Journal* did not daunt Bok's interest in snaring the purveyors of patent medicines, and Curtis did not try to prevent Bok from continuing his project. Bok simply continued to ask his contributors for accurate facts. [13]

Advertising trade journals angrily denounced the *Journal* attacks on patent-medicine manufacturers. *Profitable Advertising* informed its readers that many "high-grade" magazines refused to publish nostrum advertisements and that the Post Office Department was considering a plan to eliminate some of the advertisements from the mails. It also expressed concern about the repercussions if Dr. Pierce should lose his suit against the *Ladies' Home Journal*. When the *Journal* lost its case, *Profitable Advertising* was jubilant. Referring to Bok's July editorial, "Doctor Pierce's Favorite Prescription—A Retraction," the trade journal chided Bok's editorial carelessness and insinuated that he lacked the "true editorial instinct" that demanded "the up-to-dateness of facts." [14]

A year later, the other leading trade journal, *Printers' Ink*, showed that the *Journal* refused to advertise the Keely cure for drug and alcohol addiction only because "its readers are not supposed to be slaves to either the liquor or drug habit." Compared to the criticisms levied by other trade journals, this explanation of the *Journal*'s battle against the nostrums was unusually kind. Although Bok's contributions to publicizing the dangers of the nostrum were often minimized by later generations, his contemporaries at *Printers' Ink* generally referred to him as a zealous reformer. [15]

Bok extended his publicity campaign against patent

medicines by asking eight medical journals to publish a letter he had written to the *Journal of the American Medical Association*. As his managing editor explained, Bok wanted "the earnest co-operation of the medical profession in the work he had undertaken for the good of the public." Although the American Medical Association had been among the first groups to fight against the nostrum, its journal was at this time still a haven for some proprietary advertising.[16]

Bok expressed his surprise that the religious press also advertised patent medicines. He publicized the curious fact that a distilling company's whiskey ads were banned by a church periodical, though its remedy ads were accepted. One church periodical refused patent-medicine advertising, and Bok singled it out for praise. Bok's critics accused him of distortion and slander, but he cited specific papers, such as the *Christian Advocate* (Methodist), the *Watchman* (Baptist), and the *Christian Endeavor World*, which published nostrum advertisements. He declared that the Episcopal paper, the *Churchman*, "gayly leaps over the fence and prints advertisements of 'Muir's Scotch Ale,' which we are delightedly told is 'a delicious sparkling nut-brown ale that's a feast in itself.'"[17]

In 1906 the *Journal* tried to enlist its readers' support for legislation to curb some of the evils of nostrums. The magazine's February issue published the text of the bill sponsored by Weldon Brinton Heyburn, the Democratic senator from Idaho. It called for the labeling of patent medicines to show alcohol percentages over 8 percent and any presence of dangerous drugs. Readers were asked to cut the text of the proposed bill out of the magazine and send it to their congressional representatives and to check the bill when it was introduced in the legislature for any changes in copy.[18]

At this critical moment in the *Journal*'s patent-medicine campaign, Bok explicitly told his readers about the advertising interests of those newspapers that opposed regulation of patent medicines: "Simply turn from the editorial or news columns of your paper to the advertising columns, and the secret of the newspaper's opposition to this or any other bill of the kind becomes apparent."[19] On assignment for the *Journal*, Mark Sullivan had investigated the influence of patent-medicine advertisers upon the editorial policy of periodicals in which they advertised. The so-called contract of silence between advertiser and newspaper editor called for the voiding of a patent-medicine advertising contract if the newspaper advocated legislation to restrict the sale or manufacture of nostrums.[20] The article was too long for the *Journal* to publish, but Bok encouraged Norman Hapgood of *Collier's* to publish it.

As late as 1911, patent-medicine manufacturers continued to use threats to keep advertising columns open to them. One letter sent to the press by the Advertisers' Protective Association (APA) showed why advertising revenues had fallen in those papers that criticized patent medicines and certain foods. The APA also urged the press to attack Dr. Harvey Wiley and the Department of Agriculture's Bureau of Chemistry.[21] Wiley was the expert in the bureau who strongly advocated pure foods and drugs.

Bok regularly emphasized that it was the public, not the magazine, with whom the burden of action rested. After the *Journal* printed Heyburn's proposed bill, he wrote that the *Journal* had done all that it could and that "it is now for the public to act." When the bill passed Congress in 1906, he warned his readers to beware of using patent medicines in the period of grace before the law was in effect on January 1, 1907.[22] Bok described the dangers still present because of the law's loopholes and showed how citizens could protect themselves. He called for state legislation and explained that "if there is alcohol in 'Peruna' that fact must, beginning with this month, be stated on the label of every bottle sold outside of Ohio [where it was manufactured]. . . . In other words, the people of the State in which a 'patent medicine' is manufactured know less than the people who live in other States."[23]

As late as 1916, the *Journal* was advising readers to read labels on patent medicines. One 1911 article advised women to look for the additives acetanilid and phenacetin in the fine print on headache powder labels. Nostrum manufacturers were no longer complaining about labeling their products because few persons read the lists of contents.[24] Bok revealed his annoyance and impatience with careless housekeepers in a 1913 editorial: "Would there ever have been occasion for a Pure Food Law if the American housekeeper had been competent? Would the present agitation about short weights and measures ever have been if the average American woman had known what came into her kitchen."[25]

Although he deplored the housekeeper's ignorance, Bok continued to publish facts to guide the inexperienced and awaken reader awareness. He described old manipulative techniques that had found new guises, such as the fraudulent impression given by some nostrum advertisements that the product was guaranteed by the United States government. The guarantee, of course, referred to the contents listed on the label, not to the curative powers of the potion. The *Journal* also exposed "free medical advice," among other related schemes of the patent-medicine makers, and the chicanery of quack doctors who exploited their prey.[26]

Bok held the opinion that the American woman's vanity matched her ignorance. The *Journal* described the foolishness of women who patronized "beauty doctors" and subjected themselves to all kinds of hazard and injury from chemical treatments in beauty parlors.[27] If the beauty cream was not a placebo, it was no doubt dangerous. In either case, a woman was tricked.

Bok hoped that the American clubwoman would get busy and tackle the serious problems. In addition, he suggested that readers request the creation of a joint department of health and education in the federal government.[28] The farmer, he said, could get all the help he needed on the health of his hog, but a woman who wanted information on tuberculosis could get none.

An important corollary of the *Journal*'s exposure of patent medicines was its publicity on adulterated foods and merchandise frauds. The reader learned how to test the purity of many products such as butter and coffee and how to detect the presence of coal-tar dyes in food products. The label was the key to consumer protection and greater business profits as well. *Printers' Ink* assessed the mood of the times when it stated that the public was learning to "be wary not only of anonymous foods, but of unnamed fabrics and every other mongrel commodity."[29] Foods and products sold in bulk were already a thing of the past. It was essential to adopt a trademark advantage as soon as feasible.

Bok's next serious venture into reform was not one of the obvious targets but a subject altogether unprecedented for a family magazine to examine. He was seriously alarmed at the unwillingness of parents to deal frankly with their children about sex education and was conscientiously gentle as he tried to inform his readers about its importance.

The *Journal*'s campaign for sex education was unique in its time owing to the risks of bad publicity. *Journal* circulation and advertising accounts were threatened, and more important, many readers' confidence in the integrity and wholesomeness of Bok and his magazine was shaken. Because Bok believed in the rightness of his crusade, Cyrus Curtis put aside his businessman's doubts and quietly endorsed Bok's work. All Curtis said to critics was, "I don't know a thing about it... Mr. Bok feels he is right, and that's all there is to it. He is the editor." [30]

Before the *Journal* undertook this most controversial topic, Bok had studied the issue for five years. In addition, he had prepared his readers, albeit tamely, by offering them occasional thoughts about marriage and the family. The *Journal* had formerly given conventional advice on these subjects. Women were told not to marry men their junior in age because they aged physically much sooner than men and because a mature woman was less likely to yield to her husband's opinions. Bok consistently opposed the double standard of morality and pooh-poohed the notion that sowing wild oats was healthful for young men. Writing about a woman's loss of chastity, he stressed the fact that she became nothing if she had sexual relations before marriage. [31]

When Bok started to publish editorials on the need for frankness with children on questions of sex education, he defied a taboo held by most of his readers. The policy of silence and the hope of innocence had long been mainstays in American families. Bok wanted to show that tragedy often resulted from these notions, which he called wrong and misguided, and feature articles deplored such "mock modesty." [32]

Bok cautioned that ignorance was not to be confused with innocence. One article presented a case study in which the pregnant girl was fourteen and the boy not yet sixteen. The writer said, "These two poor babies were not sinners; they were as far from sin as they were from virtue." A basic reality like this had to be made explicit to *Journal* readers. Parents, not schoolteachers, had to assume responsibility for their children's sex education. Although the *Journal* did not inform readers about what to tell their children, it did provide suggestions on how to do it, with articles by Jane Addams, Helen Keller, and other leaders in education and religion. In addition, Bok edited a series of books for young people that he encouraged parents and youth to read, and he expressed the hope that the Church and women's clubs would reinforce the idea that sex knowledge could protect rather than destroy innocence.[33]

The *Journal* only hinted at the problem of venereal disease in the early articles on sex education. Helen Keller wrote an article on infantile blindness, not mentioning the probable cause but emphasizing the need for placing silver nitrate solution into the eyes at birth. One editorial, which described the contraction of a lip ulcer of "unmentionable origin" from a public drinking cup, stressed the dangers of the common cup, not of venereal disease. By Bok's own admission, one editorial used tantalizing statistics to prod women to ask their husbands, "What does Mr. Bok mean?" He had written, "Over 70 out of every 100 surgical operations on women are the direct or indirect result of one cause." In the next issue an article explained the great suffering brought about by venereal disease. And the *Journal* applauded the Massachusetts ordinance barring doctors' advertisements of cures for venereal disease. Bok said that this policy gave no hope or encouragement to wrongdoers.[34]

According to Bok's autobiography, the clergyman Lyman Abbott, whom he greatly respected, urged a *Journal* discussion of venereal disease. Bok was surprised at this suggestion but finally decided that Abbott was correct; the problem was in the *Journal*'s province because it affected the basis of the magazine's existence—women and the home. Although he never fully studied or discussed venereal diseases, Bok decided to approach the problem by studying its prevention.

Later, at a 1913 advertising conference, he explained the widespread protest against the sex education campaign in this way:

> Mr. Alexander was my editor at that time, and he came into the office with two boys dragging a wash basket, each wash basket loaded with letters. He said that was the result of the first mail, containing either protests or letters stopping subscriptions. He said he could not catch my second editorial, but he could catch the third. I asked him what induced him to catch my third, and he said, "On account of those letters." I told him that proved that I was right, and that if I had not got them I would have thought that I was wrong. Here was a question that was very close to parents, and not a soul hardly expected that the Ladies' Home Journal would touch it. It was like a bolt out of the clear sky.[35]

Bok was pleased when the *Delineator*, a family magazine, decided to study the problem of venereal disease:

> As I understand from [Samuel Hopkins] Adams, the Delineator is going to allow him to mention the two diseases which I spoke of, which to my mind have no place in a woman's periodical. He was trying to find synonyms, but could not. I cannot, although I have hunted all through the language and dictionaries and encyclopedias. That is what I meant by those two causes.[36]

In spite of the initial furor caused by the *Journal*'s discussion of sex knowledge for children, the issue was resolved in seven years' time by public opinion. There was no little irony in the fact that the *Journal*'s pioneer work in the area had been forgotten. As Bok said rather bitterly in 1913, "The very social workers for whom this magazine made it possible to do their work ask us why we do not publish something on this subject that is 'so vitally important'(!) and 'can today be discussed with propriety in the most carefully edited magazine.'"[37]

The key *Journal* campaigns for patent-medicine and sex

education reform were ongoing and not confined chronologically to the muckraking period. As in the muckraking articles, however, these subjects were handled authoritatively and thoroughly and, unlike other *Journal* concerns, from one viewpoint only—the correct one. The happy combination of a serious-minded editor generally esteemed by his public and a trusting publisher financially well grounded enabled the magazine to tackle these issues with great energy and to emerge comparatively unscathed. In fact, the *Journal* became even stronger than before because issues of substance at last had been explored. Nevertheless, social workers and other experts hastily removed the problems to their own areas for further exploration. Bok estimated that at the very least, 25,000 subscribers had been lost because of the magazine's sex education campaign.[38] But the editor had held the trust of most of his audience, and he had astutely gauged its readiness to listen to the tenets of a new morality.

He always told his readers that only they could effect reforms. Of course he believed that it was the *Journal*'s job to teach readers how to observe and examine problems in their society. This mission was what he once called the *pill* he prescribed for his readers. Addressing the 1913 Curtis Company Advertising Conference, he said: "The policy of the Ladies' Home Journal has been never to publish anything unless there is an underlying reason. We will sugarcoat those pills so thick that you cannot see the pill, but the pill is there."[39] He was aware that, in carrying out his mission, he would have to face critics:

> When your purpose is decent, it makes no difference what criticism you get. Sometimes the higher your purpose, the more criticism you will receive, but if a magazine has not any backbone, for the Lord's sake, what is the use of publishing it? (Applause).
> You hear this criticism, of course you do. So do I, but it is very

often based on a misconception. Not one of you fellows would think one tenth as much of the *Journal* if it were spineless. If a thing has not got an ideal it is not worth doing, and the bigger the ideal, the better it is, provided it has both feet on the ground.[40]

On the eve of World War I it was evident that Bok and his *Journal* had traveled a long way from the taboos of the 1890s when he had been willing to court his readers on unimportant issues. His handling of the patent-medicine and, particularly, the sex education issues revealed his courage and editorial maturity.

VI ❧ Minerva in Battle

Minerva, Jupiter's daughter and the Roman goddess of wisdom, was often depicted on the *Journal* masthead. The choice of Minerva as the *Journal*'s symbolic leader was prophetic. She not only uplifted all domestic and liberal arts, but she staunchly led her subjects in war.

Edward Bok's editorial leadership in public service and reform before the war enabled the *Journal* to make an easy transition from a magazine designed to help middle-class women live better lives to a periodical that in many ways met the demands of a nation at war. Bok accomplished this transition, first, by building upon the familiar themes long emphasized by the *Journal*—better education, civic improvement, and a Beautiful America—and, second, by trying to build a bridge of understanding between the federal government and *Journal* readers. He encouraged a changing view of woman's role and the kind of commitment she had to make to her society. In wartime particularly, she was responsible for keeping a critical eye on the country and its institutions.

From the *Journal*'s perspective the war would force women to practice all those traits it had preached for so long. Efficiency, which Progressives believed guaranteed the good life, would

113

surely triumph. A new outlook on life, a new realization of what was important could not escape the citizen's perception. The magazine continued to be interested in specific social issues, many of which were directly related to wartime needs.

As the war greatly expanded the role of women in American society and provided the final impetus to the extension of the suffrage, the tasks of a woman's magazine took on a heightened importance. The serious purpose that Bok held for the magazine could now be applied to the national effort, which also provided a new unity to his vision of a better society. Thus, many of his favorite programs broadened and matured near the conclusion of his career.

One Curtis employee wrote an abbreviated company history in which he correctly observed that the *Journal* "submerged its own personality, built up over a period of many years, in its desire to do its share [of war work]." Fiction was patriotic in spirit, and articles on wartime work and economy in the home were featured.[1] The essential character of the magazine and its ideal woman remained unchanged, but the *Journal* was more eager to accept the expanding possibilities for women's work than it had been in earlier years. Of course, the ideal of service had been presented to the *Journal* reader for twenty-five years before the war began; the character of services acceptable to the *Journal* had simply matured with the editor.

Before the eve of World War I, very few *Journal* articles instructed women on important topics of international affairs.[2] After the war broke out in Europe, the *Journal* published a growing number of articles on war in general as well as the current conflict. It was, however, not yet America's battle. In one of Bok's first editorials on the war, which discussed the opportunities it created for United States economic growth, he wrote that American isolation meant "America's chance—commercially," if women would only encourage the manufacture and sale of American-made articles. In the same November, 1914, issue, Jane Addams and Secretary of State William Jennings Bryan wrote essays answering the question, "Is the Peace Movement a Failure?" Both pacifists answered no; at last, they said, people were disgusted by the follies of war and preparedness. In his Christmas editorial, Bok said he shared the confusion felt by the "clearest minds [who] have stood befogged and bewildered at the sudden transformation of a Christian world into a state of barbarity." He optimistically concluded, however, that " 'God's in His Heaven: All's right with the world.' " [3]

Bok's managing editor told Curtis Company advertisers in 1915 that Bok thought "it would be disagreeable to handle the war as such, but that he would treat the results as they affected American women." [4] Although it was plain to Bok that the war affected his readers indirectly, he took the opportunity it presented to reinforce his favorite themes. In a February, 1915, editorial, he listed many lessons and opportunities that the distant war brought to Americans. His list included stimulation of domestic industry, concern for neighbors, international interdependence, the danger of war toys for children, and the promise of a potential veto by women on all war making. The war against war, he said, had to be won by women, in the playroom, schoolroom, and the home. "Only Eve," he said, "can make the world an Eden without a Cain." In 1913 Bok had already expressed his dismay with those women who encouraged militarism by preferring "soldiers to bakers" as beaux. One writer said that her husband had questioned whether the war would be on if women had had the chance to make decisions in European councils of state. [5]

In 1915 the *Journal* concentrated on appeals for war relief. Because Bok had accepted the vice-presidency of the Belgian Relief Fund, he knew what the needs were. He appealed to his readers to send money for food and published an appeal by Elisabeth, queen of the Belgians. In June, the *Journal* printed the results of the "Queen of the Belgians Fund" drive and promised to send Her Majesty a book inscribed with the names of all contributors.[6]

Ladies' Home Journal involvement in the preparedness controversy diplomatically echoed the tug-of-war in the federal government. The *Journal's* oblique first mention of preparedness was in April, 1916, in an essay explaining the value of preparedness as national policy for avoiding war.[7] As Arthur S. Link has pointed out, many Progressives soon changed their antipreparedness opinions about the war to views that endorsed the need for "reasonable" preparedness.

As President Wilson shifted to building a large military force, Bok voluntarily tried to anticipate some of the government's needs and began to build a liaison between federal government and citizens. In February, 1916, a new department, "My Government and I," was begun. It was written by Dudley Harmon, Washington correspondent for the New York *Sun.* Opening features included an explanation of new military policies, such as conscription, and a description of the federal government's pamphlet series. Headed by Harmon, the *Journal's* Washington office was opened and made ready for any calls from the executive branch of the government.[8] Few calls, however, were expected. Bok had written to Wilson asking him to endorse the idea upon which the new department was based and to grant a five-minute interview with Harmon. Wilson denied the requests, but Bok featured the monthly column anyway.[9]

In response to readers' questions, Bok's May, 1916, editorials echoed the Wilson administration's more conventional approaches to preparedness. Under the overall heading of "Your Boy and Mine," he wrote that the nation's position on preparedness changed in wartime and that history showed preparedness to be necessary. The "real question was whether or not American boys were to be confronted with the draft without any adequate military training."[10] More specific preparedness goals appeared in subsequent issues. In June, 1916, the "My Government and I" column featured an article by the key spokesman for the American Red Cross, Mabel T. Boardman, urging American women to participate in the organization. In August, Bok urged women to organize Red Cross auxiliaries and make bandages for either domestic or overseas use.[11]

Other aspects of the war and preparedness came up in some July, 1916, guest editorials. As the first step toward preparedness, one writer called for an immediate prohibition of the sale of alcoholic beverages instead of "waiting until war has forced the necessity upon us and making frantic efforts at prohibition in the midst of a great national crisis."[12] The article related the English experience of immediate wartime prohibition of grain use for alcohol production. The urgency of readiness for war, not temperance agitation, inspired this kind of editorial.

Then, for nearly a year, the *Journal* gave little attention to the war. By 1917 the preparedness issue was plagued with controversy that left little room for advocates of reasonable preparedness. Certainly Bok's 1915 and 1916 *Journal* writing had fostered preparedness to the degree that women could understand the tumultuous world situation. In the last twelve months before the United States entered the war, he cautiously avoided the subject of preparedness altogether. Moreover, as late as June, 1916, he endorsed Theodore Roosevelt's presidential candidacy.

Not until June, 1917, did the *Journal*'s publishing schedule enable it to catch up with the events of April and the United States' declaration of war. In that issue's editorials, Bok stressed that "for months it has been apparent to all that we were drifting toward inevitable participation." The Reverend Russell H. Conwell, an inspirational writer known for his essay, "Acres of Diamonds," wrote an article, "Should the Christian Man Go to War?" Conwell answered yes to the title's question, because "war for a year, winning a victory for righteousness will save many years of bloody war in the near future. The sacrifice of a day is thus the economy of the years."[13] Harmon's "My Government and I" was changed to "Keeping Up with the Times," which presented all kinds of hints from Uncle Sam. For instance, the May, 1917, article recommended that citizens raise rabbits for meat. In the same issue, government experts who supplied information on home gardening were credited.[14]

During the war, the *Journal* preserved its characteristic level-headedness in its admonitions to readers. At the beginning of American involvement in the war and at its end, Bok urged women not to be slackers in either war relief or domestic charities. He warned particularly against lowering standards in domestic welfare programs when the war's demands seemed to threaten them. And, typically, he urged parents never to mention hate in front of their children.[15] Keeping a clear eye on government demands while maintaining keen sight of the larger perspective of humanistic values was a key *Journal* preoccupation. In all probability the *Journal*'s lack of war fever was a source of no little consternation to certain people in the administration who denounced anything less than one-sided commitment to narrow definitions of wartime patriotism.

Even with the first issue printed in response to April's events, the *Journal* exhorted clubwomen to prepare for peace. The wartime lessons of efficiency and conservation could be translated into peacetime living. In more precise terms, the *Journal* reported a few months later that the Women's Committee of the United States Council of National Defense urged clubwomen to study the war and its place in European history as a guide to understanding a future peace settlement.[16] In addition, Bok encouraged his audience to see the human sides of questions and not be waylaid by nationalistic considerations. One article centered on the autobiography of a German-born scholar, long resident in England until wartime harassment by local citizens forced him to move to the United States. In America, however, he suffered abuse by German-Americans who questioned his pro-British sentiments, and he was suspected by other Americans because of his German birth. He wrote, "Is there no one to speak a word in behalf of humanity as a whole?"[17]

A year later Bok answered those people who criticized the nation for spending so much on the Allies, saying, "We have not as yet given one dollar out of every ten that we actually made." He also reminded his readers that United States troops were still only on the sidelines and that the brunt of the war was carried by the other nations. He was dismayed because Americans tended to exaggerate the part played by the United States.[18]

The *Journal*'s custom of avoiding extremist viewpoints enabled it to bypass many propagandistic excesses of World War I and to prepare in positive ways for the postwar period. Readers were nevertheless presented with full-page drawings having such titles as "France Mourns" and "Belgium Waits." And some enemy denigration of valuable Red Cross work was answered with a charge of falsehood.[19]

A few times Bok permitted George Creel's Committee on Public Information (CPI) to enjoy full rein by publishing the claims for which it received so much postwar criticism. The May, 1918, issue carried in the first-page position an article in which the CPI listed the various lies fabricated by the enemy and the strategies used to create domestic dissension. Another *Journal* announcement for Creel's committee reminded citizens that the success of the war effort depended on every man's support of his government.[20] Occasional CPI advertisements were the worst offenders in *Journal* wartime propaganda. One advertisement for the Fourth Liberty Loan drive pictured the spiked helmet and bayonet, fierce symbols of the barbarism and treachery of the "Hun." Only rarely did the *Journal* publish references to common stories circulated by the Allies about German atrocities. In one instance, an observer who went to France broadcasted typical propaganda stories about the horrors of German wartime behavior by reporting what she was told, not what she saw.[21]

After the United States had entered the war, the *Journal* bemoaned a certain lack of seriousness about the war. With class orientation strongly entrenched among most Americans, Bok realized that even war work reflected class struggles and fashions. Women had to be warned not to exclude other women from volunteer jobs. Bok also cautioned against too much duplication of the more fashionable kinds of war work, particularly those that enabled volunteers to wear a uniform.[22] Many American women also had a thoughtless tendency to clean out their clothes closets and send shabby castoffs to needy people overseas. One account recorded what a foolish eighteen-year-old girl in California had sent to wartime France: a "soiled pair of white satin slippers, a pair of pink satin corset [sic], much worn, with two broken ribs and an old crêpe de chine combination." This was as foolish as the shoe shop that sent long, narrow, cloth-topped patent leather shoes, altogether useless for the cut and swollen feet of war sufferers. The reaction in Europe according to one reporter was, "They do not understand quite yet, over there at home in America." As late as September, 1918, Bok was obliged to write an editorial stating that the *Journal* was not a "slacker magazine" and would not "cut out" the war from its pages as some readers had requested. [23]

The *Journal's* war role before and after April, 1917, was to serve as an interpreter of the federal government's policies, especially those of the chief executive. Bok's close ties with President Wilson helped the editor define this role. Bok in fact styled himself as the president's advisor. In his second autobiography, *Twice Thirty*, he mentioned that when Wood-row Wilson was president of Princeton University, they be-came friends. In later life Bok liked to think that he and Wilson shared a great many things in common. He even al-luded to a striking physical resemblance. Bok's fondness for Wilson grew as his admiration of Theodore Roosevelt di-minished, and American participation in the war further modified his loyalties. In the course of Wilson's presidency, however, Bok's suggestions to him were generally turned down. [24]

One accepted suggestion came in the early phase of the war, when the United States was anxiously trying to preserve its neutrality. Bok's managing editor, Karl Harriman, wrote to Secretary of State Bryan pointing out that in two Philadelphia movie theaters, demonstrations had broken out when films showed mobilization of troops in the warring countries. Har-riman suggested that Wilson prepare a handwritten request on his executive letterhead asking theater audiences to "re-frain... from expression of approval or disapproval." A fac-simile of the president's request would be sent to motion pic-ture producers, who would then include this message in all their war films. Bryan endorsed this suggestion in a note to Wilson, who called it an excellent idea and implemented it. [25]

After a number of ineffective efforts to engage Wilson

directly in explaining his policies to *Journal* readers, Bok
desisted until United States entrance into the war was imminent. Wilson was then more willing, indeed anxious, to secure space for his messages. Bok obtained the president's
commitment to write one essay. When Wilson submitted his
article on Mexico to the *Journal*, Bok offered him a $250
compensation. He said that because the president had "put
aside the unwritten law that the President of the United
States shall not contribute to a general magazine during his
incumbency of office," the editor was putting aside "the unwritten law that you can offer no compensation to the President." Wilson replied that he could not accept Bok's check
because "the only use I could make of it would be to send it to
the headquarters of the Democratic National Committee for
campaign use, and I am not sure that you would approve of
that." Wilson probably was thinking of Bok's outspoken endorsement of Theodore Roosevelt in that election year. Bok
had written a publicized letter to the Roosevelt Non-Partisan
League asserting that Roosevelt was the man the nation
needed. [26]

Although Bok proposed many schemes to Wilson during
the war, the president called on him for specific help only a
few times. His most important request was that Bok stay on at
the *Journal.* Late in January, 1917, when Bok mentioned to
the president that he was planning to resign, Wilson wrote
to him, "Not now. Not for one minute. . . . This is no time to
consult your own wishes or pleasure,—not in these times." He
needed Bok and the *Journal* to concentrate on the domestic
front, if the United States entered the war. The following
month Wilson presented Bok with a twofold request. He
wanted him to encourage enlistment in the United States
Navy and to continue supporting the Red Cross. Fulfilling the
request, the *Journal*'s first war issue contained a number of lead
articles on the navy and two articles on the Red Cross. [27]

The work of the Y.M.C.A. and the Women's Committee of the United States Council of National Defense also found monthly space in the *Journal.* Bok was chairman of the Y.M.C.A. commission in Philadelphia, which was charged with recruiting men for civilian jobs in England and France.[28] Anna Howard Shaw's recurrent emphasis in her Women's Committee column was on domestic issues like child labor that threatened to be exacerbated by the war. In addition, Miss Shaw was a war work liaison between the *Journal* and those federal agencies needing a public forum. She received instructions, for example, to persuade the *Journal* to refuse advertising space for foodstuffs whose use was discouraged in wartime, since advertising was "obviously [the] most potent means of regulations [*sic*]."[29]

An important aspect of the *Journal's* war work was its promotion of the federal government's extensive food program. In World War I direct government controls were placed on wholesalers but not on consumers; therefore, national success in the food program depended on voluntary cooperation by consumers. Farm women had to be advised to stay on the farm, and town women had to learn more efficient means of food purchase, preparation, and storage. In the first phase of its food program, which emphasized food conservation, the *Journal* gave special encouragement to the woman who planned ahead. Always anticipating the imitation of the upper classes, Bok showed how "fashionable" American families saved food to prevent shortages and high prices. Readers also received information on meatless dishes, waste prevention, storage of vegetables, and gardening.[30]

"The Woman and the War" feature soon replaced the "Keeping Up with the Times" and "My Government and I" sections. At last, Bok's earlier hope had materialized; the new department was "conducted with the approval and cooperation of the Executive Departments of the United States government."[31] The feature was heralded with the comment: "New powers, new duties are being assumed daily by the government, particularly with reference to food. . . . The Washington Bureau [of the *Journal*] will assist the government to reach you, and will help you to get what the government wants you to have." It was essential to show the consumer the necessity of supporting the United States Food Administration program, headed by Herbert Hoover. Early in 1917, Wilson told Bok: "Hoover, better than any man in the world, understands the food question in the large sense. He may not see it so easily in the small family unit. There is where you come in. I want you to get back of Hoover, and give him your fullest support, and open up your magazine to him, so that he can reach the women under the most favorable auspices. There will be much to explain to them and ask of them."[32]

Beginning in the August, 1917, issue Hoover began his regular series of columns in the *Journal*, advising women to carry their own packages rather than indulge in home deliveries, to serve no young meat, and to plan a menu that included one meatless day a week and one wheatless meal a day. Included in the column was a pledge slip that readers were asked to sign and mail to Hoover as a token of their promise to abide by his suggestions. In the same issue, one of Hoover's advisors explained that the United States was sending wheat abroad to maintain bread rations among the Allies. Because it was not in the war theater, the United States was in a better position than the Allies to request changes in its citizens' daily routines and to experiment with different foodstuffs.[33] A week before the *Journal* was on the newsstands with its pledge slip, Hoover informed his staff that some of his correspondents had already observed resentment against the pledge. Women apparently were not convinced that such "revolutionary changes" were necessary, and they imagined the pledge to be a kind of criticism of them.[34] Perhaps they resented what appeared to be government-supervised efficiency in household management.

Besides providing Hoover with space for feature articles, Bok offered him his editorial chair to promote Food Administration guidelines for consumers. Bok underscored Hoover's requests for help and wrote a number of editorials on a husband's need to cooperate with his wife in managing a wartime household. In response to consumer concern about price rises during the war, the *Journal* gave its readers an idea of "fair prices" by publishing the Food Administration's list of consumer prices based on the markup from wholesale.[35]

To assist Hoover further, the *Journal* featured recipes that complied with the Food Administration's recommendations, in some cases obtaining approval statements to run with the recipes.[36] Frequently, the *Journal* had to take the initiative in war work, for the many federal agencies were unable to synchronize their activities and knew little of the realities of publishing schedules. The Food Administration occasionally recommended timetables for publicizing various phases of its program. In December, 1917, it sent to magazine editors a circular on conservation that urged the saving of wheat in January and fats in February, and the active use of dairy products in March.[37] If this circular was the first announcement of the timetable that the editors received, it arrived too late. The *Journal* reader found emphasis on the March program, but because of the time lag between preparation and publication, nothing on wheat or fat conservation appeared in the January and February numbers.[38]

The *Journal* began the second phase of its wartime food program, which promoted abstinence from certain foods, with an urgent request in June, 1918, that its two million readers abstain from using wheat during June, July, and August. An article in the next issue stressed the need for families to give up at least 25 percent of their wheat consumption if they could not abstain from wheat altogether. The food program was de-emphasized in the following months because the Food Administration found that too many casualties made the "food will win the war" theme unrealistic. (In fact, as the American casualty lists lengthened, more *Journal* copy focused on the problems of the disabled veteran.) [39]

The United States consumed only one-third of its usual wheat quota during 1917 and 1918, leaving no doubt that consumer propaganda was successful. A letter of thanks to American women from the food administrators in the Allied countries was published in the November issue. The food problem, however, remained a persistent issue. [40]

Other appeals were highlighted in the *Journal,* and they were frequently cushioned by Bok's usual optimism. He noted, for instance, that citizens who responded to the government's plea for saving fuel by lowering the heat level in their homes would benefit from the consequent disappearance of the common cold. In the same spirit, he said that contributions to the Y.M.C.A., Red Cross, and Knights of Columbus, and the purchase of Liberty bonds were not to be construed as charities but as investments. And, in an article on the scarcity of cotton and wool, Bok assured readers that the War Industries Board had promised an equitable distribution of yard goods, and citizens would "still be well dressed." [41] He continually turned the demands and costs of the war into gains.

The *Journal* actively participated in several Liberty bond campaigns. In one of its first articles on bonds, Eleanor McAdoo, Wilson's daughter and the wife of the secretary of the treasury, answered questions about government bonds; and, like Bok, she pointed up the gains rather than the costs of the war. The Curtis Company also participated by announcing that it would pay its subscription solicitors in bonds.

After Bok heard rumors that the third Liberty Loan was going to be undertaken on May 1, he composed a message based on Wilson's proclamation of the second Liberty Loan and enclosed it in full-page makeup with a letter to the president asking permission to print the message on the first page of the May *Journal.* Wilson agreed to the request. In later issues, an interpretive article and other appeals were published, including the postwar drive for a new loan. [42]

Although Bok served the Wilson administration, he also occasionally annoyed it during the war years. In one instance, he wrote an editorial saying that private home entertainments as well as the sending of sweets to soldiers and sailors should be stopped. Two *Journal* issues later, in a refutation of Bok's editorial, the chairman of the War and Navy Department's Commission on Training Camp Activities said that overdone hospitality toward servicemen was not typical. [43]

In a second incident, Bok suffered censorship and a serious loss of face with his journalistic peers because of his naïveté about soldiers on leave. When he visited the war theater, he was alarmed to find that American soldiers were "wrecked" by London prostitutes who led them to "moral crucifixion." Bok not only aired his views in the London *Times* but also sent cablegrams to leading American newspapers to report his findings. The cablegrams were intercepted by the Foreign Press-Cable Service of the CPI and delivered with the request that the dispatch not be published. According to the director of the Foreign Press-Cable Service, the Philadelphia *Public Ledger* cabled its own London correspondent "not to send further stories dealing with the subject." Propaganda agents were worried that Bok might "play up the subject" and also criticize the censorship once he discovered that his dispatches had not been published. [44] Consequently, an agent spoke with Bok in London and informed the CPI's George Creel that Bok "realized the mess he was stirring up" and that he intended to "drop the matter." As soon as the publishing schedule allowed it, the editor reversed himself. After stressing what was most important, the wanton destruction wrought by war, he told women not to worry about their soldiers' habits, because "intoxication simply does not exist and venereal diseases are negligible."[45]

There is evidence of only one instance in which Bok tried to profit from his wartime help to the administration. Legislation was pending early in 1918 to increase postal revenues by introducing a postal zone system for periodicals. In a surprisingly small-minded letter to Wilson, Bok listed some *Journal* contributions to the war effort and said, "But, frankly, Mr. President, after doing all this—and my magazine is only typical of our other two magazines, The Saturday Evening Post and The Country Gentleman—does it seem quite fair to you that a zone system should be placed upon us which is going to drive this magazine to the wall and under which it is impossible for us to operate? This is not an extravagant statement—it is a fact."[46] There was a certain veiled element of threat in Bok's closing sentence, which stated that this was a time when the government should enjoy nothing but "the heartiest cooperation" of the editors. Wilson asked the postmaster general, Albert S. Burleson, whether Bok's remarks had any foundation.[47] Burleson replied that handling and transporting the *Journal* cost the government, that is, the general public, $5 million above the amount covered by postal rates. Calculating strictly on a cash-and-carry basis, he said, "This service to Mr. Bok, or his publication, rendered by the Government without charge would many times compensate him at his regular advertising rates for all space contributed for the uses outlined in his letter." Wilson sent Bok a copy of Burleson's letter along with a note promising to "regret it very much" if "any injustice" resulted from the act of Congress.[48] Wilson's note silenced Bok for little more than one month.

Early in April, 1918, he again wrote to the president and proposed meeting with Burleson to suggest a six-month delay in enforcement of the legislation. He also suggested that the president appoint a commission to investigate whether the postal zone system threatened the stability of the publishing industry. "I think this would be satisfactory to the publishers and editors," he said, "as it would give them a chance to state their case to a commission of businessmen, and not to a group of non-comprehending Congressmen."[49] Bok claimed that he wrote about the problem independently, not as a spokesman for the industry, any organization, or even his own company. Wilson immediately wrote to Burleson, "Don't you think it would be wise to fall in with the suggestion contained in this letter? I hate to suggest it, but perhaps we had better let these men feel that they have never been denied a hearing on anything they chose to suggest."[50] The president's lack of surprise or overt hostility toward Bok suggests that perhaps he expected to have his share of politicking friends and associates. In any event, he accepted the reality that he needed popular support for his domestic program and was, no doubt, willing to make small compromises to guarantee mass magazine popularization of the administration's programs.

Bok took it for granted that *Journal* readers would serve the nation in its time of crisis. One general means of effectively aiding the war effort was a wholehearted commitment to efficiency, the crystallization of progressive hopes for a planned society. Production and distribution of commodities had to be organized to prevent shortages. Popular habits and customs could not stand in the way of wartime needs, and community efforts often had to replace older and more private ways of doing things.

Throughout its history the *Journal* had subscribed to a way of life that revered singleness of purpose and devotion to producing superior results. Bok repeatedly said that women seemed to be dissipating their energies. If only they would concentrate on household management, they would not be vulnerable to retail frauds and other means of potential waste.[51] The *Journal's* particular emphasis was on economy of time and money. If the housekeeper did not systematize her food shopping, for example, the *Journal* reminded her that she was wasteful. Women's household negligence was frequently cited as the cause of high prices. In prewar years one *Journal* writer blamed the large industrial trusts for high prices, although another had said that foolishly extravagant women were at fault. Later, when high prices beleaguered the nation, and again in 1915, when beef prices soared, Bok said he was pleased that women would have to practice economy. Too, he said, Americans ate more meat than was good for their health.[52]

High standards of efficiency also had to be observed by domestic help. In this context as well as others, Bok underscored the need for an adequate domestic wage. He reminded employers to temper their demands on domestic help with consideration, and he quoted one servant as saying, "What's the use of becoming more and more efficient in our work when the only result is that we are more and more imposed on?"[53]

Bok gave an editorial position to the president of the National Housewives League, Mrs. Julian Heath, in hopes that she would awaken American women to their wasteful ways. "I am conservative in my statement," Mrs. Heath wrote, "when I say that if one-half of our businessmen conducted their business as women do their housekeeping the country would soon be bankrupt." By pointing out that households and businesses both required management, Mrs. Heath gave the American housewife's duties a status not generally acknowledged. Furthermore, she demonstrated that housewives could influence the prices of commodities and wield economic power. Like Bok, she insisted that the rise of women's power in the marketplace depended on banishing their ignorance and apathy. In fact, she said, urban women should join economic forces with farmers, learn market conditions, and buy accordingly.[54] In *Journal* economics, this meant demanding lower prices for apples in a season of bumper crops.

The *Journal* paraded the "new housekeeping" vogue, or the use of scientific principles in household management. Bok acclaimed the practice of hiring a "visiting housekeeper" to reorganize household routines scientifically. By 1914, the businessman and farmer had incorporated many labor-, time-, and money-saving devices into the management of company and meadow. Their wives, according to the *Journal,* were still far behind. In these years the *Journal* also began to champion efficiency in the Church, in club work, and in human relationships.[55]

The coming of the war demanded new definitions of thrift and economy. For the health of the nation it was essential that hoarding, so common in troubled times, not be characteristic of American housekeepers. And because it was crucial to keep nonwar industries in production, women should not stop spending. Congresswoman Jeannette Rankin contributed an essay to the *Journal* on the necessity of avoiding foolish economies. "The whole tendency of the present time is toward large-scale production," she wrote, "and the effect of war will be to accelerate that tendency." The president of the American Society for Thrift explained that genuine thrift was "the sane administration of one's personal affairs." For the least amount of waste to occur, there ought to be the "least amount of lost motion" and the "greatest possible good to one's self and the nation." Bernard M. Baruch, chairman of the War Industries Board, echoed the *Journal*'s new definition of thrift by calling it the saving of manpower. His discussion of thrift introduced the announcement that the board had arranged to eliminate "useless varieties" such as the many colors in women's shoes.[56]

In 1918 a new *Journal* department called "How Are We Going to Live?" occasionally forecast some radical changes in American life-styles that could increase efficiency. Many ideas for revolutionizing American communities were circulated in wartime, but the concepts behind them were separate from the war effort. Bok applauded the coming of one change, the self-service food market. In the April, 1918, issue, the results of a successful experiment in a southern city were shown, illustrating that it was cheaper to shop in a supermarket because of the decreased labor costs. Articles appeared on cooperative kitchens, wherein all families would subscribe to meals that would be delivered directly to their homes and thus save on household help expenses, food, and fuel. Bok had earlier encouraged the community servant—an idea that was salvaged. Several articles touted the potential success of the "eight-hour assistant" as a replacement for live-in help. As early as 1910, a *Journal* article had proclaimed community cooperation as an answer to fighting high prices: "This is not socialism; it does not lead to paternalism; it is plain, every day, American business common-sense."[57]

The idea of the community church interested Bok. His tendency was to decry denominationalism altogether and to support united efforts like the Y.M.C.A. He published a letter, allegedly from a soldier at the front, in which the soldier said that his comrades were all in favor of the Y.M.C.A. and were coming back to the states as "strong rooters" for it. In addition, this soldier asked, "Is the church going to wake up? It can't with its present weak men." Bok also published a bishop's proposed plan for the organic union of American churches, as well as the record of cooperation between the Y.M.C.A. and the Knights of Columbus, which gave a new harmony to Roman Catholic-Protestant relations.[58]

Bok encouraged making full use of church buildings and schoolhouses every day of the week. In one article, a minister wrote that soldiers slept on cots in the church when they were on leave; and in another issue, the New York City Red Cross chapter was cited for its Junior Red Cross program, in which children made war relief items in the classrooms and received Red Cross instruction.[59]

While the nation's wartime needs were demanding careful reorganization of household routines and suggesting communal answers, growing numbers of women were needed outside their homes in the marketplace and industry. Some preparation for women and vocations had been made in the years before the war, and Bok had increasingly accepted woman's role in serving her community. In one editorial just before the nation entered the war, he wrote that a girl could do office work as well as a boy and often better.[60] The November, 1917, issue contained an article on war jobs, listing the types of factories needing workers in each state. One subheading in this article declared, "Thousands of Women Are Wanted Practically at Men's Pay."[61]

Although a woman's employment for private gain, not to mention her own wishes for a career, had long been unacceptable to Bok, he was quite willing to support the war's demand for women workers while men were at the front. The turning

point came in the first installment of a regular *Journal* feature
during the war and after, "The New Day for Women: What Its
Problems Are and How They Are Being Met." The first column casually assumed that the vote would soon be available to
all women. In June, 1918, Bok prefaced a new series, "The
After-the-War Woman: What Is She Going to Become and
Where, Too, Will Be Her Place?," by stating that "the most
startling single factor . . . coming out of the war is woman" and
that many previously held notions about women would have
to be discarded.[62] The same issue described France's provision
of nurseries for children of women who worked, and the September issue carried the unusually strong statement, "Whatever happens it seems certain that the old bondage to man's
will and mastery will cease when the war is over."[63]

After armistice, the *Journal* continued to guide women toward employment outside the home. In January, 1919, the
first column of a department called "The American Woman's
New Work" explained that factory working conditions had
improved. To combat the blue-collar stigma, Dudley Harmon
wrote, "The munitions worker of today undergoes a complete
transformation before she leaves the shop . . . she is not to be
distinguished from the 'white collar and cuff' office worker,
except that you would probably find more money in her
purse."[64] This woman was a startling change from the ideal
Journal woman of a few years earlier.

The same department contained an essay of encouragement
for the woman past forty. Not only were many jobs available
to women in their middle years, it said, but "sex and age as the
basis for selection in hiring are being superseded by efficiency." The entire work question was given new impetus
when a *Journal* writer proclaimed that it was actually healthier
for women to leave their housework to someone else and find
employment outside their households. Under this arrange-

ment, their children would benefit from longer school days and good institutionally provided food and recreation. Just how aggressively the *Journal* allowed its contributors to tackle the issue of employment for women may be deduced from Anna Howard Shaw's April, 1919, article, which called for the creation of two cabinet posts to cover a health, education, and industry department and a woman to be appointed assistant secretary of labor. According to one commentator, the "bridge and boredom" of prewar days were history.[65]

Bok showed that in going to work, American women would only be following their sisters abroad. Readers were told that Englishwomen were likely to keep up their demands for better lives and that the government had to provide solutions to the problems raised. And New Zealand was presented as a happy illustration of "socialism without the doctrine" and as a nation where women's suffrage was actively used to bring about good results.[66]

New developments in woman's role in American society had been evident even before the war. Early in 1915 Bok had written to Wilson that women's influence in national affairs was growing. For that reason he urged Wilson to clarify his attitudes on many questions of special interest to women.[67] At that time, however, Bok expressed his awareness mostly in private.

Although many reformers were willing to surrender domestic needs for wartime essentials, Bok continued asking his readers to work with their prewar charities and services as well as to take on wartime burdens. He was especially worried about backsliding in the area of child welfare, because war demands seemed to encourage longer hours and a lower minimum age for child laborers. The fight for the child labor bill had been endorsed by the *Journal,* and for the October, 1917, issue, Bok asked the president to discourage parents from listening to the pleas of children who wanted to leave school and become war workers. The president declined: "Many young people, I dare say, will be obliged to undertake the tasks which older people have generally been able to perform and I must 'go slow.' "[68]

In 1909 the *Journal* had started a feature that permitted mothers to register their babies and receive mail-order advice on the care of them. By 1918 the number of registered babies had grown to sixty thousand—all the more reason for the *Journal* to despair of the war's effects on many babies in the United States. The child mortality rate had risen because of inadequate food and shelter, milk shortages, improper maternal care, the relaxing of the child labor laws, and increased problems for rural women. The director of New York City's Bureau of Child Hygiene urged women to consider the nation's high mortality rate for children between two and six. She wrote that a slogan for all women should be "No mother's baby is safe until every mother's baby is safe" and emphasized the community's role in providing decontaminated milk and clean streets. Bok cited statistics showing the infant mortality rate at home to be fourteen out of every one hundred and the rate for soldiers at the front to be two out of every one hundred. He bitterly underscored his commentary, saying, "It may not be quite so picturesque to help an underfed American baby as a little Belgian war baby, but the need is equally great."[69]

The *Journal*'s emphasis on domestic problems in wartime enabled the magazine to enjoy a certain distance from the heat of propaganda battles and to prepare its readers for the realities of a postwar world. For example, its extensive discussion of immigration deftly contributed to wartime needs and furnished new definitions of civic-mindedness toward newcomers in a democratic society. The *Journal* handled the entire issue with sensitivity toward the several needs of immigrants, native Americans, and the nation—an improvement from the days when it had published curiosity pieces on life in the tenements.[70]

In 1903 a *Journal* article contrasted the "new" immigration (from southern and eastern Europe) with the old (from northern and western Europe). It mentioned that, although three-quarters of the new immigrants remained in eastern cities where "they swarm together," the nation could "assimilate much," and there was no need to fear a continuing stream of immigrants. One exceptional article published even before the United States entered the war addressed the tensions in immigrant life. Prefaced by Theodore Roosevelt, it narrated the story of a talented young woman educated in the United States and thoroughly Americanized. She saw the alienation suffered by the parents of the first generation in their "puzzled eyes, eyes in which there will be love but no understanding—and always an infinite loneliness."[71]

Because a growing tide of immigrants was expected in the United States, several *Journal* articles expounded the positive characteristics of migrants. For this reason one article asked the question, "Who Makes the Best American?" and concluded that the Dutch, Germans, Italians, Irish, and Hebrews did. Significantly, two of these groups suffered the most from prejudice. Moreover, the *Journal* explained that only the best people, those having "the most active, ambitious and courageous blood," migrated to the United States.[72]

The immigration question was studied by the *Journal* in several ways. Readers were told what the government expected native Americans to do for the newcomer. *Journal* women were asked to help educate and Americanize the immigrants in preparing them for citizenship and even to explain "Freedom's War" to them. After all, the army's polyglot troops testified to the assimilation of the immigrants as United States soldiers. In 1915, women's clubs were advised to examine immigrant housing conditions. Even earlier, Jane Addams had urged the federal government to help immigrants settle in places where they could find work. Women's clubs had plenty to do if they sought answers to the questions raised by Mrs. Percy V. Pennypacker: What were the immigrants' living conditions? Had they good water? How did their rent compare with that of the native Americans? Was there any "artistic talent being wasted in the mills?"[73]

Journal contributors affirmed that native Americans committed to helping aliens had much to learn from them. In fact, the reader was shown a new vision of the future in which native and immigrant Americans would all be united without dissension. Writers asked readers to study different cultures, to learn foreign languages, and to shake off their "mantle of conceit."[74]

Before too long the *Journal*'s concept of Americanization changed to meet the emphasis given to it by Secretary of the Interior Franklin K. Lane, who maintained that Americanization in the fundamental sense had to uplift native and immigrant alike. The nation, he said, had to provide education for immigrant, Negro, and Indian and also had to make Anglo-Saxon children into literate citizens. From the *Journal*'s perspective, which echoed Bok's earlier demand for relevance in the schools, the hope for a genuine Americanization rested in the nation's school system. The study of foreign languages from an early age and the development of sensitivity to different cultures were ways of realizing this hope.[75]

The September, 1919, issue introduced a department called "The New Americans," which was officially endorsed by the secretary of the interior. Esther Everett Lape's monthly feature stressed a sense of community between foreign-born and native Americans. The old style of Americanizing by forcing aliens to adopt the mainstream patterns of life was clearly unacceptable. In fact, Miss Lape said, "Those who go out to 'Americanize' in the spirit of saving the country from disaster, or of reforming the heathen by abolishing all that looks unfamiliar are less likely to Americanize the foreign-born than to provincialize America."[76] In the clatter of the Red scare, Miss Lape's column rang out fearlessly, a coda for Bok's old Beautiful America dream: "There is a negative school of Americanization abroad in the land. It would Americanize America by 'fighting Bolshevism,' by words and laws, by more police power, more restrictions, more espionage. It is right that our nation should stand on guard for the principles for which it was founded. But no campaign was ever won merely by the zealous punishing of a minority. The America of the future will be built not by our fear for it, but the belief of one hundred million citizens in it."[77]

A new kind of realism was evident in the *Ladies' Home Journal* as the war ended. Before the war, certain national groups had been singled out for possessing traits that Americans should emulate. In 1919 a significant emphasis emerged on the desirability of all people to live together with the understanding that aliens provided definite benefits to American society.

The *Journal* had reflected the comfortable sobriety of the 1890s, the exuberance and reform of the first decade of the century, and the Wilsonian idealism of the war years. Bok, like his friend Wilson, hoped that out of the pain and death of the war a new progressive and democratic era would be forthcoming. Near the end of the war the *Journal* was again encouraging citizens to examine the quality of life for all men in the United States, and Bok was wondering what lessons, if any, his readers had actually gleaned from the war. The remarkable adjustment of many women to their expanding responsibilities led Bok to alter his traditionalist beliefs about woman's role, and because wartime changes brought greater public responsibilities for citizens and government, the *Journal* placed new emphasis on cooperative ventures in reform.

Although Bok wanted the coming peace to reap the benefits of wartime measures, he became increasingly disturbed by the prospects for the postwar world. Selfishness and bigotry were as much a part of the popular response to the war as commitment to service. Bok came to recognize that his audience was not quite so high-minded as he hoped. The *Journal*'s enlightened policy towards immigration was a tribute to his greater maturity, but it was also a clear response to the intolerant mood in the nation. As Bok grew in wisdom and broadmindedness, his links to his audience could only weaken; and as his *Journal* career came to an end, his concern for international peace found new channels.

When Bok retired on September 22, 1919, he claimed that he was anxious to devote his time to philanthropy and to writing his memoirs. For the first time in thirty years, he was free of knitting needles and menus, and he expressed uncharacteristic regret over his career: "It was simply not a work which from its very character I would have chosen to express my real self. There are undoubtedly acute problems which concern themselves with the proper ingredients in cooking recipes.... These are vital points in the lives of thousands of women.... But is it too much to say that they are hardly of a nature to develop and satisfy the mental and spiritual nature of a man? At least, not for a lifetime!"[78]

Although one of his friends suggested that Bok's energies were too diffused in his post-*Journal* period to be of any genuine significance, Bok established and supported many civic activities in the 1920s, in Philadelphia and elsewhere. He endowed the Woodrow Wilson Professorship of Literature at Princeton University in 1926 and the Woodrow Wilson Chair in Government at Williams College in 1929, and he helped to found the Walter Hines Page School of the Johns Hopkins University.[79] In addition, he built a public bird sanctuary in Lake Wales, Florida, and spent time encouraging businessmen to arrange frequent winter holidays to replenish their souls and spirits.

In the 1920s, Bok's most significant activity, in terms of time, energy, money, and publicity, was working for peace. He sponsored the American Peace Award in 1923 for the "Best Practicable Plan By Which the United States May Cooperate with Other Nations to Achieve and Preserve the Peace of the World," which promised a cash prize of $100,000. The policy committee of the award included many Progressives, such as Learned Hand, Mrs. Gifford Pinchot, Eleanor Roosevelt, Henry L. Stimson, and Cornelius Bliss. On the jury of award, chaired by Elihu Root, were Edward M. House, Roscoe Pound, William A. White, and Brand Whitlock.[80] When the award was first offered, Bok was jeered by leading intellectual and liberal journals, and Walter Lippmann indicted both Bok and his plan as shams. What the young critics failed to see, according to Bok's coplanner and administrator of the project, Esther Everett Lape, was that Bok hardly dared to hope that the perfect plan for world peace would emerge from a contest held open for a few months. Instead, he wished for as many people as possible to think through complex world problems and to try to work out solutions. Or, as Miss Lape said, he tried to bring the public into what had gone on at Versailles. The 22,165 plans were submitted by a wide variety of people, from scoffing intellectuals to day laborers.[81]

Bok had written to Wilson about the contest before it was announced. Wilson said that the project would not "be of the least service in the world, and would obscure the sense of responsibility on the part of our government and people if such a project were to be realized." He added his conviction that only United States entrance into the League of Nations would provide the "rightful attitude of frank cooperation and joint responsibility with the rest of the world." [82]

The winning plan, similar to chairman Elihu Root's own interests, called for United States adherence to the Permanent Court of International Justice and to the League of Nations. Nine million referendum ballots on the winning plan were distributed; of 610,558 ballots that were returned, seven-eighths were favorable. Faithful to the winning plan, Bok endowed the American Foundation, which became the key pressure group for United States entrance into the World Court. [83]

Bok had an enormous capacity to grow. In his earliest conversations with Miss Lape about world peace, he had described his belief that extensive advertising could win minds to peace. After all, he said, had not advertising created a nation of cigarette smokers? It was some time, Miss Lape remembered, before Bok saw the naïveté of his idea and realized both the essential fickleness of convictions based on advertising campaigns and the need for more realism in human affairs, as promised by a channel like the World Court.

Conclusion

Bok planned to retire from the *Journal* at fifty, after twenty-five years of editorship, but he served an additional five years because of the war. Company events provide a more complicated story of his retirement than his own version. In 1919 it was rumored that Bok had been fired, and not until Cyrus Curtis' death in 1933 did *News-Week* disclose that Bok had refused Curtis' demand that he "modernize the magazine." "At a dramatic directors' meeting, he tendered his resignation which Mr. Curtis immediately made a motion to accept. From that moment forward, Lorimer [editor of the *Post*] has been in complete charge of all the Curtis magazines."[1]

Correspondence between Curtis and the company treasurer, C. H. Ludington, supports the *News-Week* report. One month before Bok's resignation, Curtis had written to Ludington that for several years he had thought the company would "have to make some changes and to keep up with modern progress, and yet I could not see that time had quite arrived, for as long as The Journal kept up to such a high-water mark it would be a pretty serious matter to make any radical change." Both Curtis and Lorimer liked Ludington's idea of a "new publication." As Curtis said, "The main issue was to forestall competition and to do something in the way of progress."[2] A few days later, Curtis wrote to Lorimer that the *Journal*'s future would be discussed when Curtis returned to Philadelphia in September: "I think the time has come to consider it seriously, and not to stay too long in a thirty-year old rut."[3] On September 23, Bok announced his resignation, to be effective January 1, 1920.

The publisher and his editor had long been a successful team, but when Curtis saw that a needed revitalization was not forthcoming from the editor, he severed the professional relationship. Certainly Curtis acted shrewdly in the interests of his publishing company, simply by demonstrating one of his success formulas—no exclusive reliance on any advertising agency, company administrator, or editor.

During his thirty years as editor Bok tried to adapt middle-class values to the exigencies of a changing society. From 1889 to 1919, increasing numbers of citizens were subjected to the stresses of urbanization, industrialization, and immigration. Perhaps no group more than American women experienced changes that so profoundly affected their role and status. Bok was confused about women's role. He had misgivings about suffrage for women, but he wanted them to have a civic education. He wanted women to stay at home and mind their households, so he opposed the entertaining and culturally uplifting projects of clubwomen and instead encouraged them to engage responsibly in community projects. Only the needs created by World War I properly released middle-class women from their home activities, but Bok's contributors, not he, suggested that a woman's status was automatically raised if she worked outside her household.

Bok's approach to reform was fundamentally Emersonian in that he believed in reforming man rather than the institutions of society. Like many Progressives, he demanded a wider acceptance of civic responsibility from his readers. His style of reform was geared to self-help of the middle classes. Only during the war did this emphasis change to include helping others who did not share middle-class standards. But a pragmatic tone dominated Bok's reformism, which counted its costs and measured its returns. The secular ethic had replaced the Christian in rhetoric as well as in practice. Yet, when Bok became convinced that class consciousness prevented far-reaching reform, he tried to surmount the problem by asking his readers to practice rural and Christian virtues. Indirectly, however, he reinforced class consciousness through his constant dunning of correct forms and usages. The *Journal*'s emphasis on women's fashions, home decoration, good taste over bad taste, and etiquette fostered the image of a woman whose behavior was superior to those who either could not or did not conform to the prescribed life-style. In this way Bok's *Journal* aided in the uniformity of middle-class life. The *Journal* acquainted the nation with a standardized literature and a common ethic, even as it proclaimed the virtues of standard brands. Only the *Journal*'s handling of the immigration question during the war affirmed that cultural pluralism was a desirable contribution to American life.

As a mass periodical with advertising revenues tied to circulation figures, the *Journal* seldom risked ruffling the favorite prejudices of its readers. Discussions of working-class protest, labor unrest, and sectional antagonism were avoided, and national consciousness was emphasized. The pretense of an ideal world isolated from unpleasantness was characteristic of much that the *Journal* published.

Because of Bok's commitment to a progressive philosophy, he eventually modified his earlier views on individual reform. He demanded legislation to curb abuses by business and started the clamor for a national law to guarantee pure food and drugs. He accepted the need for government controls where private controls clearly had failed. Moreover, business regulation profited consumer and producer alike. Bok published an important article on trusts, which effectively summarized a progressive view on business consolidation and combination: "If a big business is tyrannical it ought to be made to feel the heavy hand of justice; the thing to be struck at, though, is not its mere form as a corporation, or its magnitude because it is great, but its acts—or its attempts to act—with oppressive intent."[4]

Bok's broadening spirit of tolerance became evident in 1912 when the *Journal* published an anonymous essay that discussed the benefits of the socialist movement: "It has aroused ordinary men and women to their duty toward each other; made employers more humane and reasonable; infused something like a conscience into corporations we all supposed soulless; and reminded men in high positions, both public and private, that they are merely trustees for the people and must give a worthy account of their stewardship."[5]

Bok successfully converted the middle-class public's general lack of faith in the value of the growing size and complexity of industry to a profoundly held confidence in the positive qualities of large-scale enterprise. The *Journal* itself was an integral part of big business. If consumers had their doubts about the products distributed by the beef trust, they certainly were not critical of the Curtis Publishing Company's leading product. Bok always affirmed that advertising created the *Journal* and enabled it to grow. In addition, the magazine exemplified sound business and aggressively protected its consumers from bogus advertisements. These practices gave way to the readers' understanding that products advertised in the *Journal* were fully as reliable as its editorial content.

No matter how much Bok pandered the virtues of business to his readers, he never forgot his fundamental misgivings about the nature of affluence. He admonished his readers to live within their incomes, teach their children a keener value of money, and learn to resist exploitation by shopkeepers.[6]

As long as Bok had maintained his image as a middle-class editor, he was secure in his hold upon his audience. The general public, however, proved to be unable to respond to the growing element in his reform consciousness that would replace class barriers with brotherhood, and he unwisely counted on satisfied Americans to mount reform efforts. His last editorial in the December, 1919, issue revealed his disenchantment with his readers. He told them that the next generation's leaders would "be giving the same advice that you have just finished yawning over."[7] The happy camaraderie between editor and readers was gone, for it became inescapably evident that he was preaching more than listening to them. The *Journal* was a slick magazine, and it no longer pleased Bok or reflected his carefully forged combination of commerce and good works. He had failed to either anticipate or deflect the conservative mood that came to dominate American middle-class opinion in the decade after the war.

At the end of the war Bok was sorely pressed to find the Beautiful America of his dreams. He had said that the small towns and cities held the keys to a better life, but the war had illuminated some unattractive features of these towns. A field secretary for the Federal Council of Churches traveled among many small cities of 5,000 to 10,000 in population. In a *Journal* article he said that socialism was making progress because the cities' elite, the "smug, self-satisfied group," hindered change. Even the churches were dominated by "a single individual or by a comparatively small group of persons."[8] Revolution was imminent, he said, unless changes came about. Something had to be done, but *Journal* readers found no programs of action outlined for them.

In the postwar era, when extreme viewpoints seemed to prevail over the measured and precise arguments of another time, Bok urged his readers to avoid forming hasty opinions. Labels had assumed serious meanings, whether they identified beans or political parties. Bok wrote: "Read, yes, [the daily newspaper] but think and weigh, remembering that every door has two sides, if we will only go to the other side and look for it."[9] An article on city government reinforced the idea that politics explained "dirty streets and public dumps" in American cities. It was efficiency that counted in a healthy community, not any alleged "Republican way of cleaning streets" or "Democratic way of collecting refuse."[10] All that the editor wanted, he said, was for the nation to get rid of "blind spots."[11]

Bok's career had opened with much bravura, a winning cajolery of his readers to high-minded causes, and a sure faith in middle-class goodness. His career ended with doubts about the ability and willingness of his audience to effect positive changes in the postwar world. By the end of the war, Bok's audience cared as little for his idealistic rural and traditional values as they did for his progressive political views.

Bok's successes and achievements in the progressive era must be evaluated in the light of his role as a successful businessman. That he worked within the confines of a major corporation for thirty years is the salient point. He used the offices open to him to work for a better American society; at the same time, he was a responsible member of his corporation. He had neither the fervor nor the rigidity of the revolutionary, and his successful reforms were not so dramatic as some of his contemporaries'. He possessed a characteristic progressive willingness to tackle some of the occasionally trite, boring, and menial problems of his day as well as some of the larger problems. The feisty, pacesetting editor displayed wisdom and foresight on issues that still concern us—ecology, conservation, efficiency, brotherhood, and peace. Bok's growth to a broader, more humane perspective, especially on the subjects of race, sex, and class, cost him his job but established his historical importance as an often prophetic witness in a period of rapid change.

Notes

INTRODUCTION

1 Edward C. Kirkland, *Industry Comes of Age: Business, Labor and Public Policy, 1860–1897* (Chicago: Quadrangle Paperbacks, 1967), 273.

2 Theodore Peterson, *Magazines in the Twentieth Century* (Urbana: University of Illinois Press, 1964), 27.

3 Mark Sullivan, *Our Times* (5 vols.; New York: Charles Scribner's Sons, 1932), IV, 256.

4 Christopher Lasch, *The New Radicalism in America, 1889–1963* (New York: Alfred A. Knopf, 1965), xiv–xv.

5 Emily Newell Blair, "What Are We Women Going to Do?" *Ladies' Home Journal,* hereinafter cited as *LHJ,* XXXVI (May, 1919), 47, 114.

6 Edward Bok, "At Home With the Editor," *LHJ,* X (September, 1893), 12. See also "The Philadelphians," *LHJ,* XIX (August, 1902), 7.

CHAPTER I

1 "Political Advertising," *Profitable Advertising,* XIV (November, 1904), 646. See also John Adams Thayer, *Out of the Rut* (The Smart Set edition of *Astir: A Publisher's Life Story*; New York: John Adams Thayer, 1912), 51. Of course this political advertisement was an exceptional instance for the *Journal.* Cyrus Curtis to Thomas Balmer, January 21, 1898, in Cyrus Curtis Letterbooks, Historical Society of Pennsylvania, Philadelphia.

2 *LHJ,* IX (August, 1892), 12; Edward Bok, "A Woman's Laugh and a Singed Cat: Chapters in the Biography of an American Publisher," *Atlantic Monthly,* CXXXI (March, 1923), 316.

3 Curtis to W. S. Niles, December 4, 1890, Curtis to J. A. Richards, June 16, 1893, Curtis to W. H. Daniels, December 13, 1890, Curtis to Edward E. Clark, December 16, 1890, Curtis to G. H. Yenowine, December 15, 1890, Curtis to Woodward and Lothrop, February 5, 1891, Curtis to B. A. Elliott Co., December 17, 1890, all in Curtis Letterbooks.

4 Curtis to R. P. Hollander & Co., December 24, 1890, Curtis to John F. Huckle, December 21, 1891, Curtis to R. S. Penfield, February 27, 1893, Curtis to Lorin

F. Deland, December 24, 1890, Curtis to W. S. Douglas, February 5, 1891,
Curtis to Richards, June 12, 1893, *ibid.*

5   Curtis to Gorham Manufacturing Co., September 24, 1890; Curtis to Bon
Marché, November 28, 1891, Curtis to Shepard, Morwell & Co., November
6, 1890, Curtis to A. Frank Richardson, October 31, 1890, Curtis to H. C.
Brown, February 28, 1893, *ibid.*

6   Curtis to W. S. Niles, December 4, 1890, Curtis to Percy Proctor, October 31,
1891, Curtis to B. T. Henry, March 10, 1891, *ibid.*

7   Curtis to J. Walter Thompson, January 16, 1892, in Curtis Letterbooks; Curtis
to Messrs. J. & J. Cash, February 10, 1892 in Curtis Letterbooks (intake volumes). See also Curtis to W. S. Niles, September 10, 1891, in Curtis Letterbooks.

8   Nathaniel C. Fowler, Jr., "Advertising for Women," *Printers' Ink*, V (August
26, 1891), 174–75; see Curtis to Deland, December 24, 1890, and Curtis to
George P. Rowell, April 2, 1894, in Curtis Letterbooks.

9   E. E. Calkins, *Business of Advertising* (New York: D. Appleton, 1915), illustrations following p. 118.

10 Ellery Sedgwick, *The Happy Profession* (Boston: Little, Brown, 1946), 294.

11 Curtis to N. W. Ayer, January 17, 1903, Curtis to L. M. Seaver, November 15,
1890, in Curtis Letterbooks.

12 Curtis Publishing Co., Condensed Report of the 1915 Advertising Conference
(Typescript in Charles Coolidge Parlin Papers, University of Pennsylvania Library, Philadelphia).

13 Sidney A. Sherman, "Advertising in the United States," *Publications of the
American Statistical Association*, VII (December, 1900), 140.

14 Edward Bok, *A Man from Maine* (New York: Charles Scribner's Sons, 1923),
107; Curtis to Balmer, January 12, 1892, Curtis to N. C. Fowler, Jr., November
24, 1890, Curtis to publisher, New York *Times*, January 11, 1899, January 24,
1899, Curtis to N. W. Ayer, January 18, 1899, October 19, 1899, all in Curtis
Letterbooks. Later Curtis ventured into one advertising innovation. Streetcar
posters temporarily advertised the *Saturday Evening Post* in Boston. Curtis
frowned on the expense and the lack of variety in exposure. After taking some
trips on Boston streetcars, he decided that he wanted no more to do with the
transit poster medium. The posters were badly illustrated and crude in spirit. See
Curtis to Charles M. Snyder, April 15, 1899, April 27, 1899, in Curtis Letterbooks.

15 Edward Bok to Messrs. C. L. MacArthur & Sons, April 15, 1890, in Edward
Bok Letterbooks, Historical Society of Pennsylvania; Curtis to Balmer, January
17, 1898, Curtis to Cornish & Co., September 25, 1890, in Curtis Letterbooks;
"The Editorial Point of View," *Advertising and Selling* [XIX], (May, 1910),
1619; *Profitable Advertising*, VII (January 15, 1898), 314.

16 Curtis to N. W. Ayer & Son, November 4, 1890, January 9, 1893, January 23,
1903, in Curtis Letterbooks.

17 Curtis to W. W. Hallock, January 12, 1893, *ibid.* Ten years later, American
advertisers organized a National Society for the Investigation and Suppression of
Fraudulent Advertising. Although the movement for the society had been
started by former Curtis employee John Adams Thayer, E. W. Spaulding, the

advertising director of the Curtis Publishing Company, was not interested in it. He wrote a letter to the editor of *Profitable Advertising* in which he said that no society could help matters if a reputable advertiser did not care whether bogus ads surrounded his own announcement. And, Spaulding asked, what job did a society fulfill, when an advertiser already refused to do business with those greedy publishers who were hungry for any scrap of advertising they could grab. See "In Pursuit of the Fraud," *Profitable Advertising*, XII (January, 1903), 632; and in the same issue, see letters from Spaulding and Oscar E. Binner, both on p. 643.

18   Curtis to N. W. Ayer & Son, January 12, 1893, February 17, 1892, in Curtis Letterbooks.

19   Ralph M. Hower, *The History of an Advertising Agency: N. W. Ayer & Sons at Work, 1869-1929* (Cambridge, Mass.: Harvard University Press, 1939), 90; Curtis to C. L. MacArthur and Son, December 4, 1890, Curtis to Daniels, February 20, 1891, both in Curtis Letterbooks.

20   Curtis to W. H. Maule, January 20, 1891, Curtis to editor, *Printers' Ink*, December 10, 1891, in Curtis Letterbooks.

21   Bok, *A Man from Maine*, 112-16; E. E. Calkins, *And hearing not. . . Annals of an Adman* (New York: Charles Scribner's Sons, 1946), 211-12. On a trust agreement between Curtis and Ayer, see N. W. Ayer to T. Seymour Scott, August 14, 1891, in Curtis Letterbooks (intake volumes). See also, Bok, "A Woman's Laugh," 319.

22   Fowler to Curtis, May 4, 1892, in Curtis Letterbooks (intake volumes).

23   Curtis to Lord & Thomas, January 18, 1892, in Curtis Letterbooks.

24   Bok to W. I. Way, December 3, 1889, in Bok Letterbooks; Curtis to W. H. Rowson, September 25, 1890, Curtis to L. G. Jones, December 2, 1901, in Curtis Letterbooks.

25   Curtis Publishing Co., *Intensive Methods for Sales Promotion by Curtis District Agents* (Philadelphia: Curtis, 1911); Curtis to Joseph P. Smith, December 1, 1890, in Curtis Letterbooks.

26   Curtis to H. N. McKinney, November 11, 1902, in Curtis Letterbooks.

27   Curtis to Central News Company, March 26, 1891, *ibid.*

28   William V. Alexander to W. Keen, March 14, 1910, in William V. Alexander Letterbooks in the Parlin Papers. See also an earlier reference: "The Magazine with a Million," *LHJ*, XX (February, 1903), 16; U.S. Federal Trade Commission, *FTC v. The Curtis Publishing Co., Respondent* (Washington, D.C.: Government Printing Office, 1918), 3-4.

29   John Walsh to Joseph Tumulty, October 26, 1920, in Edward Bok Foundation, Woodrow Wilson Papers, Manuscripts Division, Library of Congress.

30   Curtis to Grace Patterson, February 26, 1891, Curtis to J. Ralph Brown, August 9, 1893, Curtis to John M. Dandy, November 22, 1890, Curtis to Proctor, October 9, 1891, all in Curtis Letterbooks; *LHJ*, XI (November, 1894), 14.

31   "The Magazine with a Million," 16. See also *Profitable Advertising*, XV (November, 1905), 544. Curtis to E. H. Johnson, October 7, 1904, in Curtis Letterbooks; Edward Bok, "Editor's Personal Page," *LHJ*, XXIII (August, 1906), 1.

32   Curtis to T. Warren Gould, August 5 and August 8, 1893, Curtis to Balmer,

June 16, 1893, in Curtis Letterbooks.
33   Curtis to Canfield Rubber Co., June 8, 1889, in Curtis Letterbooks (intake volumes).
34   Peterson, *Magazines in the Twentieth Century*, 27–28; William H. Boyenton, *Audit Bureau of Circulations* (Chicago: Audit Bureau of Circulations, 1948), 12.
35   Curtis to Omaha *Bee*, September 30, 1890, Curtis to J. W. Heaton, October 8, 1891, Curtis to Gould, April 23, 1894, Curtis to W. H. Danforth, March 28, 1904, all in Curtis Letterbooks; Edward Bok to Edwin C. Madden, April 17, 1901, in Bok Letterbooks.
36   Bok proposed this plan to the president of Vassar College, J. M. Taylor, on December 18, 1889, and on February 14, 1890 he wrote to the presidents of Columbia, Dartmouth, Princeton, Yale, and Harvard to ask help in extending the idea to include boys, all in Bok letterbooks; Bok, *A Man from Maine*, 132–34.
37   Curtis to Elizabeth Morrell, February 3, 1891, January 22, 1891, in Curtis Letterbooks.
38   Curtis to Henry S. Mustin, November 28, 1890, Curtis to J. E. McDermott, September 30, 1890, *ibid.* Not every advertiser enjoyed good results. A perfume manufacturer caustically replied to Curtis' inquiry: "We have had two (2) responses. Cost of Adv. $395.43 result in sales $1.00 difference charged to 'Experience a/c'—This same peculiar barrenness of reach has characterized all our Home Journal advertising during 1890–1891 during which time we have paid you some $1500 or $2000. without any adequate resulting benefit either direct or indirect. . . . As our contract (to which you held us after we discovered it did not yield results) is now complete we must cease to be among your Advertisers." Lazell, Dalley, & Co. to Curtis, December 23, 1891, in Curtis Letterbooks (intake volumes).
39   Curtis to Woodard and Lathop [*sic*], October 20, 1890, Curtis to E. T. Burrowes & Co., March 13, 1891, Curtis to Proctor, October 15, 1902, Curtis to W. F. Holloway, December 9, 1891, in Curtis Letterbooks; Frank Presbrey, *The History and Development of Advertising* (Garden City, New York: Doubleday, Doran, 1929), 481. Also see Curtis to Holloway, December 9, 1891, in Curtis Letterbooks.
40   Bok, *A Man from Maine*, 120; Curtis to H. C. Brown, June 25, 1891, Curtis to Proctor, October 9, 1891, October 26, 1891, Curtis to W. S. Niles, December 10, 1891, February 10, 1892, all in Curtis Letterbooks.
41   Curtis to Balmer, July 2, 1900, Curtis to W. S. Niles, September 10, 1900, *ibid.*; see p. 727, following Alexander to Doubleday, Page, February 1901, in Alexander Letterbooks.
42   Curtis to W. S. Niles, September 10, 1900, Curtis to W. W. Haen, October 29, 1901, in Curtis Letterbooks.
43   Many letters refer to shortness of cash, as in Curtis to Proctor, April 22, 1891, and Curtis to Herbert Booth King & Bros., April 22, 1891; see also Curtis to Seaver, September 21, 1891, *ibid.*
44   Curtis to W. S. Niles, December 29, 1891, Curtis to D. E. Dallum, March 14, 1891, Curtis to Mr. Childs, March 17, 1891, *ibid.*
45   Curtis to Ernest Birmingham, June 15, 1894, Curtis to E. Press, January 5,

1891, *ibid.*

46 Curtis to Proctor, October 9, 1891, Curtis to George M. S. Horton, February 17, 1898, *ibid.*

47 Alexander to Augusta Lawrence, September 17, 1898, in Alexander Letterbooks; Bok to J. G. Kitchell, January 4, 1905, in Bok Letterbooks; Alexander to Louis Sibthorp, December 26, 1901, in Alexander Letterbooks.

48 Curtis to Marietta Holly, October 26, 1897, Curtis to Birmingham, January 3, 1898, Curtis to Balmer, July 12, 1899, February 10, 1898, June 6, 1898, June 20, 1898, Curtis to William H. Maher, April 1, 1899, all in Curtis Letterbooks; Peterson, *Magazines in the Twentieth Century*, 12.

49 Lord & Thomas, *America's Magazines and Their Relation to the Advertiser* (Chicago: Lord & Thomas, 1895), 8; Walter A. Gaw, "Some Important Trends in the Development of Magazines in the United States as an Advertising Medium," (Ph.D. dissertation, New York University, 1942), 177, 177n.

50 Quoted in Hugh E. Agnew and Warren B. Dygert, *Advertising Media* (New York: McGraw-Hill, 1938), 31.

51 Curtis to Flora Jones, February 5, 1891, Curtis to B. T. Henry, December 5, 1890, Curtis to George P. Rowell & Co., February 12, 1891, Curtis to Gervaise Graham, January 20, 1891, Curtis to B. T. Henry, February 9, 1891, all in Curtis Letterbooks.

52 Curtis to R. L. Watkins, September 30, 1890, Curtis to George P. Rowell & Co., February 12, 1891, in Curtis Letterbooks. The publisher was a little surprised that *Journal* readers so strenuously objected to hair and complexion advertisements. In *A Man from Maine,* Bok said that it was Curtis' own convictions that led to the omission of cosmetics advertising from the *Journal* (pp. 130–31). Curtis' reasons, however, seem to have been based on *Journal* readers' wishes.

53 Curtis to H. W. Seiter, September 25, 1890, Curtis to Watkins, September 30, 1890, Curtis to George P. Rowell & Co., October 2, 1890, November 9, 1891, Curtis to Lord and Thomas, October 2, 1890, Curtis to Herbert Booth King and Bro., February 22, 1891, all in Curtis Letterbooks. Thayer, in *Out of the Rut,* inaccurately claimed to have convinced Curtis to omit patent-medicine advertising after Thayer joined the company in 1892 (p. 41). Presbrey, in *History and Development of Advertising* (p. 481), said 1893 was the year for exclusion of medical advertising, not 1892 as Bok said, in *The Americanization of Edward Bok* (New York: Pocket Books, 1965), 246. Most students, up to now, have used either 1892 or 1893 as the date for medical advertising exclusion. R. S. Thain to Curtis, March 16, 1889, in Curtis Letterbooks (intake volumes).

54 Curtis to Lord & Thomas, February 19, 1891, Curtis to E. N. Erickson, February 21, 1891, Curtis to Thompson, December 18, 1890, Curtis to Lord & Thomas, October 2, 1890, all in Curtis Letterbooks. See also "Do You Read Advertisements?," *LHJ,* V (November 1888), 10; Curtis to Balmer, March 4, 1892, Curtis to Remington Bros., September 9, 1892, Curtis to N. W. Ayer & Son, September 16, 1892, all in Curtis Letterbooks.

55 George Burton Hotchkiss, *Milestones of Marketing: A Brief History of the Evolution of Market Distribution* (New York: Macmillan, 1938), 205; Presbrey, *History and Development of Advertising,* 364; Curtis Publishing Co., *Ladies' Home Journal*

Annual Trend of Columns and Lineage by Offices from 1892 to Date and Annual Trend of Revenue by Offices from 1892 to Date:

Year	Lines	Revenue
1892	97,197	$258,972.73
1893	105,793	301,431.38
1894	92,553	314,540.00
1895	99,230	389,136.00
1896	101,929	448,054.75
1897	100,119	500,630.00
1898	107,259	536,795,00
1899	129,249	646,245.00

56   Curtis to J. W. Pyle, December 20, 1890, Curtis to Mrs. Lonlowry Elkhenlly, January 21, 1891, Curtis to Mrs. A. K. T. Carey, November 22, 1890, all in Curtis Letterbooks.

57   Alexander to Messrs. Cordley and Hayes, June 29, 1899, in Alexander Letterbooks; Curtis to Montague Marks, February 25, 1891, Curtis to J. Q. Bradish & Co., December 13, 1890, both in Curtis Letterbooks; Bok to L. L. Roush, October 21, 1899, in Bok Letterbooks.

58   Alexander to Sarah Tyson Rorer, April 17, 1901, in Alexander Letterbooks; Bok to O. C. Harn, February 12, 1907, in Bok Letterbooks.

59   *LHJ*, XI (November, 1894), 27. See the trade announcement in *Profitable Advertising*, III (March 15, 1894), 304.

60   Quoted in Max A. Geller, *Advertising at the Crossroads: Federal Regulation vs. Voluntary Controls* (New York: Ronald Press, 1952), 216.

61   Curtis to Emily Vaughn, October 15, 1891, in Curtis Letterbooks; Bok to Eben E. Rexford, May 8, 1900, Bok to E. Warman, February 19, 1901, both in Bok Letterbooks; Alexander to all editors and magazine contributors, first sent February 1, 1901, in Alexander Letterbooks.

62   Edward Bok, "At Home with the Editor," *LHJ*, XII (August, 1895), 12; Bok, "Fifteen Years of Mistakes," *LHJ*, XV (November, 1898), 18; Curtis to Lyman D. Morse, December 17, 1889, in Curtis Letterbooks; Bok to Rexford, December 13, 1889, in Bok Letterbooks; Alexander to Emelyn L. Coolidge, December 15, 1903, in Alexander Letterbooks.

63   See series of letters from Alexander to Mound City Dishwasher Co., November 5, 1908, November 28, 1908, to A. F. Naylor, June 28, 1909, and to R. H. Dallugs, January 19, 1910, in Alexander Letterbooks; Curtis to Balmer, March 14, 1892, Curtis to Mrs. A. L. Twining, October 23, 1890, Curtis to publishers of *Farm and Home*, June 25, 1901, Curtis to Publishers' Collections Agency, June 28, 1901, all in Curtis Letterbooks.

64   Curtis to W. S. Niles, October 27, 1891, Curtis to B. T. Henry, January 13, 1892, and see also Curtis to Meriden Britannia Co., January 7, 1901, soliciting an advertisement because of some planned "Chafing Dish" articles, *ibid.* N. W. Ayer was the main agency through whom Curtis placed advertising; Niles was a salaried Curtis employee.

65   Alexander to International Silver Co., May 21, 1901, in Alexander Letterbooks; *Profitable Advertising*, XI (November, 1901), 465, and VIII (June 15, 1898), 50; Curtis to Franklin Mills Co., January 7, 1901, in Curtis Letterbooks.

66 Hower, *History of an Advertising Agency,* 426–30; 622 n83.
67 Curtis Publishing Co., *Curtis Advertising Code with Digest of Rulings (For Use of Representatives Only)* (Philadelphia: Curtis, 1914), p. 25 of digest and p. 14 of code, in Parlin Papers.
68 Curtis Publishing Co., *Selling Forces* (Philadelphia: Curtis, 1913), 86; Curtis Publishing Co., *Two Color Advertising: Its Advantages and Uses, with Some Examples of Effective Arrangement, Combination and Treatment* (Philadelphia: Curtis, 1917), 3, in Parlin Papers.
69 Curtis to Flora Jones, December 8, 1891, Curtis to J. McDermott, September 30, 1890, in Curtis Letterbooks.
70 Bok to L. E. Howard, June 27, 1890, in Bok Letterbooks; Curtis to S. R. Niles, May 15, 1891, Curtis to F. A. Ferris & Co., April 2, 1891, Curtis to T. B. Browne, August 3, 1892, Curtis to S. H. Parvin's Sons, January 8, 1891, Curtis to Remington Bros., December 12, 1891, all in Curtis Letterbooks; see Thayer, *Out of the Rut,* 49–50; Presbrey, *History and Development of Advertising,* 437; see list of advertising rates per page in *Advertising and Selling* (January, 1914), 28.
71 Curtis to R. P. Tillman, October 25, 1890, Curtis to B. T. Henry, April 22, 1891, both in Curtis Letterbooks.
72 Curtis to B. T. Henry, November 18, 1891, in Curtis Letterbooks; Otis Pease, *The Responsibilities of American Advertising: Private Control and Public Influence, 1920–1940* (New Haven, Conn.: Yale University Press, 1958), 7.
73 Curtis to Royal Baking Powder Co., December 24, 1890, Curtis to Messrs. G. & C. Merriam Co., September 26, 1892, both in Curtis Letterbooks. Curtis' man in charge of the Boston advertising office, B. J. Henry, wanted the *Journal* to give special consideration to rates for major advertisers interested in monthly insertions. See B. J. Henry to Curtis, November 21, 1891, in Curtis Letterbooks (intake volumes).
74 Royal Baking Powder Co. to *Ladies' Home Journal,* April 23, 1892, in Curtis Letterbooks (intake volumes); Curtis to Balmer, March 14, 1892, in Curtis Letterbooks; *Printers' Ink,* VI (January 27, 1892), 125.
75 James W. Young, *Advertising Agency Compensation in Relation to the Total Cost of Advertising* (Chicago: University of Chicago Press, 1933), 33; Curtis to A. R. Elliott, December 22, 1891, Curtis to E. H. Baker, January 22, 1891, Curtis to Robinson-Baker Advertising Bureau, September 30, 1890, all in Curtis Letterbooks.
76 Curtis to E. W. Spaulding, January 17, 1898, in Curtis Letterbooks.
77 The advertising offices of the *Journal* at this time were in Chicago, New York, Philadelphia, and Boston. The San Francisco office opened in 1914. See Thayer, *Out of the Rut,* 52–53; Calkins, *And hearing not,* 247; Curtis to W. S. Niles, December 6, 1892, in Curtis Letterbooks; Hower, *History of an Advertising Agency,* 408–409.
78 Curtis to Lord and Thomas, November 2, 1898, in Curtis Letterbooks.
79 See *Profitable Advertising,* III (July 15, 1893), 48, 51, and "Dry Goods Advertising in Boston," *Profitable Advertising,* VII (May 15, 1898), 460; Oscar Binner, "Illustrated Advertising," *ibid.,* VIII (June 15, 1898), 42–43; Curtis to Balmer, March 14, 1892, in Curtis Letterbooks; Nathaniel C. Fowler, Jr., to Curtis, September 10, 1890, in Curtis Letterbooks (intake volumes); "Designing for Advertisers: Interesting Facts About the Commercial Art Bureau of the 'Ladies'

Home Journal'...," *Profitable Advertising,* XI (January, 1902), 663; *Printers' Ink,* LI (June 28, 1905), 12; Bok, "At Home" *LHJ,* XII (August, 1895), 12; "The Magazines and Their Cover Designing," *Profitable Advertising,* XVII (July, 1907), 184. In "Some Important Trends," p. 85n, Gaw said that he found no evidence to contradict the Curtis claim to be the first American magazine to introduce monthly cover changes. Curtis to Humphrey Advertising Agency, November 29, 1890, Curtis to W. S. Niles, February 21, 1891, Curtis to Herbert Booth King and Bro., March 14, 1891, Curtis to Charles A. Stevens & Bros., September 27, 1890, all in Curtis Letterbooks.

80   Curtis to National Cloak Co., October 1, 1890, Curtis to Woodard and Lathop [sic], October 20, 1890, in Curtis Letterbooks. Percentages are based on tallies in Gaw, "Some Important Trends," p. 76n.

81   Thayer, *Out of the Rut,* 38; *Profitable Advertising,* III (December 15, 1893), 198; Curtis to W. S. Niles, February 25, 1891, in Curtis Letterbooks; Louis Asher and Edith Heal, *Send No Money* (Chicago: Argus, 1942), 35–36. Curtis' rejection of Sears, Roebuck advertising copy antedated the exclusion of all mail-order general merchandise advertising; Curtis to Messrs. George Batten & Co., February 3, 1900, in Curtis Letterbooks.

82   Curtis to H. C. Brown, January 19, 1893, Curtis to Robert P. Tillden, February 18, 1893, both in Curtis Letterbooks.

83   Bok, "Fifteen Years," *LHJ,* XV (November, 1898), 18; Curtis to E. M. White, March 29, 1892, Curtis to Balmer, July 12, 1899, in Curtis Letterbooks; Gaw, "Some Important Trends," 161–62.

84   Curtis Publishing Co., Condensed Report of the 1915 Advertising Conference (Typescript in Parlin Papers), 75–76.

85   Curtis to W. S. Niles, March 26, 1892, in Curtis Letterbooks.

86   Bok to Proctor, June 7, 1901, in Bok Letterbooks.

87   Advertising Department, Curtis Publishing Co., "An Estimate of the Trading Population, Volume of Business and *Ladies' Home Journal* Pattern Sales in all Cities of the United States of 5,000 Population and Over" (Typescript, 1913, in Parlin Papers).

88   Charles Coolidge Parlin, "The Philosophy of Buying," June 23, 1914 (Text of speech, in speech file on *Ladies' Home Journal,* in Parlin Papers).

89   "Testimonial Dinner for Charles Coolidge Parlin" (Transcript in Parlin Papers).

CHAPTER II

1   Interview with Mrs. Curtis Bok, Edward Bok's daughter-in-law, June, 1966.

2   Flora M. Holly, "Notes on Some American Magazine Editors," *Bookman,* XII (December, 1900), 360.

3   "The Story of a Magazine," *Chatauquan Advertising Supplement* [1890], in Parlin Papers. See also Philadelphia *Evening Public Ledger,* January 9, 1930. Mrs. Curtis Bok rejects Bok's estimate of the family's position in the Netherlands. She said in a June, 1966, interview that William Bok was a public notary and in that way served the crown.

4   Edward W. Bok to Benjamin Harrison, December 16, 1896, in Benjamin Harrison Papers, Manuscripts Division, Library of Congress.

5   Marvin Ferree, "Mr. Bok," *Independent,* LXXXIII (July 5, 1915), 19; George

Britt, *Forty Years–Forty Millions: The Career of Frank A. Munsey* (New York: Farrar & Rinehart, 1935), 62.

6 Ishbel Ross, *Ladies of the Press* (New York: Harper & Bros., 1936), 21. See back of Bok to Cyrus Curtis, June 25, 1889, in Curtis Letterbooks (intake volumes). William G. Bleyer, *Main Currents in the History of American Journalism* (Boston: Houghton Mifflin, 1927), 399; Bok, *Americanization*, 103, 104. Edwin Emery, *The Press and America: An Interpretive History of Journalism* (Englewood Cliffs, N.J.: Prentice-Hall, 1962), 566.

7 Bok to Curtis, [summer, 1889], in Curtis Letterbooks (intake volumes); Bok to A. B. Frost, May 5, 1890, in Bok Letterbooks; *Profitable Advertising*, III (October 15, 1893), 145.

8 Bok to Amelia Barr, October 11, 1890, Bok to Jessie Benton Fremont, July 8, 1890, Bok to Mrs. S. D. Power, September 6, 1890, in Bok Letterbooks.

9 Interview with Mrs. Curtis Bok, August, 1964. See also Bok to Mrs. Bunce, February 7, 1890, in Bok Letterbooks; William V. Alexander to Emelyn Coolidge, August 4, 1905, Alexander to E. Saxton Winter, August 4, 1905, in Alexander Letterbooks.

10 Edward Bok, *The Young Man in Business* (Boston: L. C. Page, 1900), 17, 21, 27.

11 *Ibid.*, 12. Bok modified this viewpoint. In 1913 he urged his *Journal* readers to provide youth with "special training" for the "complicated days of bitter competition and economic unrest." He seemed to be suggesting that, by 1913, it would take more than "hustling" for young people to succeed. See *LHJ*, XXX (February, 1913), 6.

12 Bok, *Young Man in Business*, 7, 18, 22, 30; Edward Bok, *Successward* (New York: F. H. Revell Co., 1895), 53–54; Edward Bok, *Why I Believe in Poverty as the Richest Experience That Can Come to a Boy* (Boston: Houghton Mifflin, 1915), 16. Also available in *LHJ*, XXXII (April, 1915), 6.

13 "Simple Faith," *The New Republic*, V (December 4, 1915), 111.

14 Edward Bok, *The Young Man and the Church* (Philadelphia: Henry Altemus, 1896), 28.

15 *Ibid.*, 8, 10–11; Edward Bok, *You: A Personal Message* (Boston and New York: Medici Society of America, 1926), 20.

16 Bok, *Young Man and the Church*, 22, 23.

17 Edward Bok, *Twice Thirty: Some Short and Simple Annals of the Road* (New York: Charles Scribner's Sons, 1925), 496.

18 Bok to George P. Morris, November 15, 1889, Bok to Margaret Bottome, July 11, 1890, both in Bok Letterbooks. Ten years later, Bok was urging less didacticism. See Bok to Joseph Jefferson, December 14, 1900, *ibid.*

19 *LHJ* XII (May, 1895), 14, and (July, 1895), 26.

20 Edward Bok, "At Home with the Editor," *LHJ*, XII (May, 1895), 12. In 1891 Parkhurst was president of the Society for the Prevention of Crime and later led the agitation for investigation of the New York City police force by the state legislature.

21 *LHJ*, XII (January, 1895), 6.

22 Alexander to Charles M. Sheldon, June 5, 1899, in Alexander Letterbooks; Bok to Sheldon, June 12, 1899, Bok to Francis E. Clark, June 11, 1900, both in Bok Letterbooks.

23 Edward Bok, *Dollars Only* (New York: Charles Scribner's Sons, 1926), 83.

24 *Ibid.*, 79; Bok, *Americanization*, 258.

25 Edward Bok, "Where I Think Glenn Frank Is Wrong," *Century*, CVI (July, 1923), 450.

26 Bok, *You: A Personal Message*, 15–16.

27 Edward Bok, "The Blot on Our American Life," *LHJ*, XII (July, 1895), 14; *LHJ*, XI (November, 1894), 14.

28 Bok, "At Home," *LHJ*, XII (March, 1895), 12.

29 Bok to Maurice Hewlett, January 1, 1908, Bok to Maud Howe Elliott, May 22, 1890, both in Bok Letterbooks.

30 *LHJ*, XXIV (February, 1907), 6. Bok once asked a writer to prepare an article on the graceful way to ring a doorbell. See Bok to Florence Howe Hall, November 7, 1890, in Bok Letterbooks.

31 Owen Kildare, "Christmas with Us in the Tenements," *LHJ*, XXIV (December, 1906), 26.

32 Alexander to Mrs. John C. Wyman, September 22, 1898, Alexander to Mary E. Trueblood, August 1, 1899, Alexander to David Paulson, March 7, 1910, all in Alexander Letterbooks; Bok to Mrs. Ballington Booth, September 30, 1898, October 18, 1898, in Bok Letterbooks.

33 Alexander to C. F. Ray, August 2, 1901, in Alexander Letterbooks.

34 *LHJ*, XXIV (July, 1907), 35.

35 John F. a'Beckett, "Blind Tom as He Is To-Day," *LHJ*, XV (September, 1898), 13.

36 Emil G. Hirsch, "How the Jew Regards Christmas," and Joseph Krauskopf, "What the Great Jewish Festival Means," *LHJ*, XXIV (December, 1906), 10.

37 *LHJ*, XXVI (July, 1909), 3; Bok, *Dollars Only*, 181.

38 Edward Bok, "Editor's Personal Page," *LHJ*, XXX (September, 1913), 1, and XXXI (March, 1914), 1.

39 "After the Jew Again," *LHJ*, XXXII (May, 1915), 4.

40 William G. Jordan [Bok's managing editor before Alexander] to the Rev. Gottheil, June 18, 1897, in Alexander Letterbooks.

41 "Our Schools and Our Teachers," *LHJ*, XII (September, 1895), 12.

42 Lola D. Wangner, "Into Such Hands Do We Commit Our Children," *LHJ*, XXIV (May, 1907), 63; *LHJ*, XXIV (June, 1907), 5.

43 See Bok to H. E. Rood, February 18, 1890, Bok to Edward Warman, January 20, 1899, in Bok Letterbooks. Bok tried to negotiate an article on convent life to refute "the popular fallacies that there exists some secretive work in convents." See Bok to A. G. Lanigan, May 16, 1890, *ibid.* Bicycling, although popular in the 1890s, was also controversial because of the special dress that had to be worn by women; Emily LaFarge Clayton, "The Pope and the Man," *LHJ*, XXIV (January, 1907), 36–37.

44 John Higham, *Strangers in the Land* (New York: Atheneum, 1963), especially Chap. 5.

45 Interview with Esther Everett Lape, May 11, 1966; Edward Bok, "Why Are We Building a 350 Million Dollar Canal," *LHJ*, XXVIII (October, 1911), 21; Arthur Bullard, "The Appalling Jungle at America's Door," *LHJ*, XXXI (November, 1914), 16; Woodrow Wilson, "The Mexican Question," *LHJ*, XXXIII (October, 1916), 9.

46 Karl Harriman to Joseph Tumulty, April 26, 1916, and June 22, 1916, with Wilson's penciled "no," in Edward W. Bok Foundation, Wilson Papers.

CHAPTER III

1   Bok, *Americanization*, 271; Bok, *Twice Thirty*, 372; Sedgwick, *Happy Profession*, 294; William Dana Orcutt, *Celebrities Off Parade* (Chicago: Willett, Clark, 1935), 234.
2   Edward Bok to Margaret Bottome, July 16, 1890, Bok to Mrs. M. B. H. Williams, March 27, 1890, both in Bok Letterbooks.
3   Peter Lyon to author, postal card, October 20, 1965; Bok to Emily Meigs Ripley, October 15, 1890, in Bok Letterbooks.
4   "The Ladies' Home Journal—The Saturday Evening Post and the New Building for the Curtis Publishing Co.," *Profitable Advertising*, XVIII (October, 1908), 469; Edward Bok, *Explaining the Editor* (N.p., January 19, 1901), 12, 31; Bok, "Editor's Personal Page," *LHJ*, XXIII (September, 1906), 1; Bok, *Americanization*, 118.
5   Curtis Publishing Company, Minutes of the Tenth Annual Conference, Advertising Department of the Curtis Publishing Company (Typescript, October, 1913, in Parlin Papers), 334–36.
6   Bok to Curtis Brown, December 23, 1907, one of Shaw's agents, in Bok Letterbooks; Cyrus Curtis to E. L. Philbrook, March 20, 1895, in Curtis Letterbooks; Bok to Benjamin Harrison, June 29, 1896, in Harrison Papers; William V. Alexander to Ida Shaper Hoxie, July 24, 1901, in Alexander Letterbooks.
7   Bok to R. C. Coldwell, July 14, 1898, Bok to Arthur C. Coit, March 22, 1905, in Bok Letterbooks. Bok maintained a strict separation between his private life and his editorial person. His family, hobbies, and interests were never directly revealed in the pages of the *Journal*. Bok, *Americanization*, 228.
8   Bok to Florence E. French, November 13, 1889, Bok to Kate T. Woods, March 14, 1890, Bok to Ella Wheeler Wilcox, June 6, 1890, Bok to Mrs. John H. Mason, March 31, 1902, Bok to Hamlin Garland, August 4, 1899, all in Bok Letterbooks.
9   Bok to Samuel L. Clemens, September 29, 1898, *ibid.* For a writer's response to office rules, see Rudyard Kipling to Bok, May 11, 1895, in Carpenter Kipling Papers, Rare Books Division, Library of Congress. Kipling wrote that if he had known about the policy of no reference to intoxicating beverages, he would not have submitted his manuscript to the *Journal*.
10 Bok to Rebecca Cameron, September 20, 1890, in Bok Letterbooks.
11 Bok to Florence Marryat, October 9, 1890, *ibid.*
12 Bok to Kate Tannett Woods, June 11, 1890, Bok to Eben Rexford, November 8, 1890, Bok to Leigh Mitchell Hodges, May 31, 1899, *ibid.* (Hodges was to receive $50 per month for scouting in New York City.) See also Alexander to Florence E. Bate, November 25, 1903, in Alexander Letterbooks; Edward Bok, "Fifteen Years of Mistakes," *LHJ* XV (November, 1898), 18.
13 Bok to the National Cloak Co., June 4, 1890, in Bok Letterbooks; Curtis to George H. Lewars, April 9, 1901, in Curtis Letterbooks.
14 Bok to Mrs. William M. Martin, August 6, 1901, Bok to Emma Haywood, August 24, 1898, in Bok Letterbooks; Bok, *Americanization*, 121–23.
15 Curtis Publishing Co., Minutes of the Tenth Annual Conference, 320, 321,

324, 325; Curtis Publishing Co., Condensed Report of 1915 Advertising Conference (Typescript in Parlin Papers).

16   Curtis to Edward Brown, September 26, 1892, in Curtis Letterbooks; Bok, *Americanization*, 314; Bok, *Dollars Only*, 94; Curtis Publishing Co., Minutes of the Tenth Annual Conference, 344–45.

17   See Walter Davenport and James Derieux, *Ladies, Gentlemen and Editors* (Garden City, N.Y.: Doubleday, 1960), 177; Britt, *Forty Years—Forty Millions*, 62.

18   Alexander to Mrs. John Dawson Follett, December 11, 1903, in Alexander Letterbooks.

19   Alexander to Follett, May 20, 1904, Alexander to Elizabeth Harrison, February 8, 1909, Alexander to Alice B. Snyder, October 10, 1900, Alexander to Mrs. S. T. Rorer, April 7, 1899, *ibid.*

20   On Alexander's authority, see Alexander to Lillian Whitney Babcock, July 21, 1909, *ibid.*

21   Alexander to Follett, May 20, 1904, June 6, 1905, *ibid.*

22   Alexander to E. Saxton Winter, January 16, 1909, *ibid.*

23   Alexander to Mrs. Francis W. Ralston, May 3, 1905, Alexander to Follett, September 15, 1904, *ibid.*

24   Interview with Esther Everett Lape, May 11, 1966, New York City.

25   Alexander to Anna Barrons, January 13, 1909, Alexander to Mrs. Thaddeus Horton, March 19, 1900, in Alexander Letterbooks.

26   Bok often mentioned this to prospective contributors. See Bok to Robert Collyer, November 19, 1889, in Bok Letterbooks.

27   Bok to Helen Moody, September 5, 1898, Bok to Mrs. Humphry, October 21, 1899, *ibid.*; see also Edward Bok, "Modern Literary King," *Forum*, XX (November, 1895), 334–43; Bok to George W. Elliott, November 20, 1889, Bok to Mrs. Henry Ward Beecher, November 20, 1889, Bok to Annie Hector, December 5, 1889, Bok to Miss Scidmore, May 1, 1890, all in Bok Letterbooks; Alexander to G. E. Lumsden, September 17, 1898, in Alexander Letterbooks.

28   Bok to Benjamin Harrison, August 1, 1896, September 10, 1896, Harrison to Bok, August 4, 1896, August 10, 1896, in Harrison Papers.

29   Bok to Finley Peter Dunne, correspondence from December, 1899, to January, 1900, in Bok Letterbooks.

30   See the following letters on one instance of plagiarism: Alexander to John Northern Hilliard, October 13, 1899, October 20, 1899, Alexander to William A. Taylor, October 20, 1899, November 22, 1899, Alexander to Francis B. Mitchell, November 2, 1899, in Alexander Letterbooks; Bok to Frank E. Holiday, June 6, 1890, in Bok Letterbooks.

31   Alexander to the Fashions Publishing Co., January 22, 1904, in Alexander Letterbooks. See also Curtis to the editor-in-chief, Detroit *Journal*, October 23, 1890, in Curtis Letterbooks.

32   Edward Bok, "The American Business Man," *LHJ*, XXXIII (October, 1916), 8. See Chap. 4, herein.

33   Curtis to Lewars, April 9, 1901, in Curtis Letterbooks.

34   Curtis to W. S. Niles, November 20, 1891, December 29, 1891, Curtis to N. W. Ayer & Sons, January 9, 1893, *ibid*; Bok to C. A. Page, December 5, 1889, Bok to D. S. Knowlton, November 8, 1889, in Bok Letterbooks; Curtis to

Thomas Balmer, February 19, 1898, Curtis to C. E. Staples, July 11, 1892, in Curtis Letterbooks.

35   Curtis to Mrs. K. M. Tyson, April 25, 1894, Curtis to Messrs. Katz and Freeman, February 17, 1898, Curtis to Balmer, February 23, 1898, Curtis to William D. Moffatt, June 19, 1899, in Curtis Letterbooks.

36   Bok, *Americanization*, 143; Curtis to H. N. McKinney, December 13, 1901, in Curtis Letterbooks.

37   Edward Bok, "The Day of the Advertisement," *Atlantic Monthly*, CXXXII (October, 1923), 534, 536; Presbrey, *History and Development of Advertising*, 586; George Burton Hotchkiss, *An Outline of Advertising* (New York: Macmillan, 1933), 456.

38   Frank Luther Mott, A *History of American Magazines* (4 vols.; Cambridge, Mass.: Belknap Press of Harvard University Press, 1957), IV, 32; Bok, *Americanization*, 168–69; Bok to Benjamin Harrison, September 11, 1895, in Harrison Papers.

39   Editorial, *LHJ*, XIII (September, 1896), 14. Almost a decade later, an excerpt from the June, 1905, *Mail-Order Journal* was printed, encouraging magazines to publish editorials on "'the value to readers in studying the offers made by advertisers.'" See "Educating Readers," *Printers' Ink*, LI (June 14, 1905), 35; in 1905, readers' confidence in magazines still seemed to be limited to giants like the *Journal*, the *Saturday Evening Post*, the *Woman's Magazine*, and *Collier's* according to this article.

40   Bok, "Fifteen Years," *LHJ*, XV (November, 1898), 18; for an early statement, see Edward Bok, "The Story of the Journal," *LHJ*, X (November, 1893), 13; see Bok, "Personal from the Editor," *LHJ*, XVI (November, 1899), 16. See also: S. H. Goddard, "Gotham Notes," *Profitable Advertising*, IV (May 15, 1895), 367.

41   Bok, "Personal," *LHJ*, XIX (December, 1901), 18; "A Magazine Question," *LHJ*, XXVIII (May 1, 1911), 5. Also see an earlier comment on the profits advertising brought to the magazine, in Bok, "Story of the *Journal*," *LHJ*, X (November, 1893), 13; Bok, "Editor's Personal Page," *LHJ*, XXXII (April, 1915), 49.

42   Curtis Publishing Co., Minutes of the 1915 Advertising Conference (Typescript in Parlin Papers); Alexander to Avery L. Rand, May 27, 1903, June 22, 1903, in Alexander Letterbooks.

43   Interview with Mrs. Curtis Bok, April 15, 1966.

44   George French, "Masters of the Magazine," *Twentieth Century Magazine*, V (April, 1912), 15.

45   Upton Sinclair, *The Brass Check: A Study of American Journalism* (Pasadena, Calif.: published by the author, 1920), 299.

46   The Country Contributor, "The Ideas of a Plain Country Woman," *LHJ*, XXXIV (June, 1917), 34; "Both Sides of Live Questions," *LHJ*, XXVII (December 1, 1910), 23, 42.

47   J. R. T. Hughes, "Eight Tycoons: The Entrepreneur and American History," in Ralph Andreano (ed.), *New Views on American Economic Development* (Cambridge, Mass.: Schenckman, 1965), 275–76.

48   Alexander to F. P. Dunne, May 22, 1899, in Alexander Letterbooks. A letter was originally sent to Frank Doubleday to give to Dunne, but a few days later

Bok requested that Doubleday not show Dunne the letter because he had by then learned that "Mr. Dooley had said that he was a bachelor and glad of it." Alexander to Frank Doubleday, May 24, 1899, in Alexander Letterbooks; Sedgwick, *Happy Profession*, 294.

49   Ferree, "Mr. Bok," 20; Bok, *Americanization*, 121; "The Rush of American Women," *LHJ*, XVI (January, 1899), 14. In fact, Bok once suggested that women just were not intelligent. Frederic W. Ayer asked Bok about the possibility of selling Curtis Company bonds to *Journal* readers through the magazine. Bok replied, "It would be practically impossible to make a statement simple enough to intelligently and convincingly explain the purchase of a bond in the Curtis Company as an investment in the Curtis Publishing Company." Bok to Ayer, August 2, 1900, in Bok Letterbooks. Despite this view, Bok had written five years earlier in the *Journal* that woman's intellectual equality with man had never been questioned. Bok, "A Third Sex," *LHJ*, XII (June, 1895), 14. Also, see Bok to Moody, September 5, 1898, in Bok Letterbooks.

50   Bok to Maurice Hewlett, January 1, 1908, in Bok Letterbooks.

51   Edward Bok, "At Home with the Editor," *LHJ*, XII (March, 1895), 12, and (November, 1895), 14; *LHJ*, VII (March, 1890), 8; "Woman's Mission of the Future," *LHJ*, IX (August, 1892), 12.

52   Bok to Benjamin Harrison, November 5, 1894, Harrison to Bok, November 12, 1894, Bok to Harrison, June 8, 1895, in Series II, Harrison Papers; Bok, "At Home," *LHJ*, XII (August, 1895), 12.

53   Edward Bok, "Een dracht maakt macht," *LHJ*, XV (September, 1898), 14; Grover Cleveland, "Woman's Mission and Woman's Clubs," *LHJ*, XXII (May, 1905), 3–4; "The Sane Woman's Club," *LHJ*, XXV (March, 1908). 5; "Invalids: Not Leaders," *LHJ*, XXV (September, 1908), 5; "A Town of Six Woman's Clubs," *LHJ*, XXVI (May, 1909), 3; Bok, "My Quarrel with Woman's Clubs," *LHJ*, XXVII (January, 1910), 5.

54   See Bok's speech, in Curtis Publishing Co., Minutes of the Tenth Annual Conference, 333; Mary I. Wood, "How to Organize a Woman's Club," *LHJ*, XXXI (October, 1914), 2.

55   Bok, "At Home," *LHJ*, XII (August, 1895), 12; Grover Cleveland, "Would Woman Suffrage Be Unwise," *LHJ*, XXII (October, 1905), 7–8; Edward Bok, "Behold the Emancipated Woman," *LHJ*, XXIII (April, 1906), 20; *LHJ*, XXVIII (January 1, 1911), 17; Bok, "Editor's Personal Page," *LHJ*, XXIX (March, 1912), 1.

56   For major articles opposed to suffrage, see the following in *LHJ*: XXVIII (January 1, 1911), 17; XXVIII (April 1, 1911), 6; XXIX (October, 1912), 24; XII (June, 1895), 15; XXII (October, 1905), 7–8. See the following editorials in *LHJ*: XXVI (February, 1909), 5–6; XXVII (March, 1910), 6; XXVII (June, 1910), 5; XXVIII (February 1, 1911), 5; XXVIII (September, 1911), 5; XXIX (June, 1912), 6; XXIX (July, 1912), 3.

57   Aileen Kraditor, *The Ideas of the Woman Suffrage Movement, 1890–1920* (New York: Columbia University Press, 1965), 67–69, 71.

58   *Ibid.*, 68. The Addams article was presented in the series, "Both Sides of Live Questions," *LHJ*, XXVII (January, 1910), 21–22. In the February, 1910, number, Lyman Abbott presented the other side, "Why the Vote Would Be Injurious to Women," 21–22. He asked women if they wanted the responsibility of governing all the citizens of the United States and "the millions of people in

the colonies which it has and is likely to have in the future." See Curtis Publishing Company, Minutes of the Tenth Annual Conference, 332, 334.

59   H. G. Wells, "The Woman and the War," *LHJ*, XXXIII (June, 1916), 10, 59–62; Sarah Bernhardt, "My France," *LHJ*, XXXIV (February, 1917), 11–12; Agnes C. Laut, "The Woman Who Has Gone and the Woman Who Has Come," *LHJ*, XXXIV (September, 1917), 32, 56. Also see Chap. VI, herein, on World War I and the *Journal*.

60   "Babies' Flannel and Parliament," *LHJ*, XXXI (November, 1914), 3; Karl Harriman to Joseph Tumulty, April 26, 1916, in Edward Bok Foundation, Wilson Papers; see also Harriman to Tumulty, June 22, 1916, *ibid*., with Wilson's penciled "no" on the letter.

61   Jane Addams, "As I See Women: In an Informal Talk with a Friend," *LHJ*, XXXII (August, 1915), 11, 54; Mary Hamilton Talbott, "Women Who Have Blazed New Trails Through the Forest of Men's Work Once Believed Closed to Their Sex," *LHJ*, XXXIV (February, 1917), 5.

62   "The Wife and Her Money," *LHJ*, XVIII (March, 1901), 16; editorial, *LHJ*, XXIV (January, 1907), 6; "Death's New Clutch on Women," *LHJ*, XXIV (October, 1907), 8; "A Wide-Open Field for Women," *LHJ*, XXVIII (January 1, 1911), 6.

63   In the 1890s, the *Journal* published a wide range of articles on employment for women. For example, see Emma Hooper, "Women as Dressmakers," *LHJ*, VIII (March, 1891), 4, and "Women as Stenographers," *LHJ*, VIII (February, 1891), 4; Charles Dumar, "Women as Typesetters," *LHJ*, VIII (June, 1891), 4; Ida M. Van Etten, "Women Behind the Counter," *LHJ*, IX (August, 1892), 9; Foster Coates, "Women in Journalism," *LHJ*, IX (September, 1892), 18; "A New Field for Women," *LHJ*, XXIX (April, 1912), 6; "Wanted: A Community Mother," *LHJ*, XXXII (May, 1915), 4; Bok's speech, in Curtis Publishing Company, Condensed Report of the 1915 Advertising Conference (Typescript in Parlin Papers).

64   "How Many of the Four Million Will Vote?," *LHJ*, XXXIII (April, 1916), 12; "Her Record," *LHJ*, XXXIII (October, 1916), 42; "A Woman's Question," *LHJ*, XXXII (March, 1915), 3.

65   Bok, *Americanization*, 216–17.

66   An American Mother, "The American Women in the Market-Place," *LHJ*, XVII (April, 1900), 19, and "What of the Woman Herself?" *LHJ*, XVIII (June, 1901), 10; J. Cardinal Gibbons, "The Restless Woman," *LHJ*, XIX (January, 1902), 6.

67   The Country Contributor, "The Ideas of a Plain Country Woman," *LHJ*, XXIII (February, 1906), 28; Edward Bok, "Shall Our Girls Go to College," *LHJ*, XV (August, 1898), 14, "Three Thousand Sensible Girls," *LHJ*, XVII (May, 1900), 16, and "The College Girl and the Stove," *LHJ*, XX (April, 1903), 16; Bok to Hewlett, January 1, 1908, in Bok Letterbooks.

68   Curtis Publishing Company, Minutes of the Tenth Annual Conference, 347.

69   Bok to Alice G. Lannigan, November 23, 1889, in Bok Letterbooks.

CHAPTER IV

1   Bok, *Americanization*, xv.

2   Sullivan, *Our Times*, I, 399.

3   Edward Bok to Maurice Hewlett, January 1, 1908, in Bok Letterbooks.

4. Cyrus Curtis to E. L. Philbrook, March 20, 1895, in Curtis Letterbooks.
5. Edward Bok, "Thirty Years," *LHJ*, XXXVII (January, 1920), 1; an advertise-ment for the *LHJ*, "The Open Secret of the *Journal*," *LHJ*, XXXII (October, 1915), 79; Curtis Publishing Co., Minutes of the 1915 Advertising Conference (Typescript in Parlin Papers).
6   *LHJ*, XXXI (June, 1914), 3; Richard Pratt, "Friend of the Family," *Quill*, XXIV (July, 1936), 7.
7   Edward Bok, "What Makes for American Men," *LHJ*, XXX (April, 1913), 5.
8. "Ill-Advised Charities," *LHJ*, XV (September, 1898), 14; "What One Woman Found Out," *LHJ*, XXXI (September, 1914), 6; "The First Social Service," *LHJ*, XXXI (October, 1914), 8.
9   "The Girl and the Waitress," *LHJ*, XXVII (July, 1910), 3; Clara E. Loughlin, "Bad Manners to the Poor," *LHJ*, XXXVI (June, 1919), 118; "Is This True?," *LHJ*, XXVIII (March 1, 1911), 6; Gerald Mygatt, "The Chambermaid in Your Hotel: The Tragedy of Her Life and Your Share in It," *LHJ*, XXXII (August, 1915), 14; "For Women of Leisure," *LHJ*, VII (January, 1890), 8.
10 "Where Shall These Girls Go?," *LHJ*, XXVII (June, 1910), 5.
11 William V. Alexander to Mrs. John C. Wyman, September 22, 1898, Alexan-der to Mary E. Trueblood, August 1, 1899, in Alexander Letterbooks.
12 "The New Servant Question," *LHJ*, XXX (March, 1913), 5; see also Curtis Publishing Co., Condensed Report of the 1915 Advertising Conference.
13 Edward Bok, "Respectable Religious People," *LHJ*, XXX (April, 1913), 6.
14 "A Stranger in the Church: The Experiences of a Young Woman in One Hundred and Fifty Churches," *LHJ*, XXIV (September, 1907), 9–10, 47; *LHJ* XXIV (October, 1907), 15–16, 84; *LHJ*, XXIV (December, 1907), 17; Albert F. McGarrah, "The Woman in the Up-to-Date Church," *LHJ*, XXX (September, 1916), 30.
15 Joseph H. Odell, "The King's Business: What Really Is the Minister's Job?" *LHJ*, XXXII (October, 1915), 13–14, and "Why I Cannot Preach My Old Sermons Now," *LHJ*, XXXV (March, 1918), [8], 88; "The Golden Rule for the American Church," *LHJ*, XXXIV (January, 1917), 7.
16 "The Church That Seems A-Coming," *LHJ*, XXXIII (November, 1916), 7; Charles M. Sheldon, "Is Christianity Practical in Worldly Affairs," *LHJ*, XVI (November, 1899), 10.
17. See especially Helen Christine Bennett, "An Effective Suburban Church," *LHJ*, XXXI (October, 1914), 22, 94–95; G. C. Shane, "The King's Business: How It Can Be More Effectively Done: Should a Church Advertise?" *LHJ*, XXXIII (January, 1916), 19, 55; Richard Orme Flinn, "Wanted: A Church Conscience: The Chart Needed to Steer Clear of Financial Rocks," *LHJ*, XXXIII (March, 1916), 25–26; James O'Donnell Bennett, "The Church That Found Itself Downtown: How Old Immanuel Outrode the Flood of Business," *LHJ*, XXXI (November, 1914), 10, 68–69.
18 "The Minister on 55 Cents a Day," *LHJ*, XXXIV (February, 1917), 10; "The Preacher and His Salary," *LHJ*, XXXIV (April, 1917), 8.
19 "Long Memories of Devout Women," *LHJ*, XXVIII (November, 1911), 6.
20 Editorial, "The Girl Who Feels Isolated," *LHJ*, XXVIII (November, 1911), 6; Helen Jay, "The Baby on the Farm," *LHJ*, XII (July, 1895), 26; "Summers of

Our Discontent," *LHJ*, XVIII (May, 1901), 16; "The Passing of the Farm," painting by W. L. Taylor, *LHJ*, XVIII (June, 1901), 5; and Edward Bok, "Two Little Books of Green Fields," *LHJ*, XIX (April, 1902), 16.

21 Bok to Sarah Woolsey, April 29, 1890, Bok to Marietta Holly, August 28, 1899, both in Bok Letterbooks; Alexander to G. E. Hamilton, October 7, 1903, in Alexander Letterbooks.

22 Helen Jay, "The Farmer's Wife and Her Boys," *LHJ*, XI (September, 1894), 18; "The Work of a Farmer's Wife," *LHJ*, XI (November, 1894), 22, "The Mental Life of a Farmer's Wife," *LHJ*, XII (March, 1895), 25, and "The Social Life of a Farmer's Wife," *LHJ*, XII (May, 1895), 22. This type of service article appeared again in the *Journal*'s "Twentieth Century Village" series, which included articles like John Gilmer Speed's "Good Country Roads," *LHJ*, XV (August, 1898), 20; Neltje Blanchan, "Starting a Village Library," *LHJ*, XV (October, 1898), 28; Mrs. John B. Sims, "Manual Training Schools," *LHJ*, XV (November, 1898), 26; "The Sleeping-Room on the Farm," *LHJ*, XVI (January, 1899), 26.

23 "Copy for the Farmer," *Printers' Ink*, LI (June 21, 1905), 9, 12.

24 Results of questionnaire sent out by P. V. Collins of Minneapolis, as reported at the meeting on agricultural publications at the *Seventh Annual Convention of the Associated Advertising Clubs of America* (Boston: Pilgrim Publicity Association, 1912), 2.

25 Curtis Publishing Co., Minutes of the Tenth Annual Conference of the Advertising Department of the Curtis Publishing Co. (Typescript, October, 1913, in Parlin Papers), 303. According to the company files, the *Journal* received 250,000 letters from the farm and country sectors in the first half of 1913. See Curtis Publishing Co., *Selling Forces*, 235, an intracompany publication, in Parlin Papers.

26 Curtis Publishing Co., *The Farm Market* (Philadelphia: Curtis, 1918), 68; C. C. Parlin, Speech, *ca.* 1926 (Text of speech in speech file on *Ladies' Home Journal*, in Parlin Papers).

27 Interview with Mr. Newman of Fresno, Calif. by C. C. Parlin, February 21, 1918, in Division of Commercial Research, Advertising Dept., Curtis Publishing Co., *Farm Market*, Vol. A, Interviews, 1917, in Parlin Papers.

28 Interview with Mr. Gregory, editor of *Prairie Farmer*, by Henry Sherwood Youker, January 17, 1918, *ibid.*

29 Edward Bok, "Where American Life Really Exists," *LHJ*, XII (October, 1895), 14; Bok to Harrison, July 5, 1897, in Harrison Papers.

30 "The Wisdom of New York," *LHJ*, XIX (May, 1902), 16; "A Few Days in New York," *LHJ*, XXI (April, 1904), 18; "What Surprises New York," *LHJ*, XXIII (April, 1906), 20; "In an Editorial Way," *LHJ*, XXIII (November, 1906), 5; editorial, *LHJ*, XXIV (September, 1907), 7; "The New York Mind," *LHJ*, XXXIII (November, 1916), 8; "Something Good for Once," "No Light No Bath No Nothing," and "Just Knew Them Slightly," in *LHJ*, XXV (February, 1908), 5; "Where American Life Really Exists," *LHJ*, XII (October, 1895), 14.

31 In *LHJ*: XV (September, 1898), 14; XVI (February, 1899), 14; XVII (January, 1900), 16; XX (September, 1903), 17. For other articles and editorials on the

abolition of homework, see *LHJ*: XXIX (March, 1912), 5; XVII (October, 1900), 16; XVIII (September, 1901), 16; XIX (January, 1902), 18; XXIV (January, 1907), 19.

32   In *LHJ*: XVII (January, 1900), 20–21; XVII (March, 1900), 4; XXVIII (March 1, 1911), 21; XXVIII (April 1, 1911), 30; XXIX (November, 1912), 30; XXXIII (October, 1916), 25.

33   "The Case of 17 Million Children: Is Our Public-School System Proving an Utter Failure?," *LHJ*, XXIX (August, 1912), 3; also in *LHJ*: XXIX (August, 1912), 4–5; XXIX (September, 1912), 5–7, 66; XXIX (October, 1912), 7–8; XXIX (November, 1912), 9; XXX (January, 1913), 3–4; XXX (February, 1913), 7–8, 58; XXX (March, 1913), 19–20, 74–75; XXX (April, 1913), 19–20, 72; XXX (May, 1913), 10, 75–77; XXX (June, 1913), 22, 60–62; XXX (August, 1913), 24; XXX (September, 1913), 24; Edward Bok, "At Home with the Editor," *LHJ*, XI (January, 1894), 12.

34   Edward Bok, "Our Schools and Our Teachers," *LHJ*, XII (September, 1895), 12. The *Journal* did endorse a special state commission to supervise high schools in order to free them from university accreditation and "substitute the standards of a modern scholarship, based upon world efficiency." See Frederic Burk, "Are We Living B. C. or A. D.?" *LHJ*, XIX (September, 1912), 6.

35   See the following editorials in the *Journal of Education*: "Is the Public School a Failure?," LXXVI (September 19, 1912), 296; LXXVI (October 3, 1912) 341–44; J. P. Womack, "Is the Public School a Failure? A Review," LXXVI (October 24, 1912), 426–28; Payson Smith, "Is the Public School a Failure?," LXXVII (January 9, 1913), 35–36.

36   Curtis Publishing Co., Minutes of the Tenth Annual Conference, 345, 347.

37   Bok, "At Home" *LHJ*, XII (March, 1895), 12; "Suppose America Goes Dry," *LHJ*, XXXIV (February, 1917), 9; Henry Smith Williams, "Is Prohibition the Remedy for the Liquor Evil?" *LHJ*, XXVIII (January 1, 1911), 21, 41; Alexander to editor, *New Voice*, January 28, 1899, in Alexander Letterbooks, on Bok's advice about abstinence for young businessmen.

38   Edward Bok, *The Keys to Success* (Philadelphia: John D. Morris, 1900), 111; Bok, "Wine at Women's Luncheons," *LHJ*, IX (January, 1892), 6.

39   "Bad Policy and Bad Manners," *LHJ*, XV (May, 1898), 14; "One Thing Men are Doing," *LHJ*, XXIV (October, 1907), 8; editorials, *LHJ*, XXXI (September, 1914), 6, *LHJ*, XXXI (November, 1914), 3. Forrest Crissey, "What Happens When a Town Goes 'Dry'—," *LHJ*, XXXII (January, 1915), 20; Charles Stelzle, "Suppose All the Saloons Were Closed: What Would Happen to Those Employed by the Liquor Trade?" *LHJ*, XXXII (September, 1915), 14.

40   Editorials in *LHJ* XXIX (February, 1912), 6, *LHJ*, XXVIII (October, 1911), 5, *LHJ*, XXXII (April, 1917), 8; Charles Stelzle, "Why Do Men Go Into Saloons," *LHJ*, XXXII (October, 1915), 22; "One Reason for the Saloon," *LHJ*, XXX (October, 1913), 6.

41   *LHJ*, XXXIV (February, 1917), 9. Bok said that prohibition would bring a host of new problems including greater use of opiates and narcotics. William H. Taft, "Is Prohibition a Blow at Personal Liberty?" *LHJ*, XXXVI (May, 1919), 31, 78.

42   Bok, "What is the Church Going to Do?," *LHJ*, XXVIII (March 1, 1911), 6; *LHJ*, XXXIII (October, 1916), 42. See Bok to Edward P. Warman, October 3, 1898, in Bok Letterbooks, a typical solicitation for a health article, "Five-

Minute Lessons in Good Health."

43   Editorials in *LHJ*: XXII (June, 1905), 18; XXIV (June, 1907), 5; XXV (July, 1908), 3; XXVI (April, 1909), 5; XXVI (July, 1909), 3; pictorial essay on some of the tragic episodes of 1909 in the April, 1910, issue, 27–30 and editorial on p. 5. Also in *LHJ*: XXVIII (March 1, 1911), 5; XXIX (May, 1912), 5; XXIX (July, 1912), 3; XXXI (July, 1914), 3; XXXI (March, 1914), 5.

44   Samuel Hays, *Conservation and the Gospel of Efficiency: The Progressive Conservation Movement, 1890–1920* (Cambridge, Mass.: Harvard University Press, 1959), introduction and 194–95, 197, for the Pinchot-McFarland controversy.

45   Bok, *Americanization*, 254–55; *LHJ*: XXII (September, 1905), 19; XXIII (January, 1906), 27; XXIII (October, 1906), 39.

46   *LHJ*, XXI (December, 1903), 15; Hays, *Conservation*, 143n; Bok, *Americanization*, 182; *Profitable Advertising*, XVII (April, 1908), 1149–56; Gifford Pinchot to J. Horace McFarland, November 18, 1909, in Gifford Pinchot Papers, #1809, Special File C, Controversial, Manuscripts Division, Library of Congress.

47   *LHJ*, XXI (December, 1903), 15.

48   Bok, *Americanization*, 183. There seems to be no evidence to identify the threatening advertisers or their overall relation to *Journal* advertising.

49   *LHJ*, XX (July, 1903), 16.

50   Bok, *Americanization*, 182; *Printers' Ink*, LI (May 31, 1905), 54; *Profitable Advertising*, XI (May, 1902), 988–89.

51   *Printers' Ink*, LII (August 16, 1905), 35. Outranking the billboards in importance were daily papers, weeklies, magazines, and streetcars, in that order; " 'Dooming the Billboard Again,' " *Advertising and Selling*, XIX (February, 1910), 1223; in *Profitable Advertising*, "The Future of the Billboard," XVI (April, 1907), 1203, and "The Legal Status of the Billboards," XVII (March, 1908), 1064–65.

52   *LHJ*, XXI (July, 1904), 27; *LHJ*, XXII (January, 1905), 21; J. Horace McFarland, "Beautiful America: A Direct Talk About Billboards," *LHJ*, XXII (July, 1905), 18; "Beautiful America: The Last Call on Billboard Removal," *LHJ*, XXII (August, 1905), 28; Bok to Guy A. Brackett, May 1, 1905, in Bok Letterbooks; *LHJ*, XXII (March, 1905), 23.

53   Alexander to J. H. McFarland, May 10, 1905, in Alexander Letterbooks.

54   *LHJ*, XXII (July, 1905), 16; on billboards, see *LHJ*: XXV (February, 1908), 6, XXV (March, 1908), 6, XXVII (July, 1910), 3; "What Very Few Farmers Realize," *LHJ*, XXXIII (January, 1916), 9.

55   In *LHJ*: XXI (June, 1904), 21; XXII (January, 1905), 21; XXII (February, 1905), 27; XXII (April, 1905), 28–29, 31; XXII (May, 1905), 33–34; XXII (June, 1905), 33.

56   Alexander to McFarland, May 11, 1904, in Alexander Letterbooks. J. Horace McFarland, "Where the Telegraph-Poles Come From: Which Do You Prefer: Trees with Life Giving Leaves or Poles with Death-Dealing Wires?", *LHJ* XXIV (February, 1907), 35.

57   Alexander to McFarland, May 10, 1905, in Alexander Letterbooks. Bok to McFarland, July 22, 1905, in Bok Letterbooks, and the resulting article, *LHJ*, XXII (November, 1905), 34.

58   "Why Does Wilkes-Barre Allow This?," *LHJ*, XXIII (February, 1906), 25.

59   In *LHJ*: XXIII (March, 1906), 29; XXIII (April, 1906), 31; XXIII (June, 1906), 29; XXIII (July, 1906), 21; XXIII (September, 1906), 19; XXIV (January, 1907), 29; "What Some Readers Do Not Like," *LHJ*, XXIII (April, 1906), 20; *LHJ*, XXVII (March, 1910), 37; Alexander to James H. Malone, March 4, 1910, in Alexander Letterbooks.

60   In *LHJ*: XXV (April, 1908), 5; XXVI (November, 1909), 6; XXVII (April, 1910), 6; XXVII (June, 1910), 5; XXVIII (February 1, 1911), 5; XXVIII (October, 1911), 6.

61   In *LHJ*: XXVIII (November, 1911), 23, 95; XXIX (April, 1912), 43; XXIX (October, 1912), 25; XXIX (November, 1912), 31; XXXI (April, 1914), 43ff; XXXI (May, 1914), 30, 31; XXXIII (February, 1916), 5; XXXIII (March, 1916), 12; XXXI (September, 1914), 18, 55, 37; XXXII (May, 1915), 27; XXXII (June, 1915), 3.

62   Curtis Publishing Co., Minutes of the 1915 Advertising Conference (Typescript in Parlin Papers).

CHAPTER V

1   Hotchkiss, *Milestones of Marketing*, 205–206; "Answer to an Inquirer," *Profitable Advertising*, XIV (November, 1904), 570.

2   Hotchkiss, *Milestones of Marketing*, 205; Presbrey, *History and Development of Advertising*, 364.

3   Edward Bok, "Personal," *LHJ*, XIX (December, 1901), 18.

4   Edward Bok, "Editor's Personal Page," *LHJ*, XXIV (July, 1907), 1.

5   "How Women Can Be Good Americans," *LHJ*, XX (July, 1903), 16; also see "The 'Patent-Medicine' Curse," *LHJ*, XXI (May, 1904), 18.

6   William V. Alexander to Arthur Newman, April 19, 1907, Alexander to Winfred T. Denison, December 13, 1910, in Alexander Letterbooks.

7   "For the Country Woman," *LHJ*, XXV (January, 1908), 6; see also the editorial in *LHJ*, XXIV (March, 1907), 5, and Edward Bok, "To You: A Personal Word," *LHJ*, XXIII (February, 1906), 20.

8   "Why 'Patent Medicines' are Dangerous," *LHJ*, XXII (March, 1905), 18. See also "Women as 'Easy Marks,'" *LHJ*, XXVII (June, 1910), 6.

9   "How the Private Confidences of Women Are Laughed At," *LHJ*, XXI (November, 1904), 18; Mark Sullivan, "Did Mr. Bok Tell the Truth?," *LHJ*, XXIII (January, 1906), 18; "What Madness Seizes Women the Moment Their Fingers Clutch a Pen," *LHJ*, XXIV (April, 1907), 5; Edward Bok, "Editor's Personal Page," *LHJ*, XXVI (March, 1909), 2.

10   In *LHJ*: "Pictures That Tell Their Own Stories," XXII (September, 1905), 15; "A Diabolical 'Patent-Medicine' Story," XXII (April, 1905), 20; "A Danger in Illinois," XXII (June, 1905), 18; Bok, "To You: A Personal Word," XXIII (February, 1906), 20; "The Most Wonderful of All" and "Why Forty-five Women Died," XXIII (July, 1906), 16; "Women's Penny-Wise Economies," XXIV (June, 1907), 6; "When Will Women Stop?," XXV (January, 1908), 6; "Just Two Little Pills," XXV (March, 1908), 5; "Another Foolish Woman," XXV (June, 1908), 6; "For the Safety of Yourself and Child," XXIII (February, 1906), 1; "When It Is Too Late," XXIV (November, 1907), 7; "Two More Babies," XXV (September, 1908), 6; "Deadly 'Soothing Syrups,'" XXVI (September, 1909), 5; "One Little Life More," XXVII (March, 1910), 5; Caroline

W. Latimer, "How Can I Keep My Baby from Crying," XXIX (January, 1912), 35, 48; William Lee Howard, "How Children Are Made Drunkards," XXIV (October, 1907), 23.

11 On this point of painstaking accuracy see Alexander to Samuel Abbott, February 11, 1903, in Alexander Letterbooks. Also see Alexander to Maud Banfield, February 11, February 19, and February 22, 1903, Alexander to Abbott, February 20, 1903, Alexander to J. Martin Rommel, March 8, 1904, Alexander to Abbott, March 22, 1904, *ibid.*, Bok to John G. Millburn, January 4, 1905, in Bok Letterbooks. See the *Journal* forecast for 1906 in the December, 1905, issue, p. 3. Mark Sullivan's autobiography included an episode in which Bok went to New York to seek out Sullivan. This surprised Sullivan, and he theorized that Bok enjoyed doing things the hard way. See *The Education of an American* (New York: Doubleday, Doran, 1928), 183. In doing so, however, Bok got the man he wanted for the job.

12 Alexander to H. P. Rank, June 22, 1904, Alexander to Rank, June 28, 1904, in Alexander Letterbooks. Rank accepted the *Journal*'s proposition.

13 Alexander to J. D. Cleaton, May 10, 1904, Alexander to William B. Bodemann, May 11, 1904, in Alexander Letterbooks; Bok, *Americanization*, 248; Bok to Millburn, January 4, 1905, in Bok Letterbooks; Alexander to Valdemar Blad, May 8, 1905, Alexander to James W. Bayard, February 1, 1907, Alexander to Charles H. LaWall, August 21, 1907, September 3, 1907, and May 5, 1910, in Alexander Letterbooks; Bok to Harvey Wiley, November 23, 1906, in Box 60, Harvey Wiley Papers, Manuscripts Division, Library of Congress; Wiley to Bok, November 30, 1906, in Letterpress books, Wiley Papers.

14 "From 'Profitable Advertising's' Point of View: Tribulations of the Medicine Men," *Profitable Advertising*, XIV (July, 1904), 130–31; "An Editorial Blunder," *Profitable Advertising*, XIV (August, 1904), 228–29; *LHJ* XXI (July, 1904), 18.

15 *Printers' Ink*, LII (July 26, 1905), 26–27; "Sensational Attacks Upon Proprietary Medicines," *Printers' Ink*, LII (August 23, 1905), 9; "Mr. Bok Has Some Live Stuff on Proprietary Medicines in the September Issue of His Periodical," *Printers' Ink*, LII (September 13, 1905), 45; George French, "The War on 'Patents': A Consideration of the Tendency on the Part of High Class Publications to Exclude Proprietary Remedies from Their Advertising Columns," *Profitable Advertising*, XV (September, 1905), 338–40.

16 Alexander to Frank P. Foster, May 23, 1905, in Alexander Letterbooks. See James Harvey Young, *The Toadstool Millionaires* (Princeton, N.J.: Princeton University Press, 1961), 207, 208n. Not many years later, the AMA excluded suspect advertisements and published a compendium of medical frauds and dangerous patent-medicines: American Medical Association, *Nostrums and Quackery: Articles on the Nostrum Evil and Quackery Reprinted, with Additions and Modifications from the Journal of the American Medical Association* (Chicago: Press of the American Medical Association, 1912).

17 In *LHJ*: XXI (May, 1904), 18; XXI (September, 1904), 16; XXIII (September, 1906), 16; XXIV (January, 1907), 5; XXIV (May, 1907), 6; XXIV (October, 1907), 8; XXV (July, 1908), 4; "Some Pious Judases," *LHJ*, XXIV (November, 1907), 7; "A Church That Points the Way," *LHJ*, XIV (Nov., 1907), 7; *LHJ*, XXIV (January, 1907), 5.

18   Bok, "To You," *LHJ*, XXIII (February, 1906), 20.

19   *Ibid.*

20   Sullivan, *Education of an American*, 191; S. H. Adams, *The Great American Fraud: A Series of Articles on the Patent Medicine Evil, Reprinted from Collier's Weekly. Also–The Patent Medicine Conspiracy Against the Freedom of the Press* (Chicago: Press of the American Medical Association, 1906), 74.

21   American Medical Association, *Nostrums and Quackery*, 669–70.

22   "What A Magazine Cannot Do," *LHJ*, XXIII (March, 1906), 18; Bok, "Editor's Personal Page," *LHJ*, XXIII (October, 1906), 1 and editorial on p. 6.

23   Editorial, *LHJ*, XXIV (January, 1907), 6; "What 'Patent-Medicines' Have Done," *LHJ*, XXV (April, 1908), 42.

24   In *LHJ*: XXVIII (November, 1911), 15, 80, 81; XXXIII (March, 1916), 17; XXXIII (May, 1916), 7; XXXIII (June, 1916), 3.

25   Editorial, *LHJ*, XXX (October, 1913), 5; Lewis E. Theiss, "How Housewives Are Cheated," *LHJ*, XXVII (March, 1910), 56.

26   See the *Journal* reprint from the Bureau of Chemistry, U.S., Department of Agriculture, "How You Can Tell a Fresh Egg," *LHJ*, XXXII (January, 1915), 35; *LHJ*, XXXI (July, 1914), 40. The particular consumer trap emphasized here was that wholesalers were required to label their wares, but not the retailers. "The Same Old Ananias," *LHJ* XXIV (September, 1907), 7; Mark Sullivan, "How the Game of Free Medical Advice Is Worked," *LHJ*, XXIII (February, 1906), 23; *LHJ*, XXX (September, 1913), 10, 58; *LHJ*, XXXII (April, 1915), 14.

27   In *LHJ*: XXIV (November, 1907), 7; XXV (January, 1908), 17–18; XXV (May, 1908), 26; XXVI (September, 1909), 6; XXVI (October, 1909), 6; XXIX (November, 1912), 14; XXXIII (October, 1916), 8; XXVII (June, 1910), 6.

28   Bok, "My Quarrel with Women's Clubs" *LHJ*, XXVII (January, 1910), 5–6; in *LHJ*: XXVI (November, 1909), 5; XXVIII (March 1, 1911), 6; XXIX (November, 1912), 5; XXX (November, 1913), 5.

29   *LHJ*, XXIV (January, 1907), 6; *LHJ*, XXIII (January, 1906), 22; "Manufacturers Are Now Interested in Advertising," *Printers' Ink*, LI (May 31, 1905), 32–33.

30   Quoted in Bok, *A Man from Maine*, 167–69.

31   Ruth Ashmore, "Side-Talks with Girls," *LHJ*, XII (June, 1895), 27; Edward Bok, "At Home with the Editor," *LHJ*, XI (June, 1894), 14; editorials in *LHJ*, XXV (June, 1908), 5; *LHJ*, XII (June, 1895), 14.

32   In 1894 Bok asked fathers to "put aside what is, after all, nothing but mock modesty, and talk frankly with their sons of those phases of their moral life which sooner or later they must learn." See Bok, "At Home," *LHJ*, XI (June, 1894), 14. See editorials in *LHJ*: XXIII (March, 1906), 18; XXIII (May, 1906), 16; XXIII (October, 1906), 5; XXIV (February, 1907), 5; XXIV (April, 1907), 5; XXIV (May, 1907), 6; XXIV (June, 1907), 1; XXIV (September, 1907), 7. See articles in *LHJ*: XXIV (January, 1907), 13; XXIV (August, 1907), 32; XXIV (March, 1907), 9.

33   "About Plain Speaking," *LHJ*, XXV (September, 1908), 6; Margaret Deland, "'I Didn't Know...'" *LHJ*, XXIV (March, 1907), 9; in *LHJ*: XXIV (September, 1907), 13–14, 26; XXIV (November, 1907), 7; XXV (January, 1908),

6; XXV (May, 1908), 1; XXV (April, 1908), 6; XXVI (January, 1909), 6, 23; XXVI (March, 1909), 5; XXVII (February, 1910), 5; XXVIII (January 1, 1911), 39; XXIX (May, 1912), 28; XXVI (November, 1909), 6; XXVII (April, 1910), 5; XXVII (October 1, 1910), 5; XXVIII (February 1, 1911), 5; XXVIII (June, 1911), 6, 63; XXXI (May, 1914), 5; XXXIV (January, 1917), 7. See the editorial reference, "The Girl's Turn with a Little Book," *LHJ*, XXX (November, 1913), 70. The Edward Bok Books of Self-Knowledge for Young People and Parents series included titles such as Winfield Scott Hall, *Instead of Wild Oats* (New York: F. H. Revell Co., 1912), and Mrs. Woodallen Chapman, *How Shall I Tell My Child?* (New York: F. H. Revell, 1912). *LHJ*, XXIV (October, 1907), 7; *LHJ*, XXVI (April, 1909), 6; *LHJ*, XXVI (July, 1909), 3.

34 Helen Keller, "Unnecessary Blindness," *LHJ*, XXIV (January, 1907), 14; "A Young Woman's Misfortune," *LHJ*, XXVII (February, 1910), 5. Bok, "Editor's Personal Page," *LHJ*, XXV (September, 1908), 1. See Curtis Publishing Company, Minutes of the Tenth Annual Conference of the Advertising Department of the Curtis Publishing Co. (Typescript, October, 1913, in Parlin Papers), 339; Abraham L. Wolbarst, "The Tragedy of the Marriage Altar," *LHJ*, XXV (October, 1908), 26; "A Splendid Safeguard," *LHJ*, XXVI (May, 1909), 4.

35 Curtis Publishing Co., Minutes of the Tenth Annual Conference, 339–40; Bok, *Americanization*, 250–51.

36 Curtis Publishing Co., Minutes of the Tenth Annual Conference, 342.

37 Bok, "Editor's Personal Page," *LHJ*, XXX (May, 1913), 1. See Helen Christine Bennett, "An Effective Suburban Church," *LHJ*, XXXI (October, 1914), 72, 94–95. By 1914, a parish church included a program in sex hygiene and was praised by the *Journal*.

38 Curtis Publishing Co., Minutes of the Tenth Annual Conference, 343.

39 *Ibid.*

40 *Ibid.*, 344.

CHAPTER VI

1 Alan C. Collins, *Something About the Ladies' Home Journal* (Philadelphia: Curtis, Ca. 1927), 35, in Parlin Papers. See also "Her Chance for Service," *LHJ*, XXXIV (June, 1917), 7.

2 In December, 1913, the *Journal* published an essay by Jane Addams on arbitration between nations: "Peace on Earth," XXX (December, 1913), 27; in 1914 and 1915, Bok gave space to a three-part essay on history and life in Panama; see also in *LHJ*: "The Key to Pan-Americanism," XXXIII (June, 1916), 29; Woodrow Wilson, "The Mexican Question," XXXIII (October, 1916), 9.

3 *LHJ*, XXXI (November, 1914), 3, 5; Catherine Van Dyke, "What This Christmas Means to the Women of Europe: An Actual Picture of the Present War," *LHJ*, XXXI (December, 1914), 6; "Toys That Are Behind the Times," *LHJ*, XXXII (September, 1915), 5; "Nevertheless," *LHJ*, XXXI (December, 1914), 1.

4 Quoted in Curtis Publishing Co., Condensed Report of the 1915 Advertising Conference (Typescript in Parlin Papers).

5 "What Is Coming Out of the War That Is Touching American Women?" *LHJ*, XXXII (February, 1915), 3; "Girls and Brass Buttons," *LHJ*, XXX (October,

1913), 6; Estelle L. Lindsey, "Running to Win: The Story of My Campaign and Election to the City Council of Los Angeles," *LHJ*, XXXIII (November, 1916), 14, 112–13.

6 *LHJ*, XXXII (January, 1915), 1, 7; *LHJ*, XXXII (February, 1915), 1; *LHJ*, XXXII (June, 1915), 47.

7 A Swiss Mother, "Why I Raise My Boy to Be a Soldier," *LHJ*, XXXIII (April, 1916), 27, 76.

8 Dudley Harmon, "My Government and I," *LHJ*, XXXIII (February, 1916), 7. Many early columns in this series contained information on the dangers of patent medicines, but the information came directly from the federal government, not from the editor. See especially, "Bottled Frauds and Poisons" and "54 Bad 'Patent Medicines,'" *LHJ*, XXXIII (March, 1916), 7; *LHJ*, XXX (May, 1916), 7; "Dangerous Doctoring," *LHJ*, XXXIII (June, 1916), 3; "The Medicine You Are Taking," *LHJ*, XXXIV (April, 1917), 26; *LHJ*, XXXIII (February, 1916), 33.

9 Edward Bok to Woodrow Wilson, November 26, 1915, Wilson to Bok, December 13, 1915, in Edward W. Bok Foundation, Wilson Papers.

10 "The Future of Our Country, Not the Past," "What Wars Have Proved," "The Real Question," all in *LHJ*, XXXIII (May, 1916), 11.

11 "The American Red Cross: An Opportunity for Women," *LHJ*, XXXIII (June, 1916), 3; "The Woman and Her Country," *LHJ*, XXXIII (August, 1916), 9; "The American Red Cross Needs You; Your Assistance Is Each Day More Imperative," *LHJ*, XXXIII (August, 1916), 5.

12 *LHJ*, XXXIII (July, 1916), 10.

13 *LHJ*, XXXIV (June, 1917), 7, 54.

14 *LHJ*, XXXIV (May, 1917), 3; Dudley Harmon, "Let Uncle Sam Help with Your Garden: Your Food Bills Can Be Kept Down with His Assistance," *LHJ*, XXXIV (May, 1917), 37.

15 "A Little Careful," *LHJ*, XXXIV (July, 1917), 7.

16 *LHJ*, XXXIV (June, 1917), 72; *LHJ*, XXXIV (December, 1917), 26; *LHJ*, XXXIV (August, 1917), 15.

17 "A Man Without a Country," *LHJ*, XXXIV (September, 1917), 45.

18 "Why?" and "Lest We Forget," *LHJ*, XXXV (November, 1918), 34.

19 Drawings by J. Pierre Nuytens, *LHJ*, XXXIV (December, 1917), 126, 127; "A Lie," *LHJ*, XXXV (February, 1918), 90.

20 Committee on Public Information, "'They Say': But They Lie: An Authoritative Announcement for the Government of the United States," *LHJ*, XXXV (July, 1918), 1, 76; *LHJ*, XXXV (May, 1918), 10.

21 *LHJ*, XXXV (October, 1918), 107; Catherine Van Dyke, "I Go and See: A Village in France and This Is What I Saw," *LHJ*, XXXV (January, 1918), 13, 14.

22 *LHJ*, XXXIV (December, 1917), 26; *LHJ*, XXXIV (September, 1917), 10.

23 *LHJ*, XXXV (January, 1918), 13, 14; "Not a 'Slacker Magazine,'" *LHJ*, XXXV (September, 1918), 34.

24 Bok, *Twice Thirty*, 337–38, 340. See the following letters from Bok to Wilson, all of which included suggestions rejected by the president: Bok to Joseph Tumulty, January 4, 1915, Bok to Wilson, June 14, 1915, November 26, 1915,

December 9, 1916, January 15, 1917, July 25, 1917, June 19, 1918, all in Edward W. Bok Foundation, Wilson Papers. For two ideas accepted by the president, see Bok to Wilson, April 11, 1917, and February 25, 1918, *ibid.*

25   Karl E. Harriman to William Jennings Bryan, September 8, 1914, in 1645 Neutrality, Wilson Papers; Bryan to Wilson, September 10, 1914, in Edward W. Bok Foundation, Wilson Papers; Wilson to Bryan, September 11, 1914, in 1645 Neutrality, Wilson Papers.

26   *LHJ*, XXXIV (July, 1917), 9; "To the Women of America," *LHJ*, XXXV (May, 1918), 11; *LHJ*, XXXV (November, 1918), 7; Bok to Wilson, August 5, 1916, Wilson to Bok, August 11, 1916, in Edward W. Bok Foundation, Wilson Papers; New York *Times*, June 1, 1916, p. 5, col. 3.

27   Quoted in Bok, *Twice Thirty*, 344–45, 346; *LHJ*, XXXIV (June, 1917), 1, 24; F. D. Roosevelt, "What the Navy Can Do for Your Boy," *LHJ*, XXXIV (June, 1917), 25, 88. On the Red Cross, see reprints from *Red Cross Magazine*, such as "The Wonder War Dogs of Mercy," *LHJ*, XXXIV (June, 1917), 13. This issue included a new department, "The American National Red Cross," edited and conducted by William H. Taft, chairman of the Central Committee.

28   John R. Mott conducted the series, "The Y.M.C.A. in War," beginning in the July, 1917, *LHJ*. Bok, *Twice Thirty*, 317.

29   Telegram, Clara Evans to Anna H. Shaw, July 26, 1917, in Ida M. Tarbell Correspondence, General Office, Home Conservation Division, Records of the U.S. Food Administration, Record Group 4, Washington National Records Center Building. Shaw replied that the issue could not be taken up until the enactment of the food administration bill. See telegram, Shaw to Evans, July 26, 1917, *ibid.*

30   *LHJ*, XXXV (May, 1918), 105; *LHJ*, XXXIV (July, 1917), 8, 27, 28–30.

31   *LHJ*, XXXIV (July, 1917), 27.

32   Quoted in Bok, *Twice Thirty*, 346.

33   *LHJ*, XXXIV (August, 1917), 25, 10.

34   Herbert Hoover, Memorandum for staff meeting, July 17, 1917, "M," in Tarbell Correspondence.

35   In *LHJ*: XXXIV (October, 1917), 8; XXXV (January, 1918), 26; XXXV (February, 1918), 33; XXXV (May, 1918), 32; XXXV (June, 1918), 32; XXXV (April, 1918), 29.

36   Gertrude B. Lane to Dr. Wilbur, August 16 [1917], in Magazine and Feature Section, Public Information Division, U.S. Food Administration, National Archives.

37   Lane to George H. Lorimer, December 11, 1917, *ibid.*

38   *LHJ*, XXXV (March, 1918), 44.

39   *LHJ*, XXXV (June, 1918), 27; *LHJ*, XXXV (July, 1918), 29; *LHJ*, XXXV (September, 1918), 31; Lane, interoffice memorandum to her staff, June 13, 1918, in Magazine and Feature Section, Public Information Division, U.S. Food Administration, National Archives; in *LHJ*: XXXIV (November, 1917), 64; XXXV (June, 1918), 107; XXXV (October, 1918), 28, 76; XXXV (November, 1918), 16, 90; XXXV (December, 1918), 99; XXXVI (February, 1919), 1.

40   *LHJ*, XXXV (November, 1918), 1, 79; *LHJ*, XXVI (January, 1919), 12.

41 The Lever Act of August, 1917, created both the Food and Fuel adminis-
    trations. See in *LHJ*: XXXIV (November, 1917), 118; XXXV (February, 1918),
    31; XXXV (September, 1918), 30; editorials in *LHJ*, XXXV (February 1918),
    30, *LHJ*, XXXV (May, 1918), 32; *LHJ*, XXXV (September, 1918), 32.
42 *LHJ*, XXXIV (September, 1917), 1; *LHJ*, XXXV (February, 1918), 34; *LHJ*,
    XXXIV (November, 1917), 1; *LHJ*, XXXV (May, 1918), 11. Bok to Wilson,
    February 25, 1918, in Edward W. Bok Foundation, Wilson Papers. See also
    Wilson to Tumulty, March 5, 1918, *ibid*. *LHJ*, XXXV (October, 1918), 38,
    64; *LHJ*, XXXVI (April, 1919), 33.
43 *LHJ*, XXXV (May, 1918), 1; *LHJ*, XXXV (July, 1918), 32.
44 Walter Rogers to George Creel, September 25, 1918, in General Corre-
    spondence of George Creel, Correspondence of the Committee on
    Public Information, Record Group 63, National Archives Building. See also
    Rogers to Creel, September 28, 1918, for elaboration, *ibid*.
45 *LHJ*, XXXV (November, 1918), 7.
46 Bok to Wilson, February 15, 1918, in 22-D, Wilson Papers.
47 Wilson to Albert S. Burleson, February 18, 1918, *ibid*.
48 Burleson to Wilson, February 22, 1918, Wilson to Bok, February 25, 1918, *ibid*.
49 Bok to Wilson, April 3, 1918, in Edward W. Bok Foundation, Wilson Papers.
50 Wilson to Burleson, April 4, 1918, *ibid*. A few days later, David Lawrence, the
    New York *Evening Post*'s Washington correspondent who had the ear of many
    publishers and also Wilson's, wrote Wilson a strong letter of praise for the
    Saturday Evening Post editor, who was "using his business to win the war." See
    Lawrence to Wilson, April 8, 1918, *ibid*.
51 *LHJ*, XIX (June, 1902), 18; *LHJ*, XXIX (June, 1912), 5; *LHJ*, XXIX (October,
    1912), 6; see editorial, *LHJ*, XXXII (March, 1915), 4.
52 In *LHJ*: VI (November, 1889), 16; XXVII (November 1, 1910), 21, 70, 71;
    XXVII (December 1, 1910), 23; XXIX (May, 1912), 5; XXIX (October, 1912),
    5; XXIX (November, 1912), 5; XXXII (April, 1915), 32; and on the use of
    inexpensive substitutes, XXXIII (March, 1916), 12.
53 *LHJ*, XXX (March, 1913), 6; *LHJ*, XXXII (March, 1915), 3.
54 *LHJ*, XXXI (January, 1914), 3; *LHJ*, XXXI (October, 1914), 17, 90.
55 See "Practical Home Economies" in *LHJ*, XXXI (November 1914), 34 (on fuel
    saving) and 35 (on reducing the meat bill); also in *LHJ*: XXXII (January, 1915),
    2; XXXII (February, 1915), 36; XXXIII (September, 1916), 34; XXIX (Oc-
    tober, 1912), 5; XXXI (October, 1914), 58; XXXI (December, 1914), 48;
    XXXII (March, 1915), 23; XXXII (May, 1915), 48; XXXIV (June, 1917), 79;
    XXXIII (November, 1916), 42; XXXII (May, 1915), 27; XXXII (October,
    1915), 27; XXXIII (March, 1916), 25–26; XXXI (June, 1914), 3.
56 *LHJ*, XXXIV (July, 1917), 7; *LHJ*, XXXV (January, 1918), 26; Jeannette
    Rankin, "What We Women Should Do," *LHJ*, XXXIV (August, 1917), 17; S.
    W. Straus, "When Peace Comes This Will Come," *LHJ*, XXXV (January,
    1918), 1; *LHJ*, XXXV (September, 1918), 29.
57 In *LHJ*: XXXIV (September, 1917), 9; XXXV (March, 1918), 42, 111; XXXV
    (September, 1918), 95–97; XXXV (April, 1918), 29; XXXVI (January, 1919),
    65; XXXV (September, 1918), 97; XXXVI (January, 1919), 66; XXXVI
    (March, 1919), 35, 50; XXXVI (June, 1919), 111; XXXVI (April, 1919), 35,
    86; XXXVI (September, 1919), 47; XXXIV (November, 1917), 121; XXVII

(December 1, 1910), 23; XXXVI (June, 1919), 41, 152, 156. In contrast, see *LHJ*, XXXV (September, 1918), 95, in which Cincinnati is illustrated as being divided into five hundred member units for maximum efficiency.

58 *LHJ*, XXXI (May, 1914), 6; *LHJ*, XXXV (October, 1918), 97, 98; *LHJ*, XXXV (June, 1918), 33, 89; *LHJ*, XXXVI (March, 1919), 39, 120; *LHJ*, XXXV (May, 1918), 20. Oftentimes, anonymous *Journal* contributions seem to be Bok's own essays in thin disguise. Also, see *LHJ*, XXXV (March, 1918), 66.

59 *LHJ*, XXXIV (November, 1917), 32; *LHJ*, XXXV (September, 1918), 3; *LHJ*, XXXIV (December, 1917), 38, 89.

60 *LHJ*, XXXIV (April, 1917), 8.

61 *LHJ*, XXXIV (November, 1917), 39, 91, 92.

62 *LHJ*, XXXV (April, 1918), 29; see Bok's note in *LHJ*, XXXV (June, 1918), 13.

63 *LHJ*, XXXV (June, 1918), 30; *LHJ*, XXXV (September, 1918), 28.

64 *LHJ*, XXXVI (January, 1919), 22.

65 *Ibid.*, 23, 69; in *LHJ*: XXXVI (March, 1919), 37, 58, 39, 156; XXXVI (May, 1919), 41, 47, 114; XXXVI (April, 1919), 35, 47, 86; XXXVI (May, 1919), 47, 114.

66 *LHJ*, XXXVI (June, 1919), 47, 48; *LHJ*, XXXVI (July, 1919), 37, 72, 74.

67 Bok to Tumulty, January 4, 1915, in Edward W. Bok Foundation, Wilson Papers.

68 *LHJ*, XXXIV (September, 1917), 9; *LHJ*, XXXIII (February, 1916), 12; Bok to Wilson, July 25, 1917, Wilson to Bok, July 26, 1917, in Edward W. Bok Foundation, Wilson Papers.

69 In *LHJ*: XXXV (April, 1918), 3; XXXV (May, 1918), 89; XXXIV (August, 1917), 3; XXXV (April, 1918), 28; XXXV (June, 1918), 1; XXXV (July, 1918), 3; XXXV (May, 1918), 32.

70 For an early example, see: David M. Steele, "The Other Side of Town," *LHJ*, XIX (December, 1901), 20.

71 *LHJ*, XX (April, 1903), 17; *LHJ*, XXXIII (October, 1916), 86.

72 *LHJ*, XXXIV (January, 1917), 3: *LHJ*, XXXIV (February, 1917), unnumbered last page; *LHJ*, XXXV (October, 1918), 94.

73 In *LHJ*: XXXIII (May, 1916), 33; XXXIII (June, 1916), 3; XXXV (August, 1918), 3; XXXV (January, 1918), 78–79; XXXII (April, 1915), 27; XXX (June, 1913), 27; XXXIII (May, 1916), 33.

74 *LHJ*, XXXII (April, 1915), 27; *LHJ*, XXX (June, 1913), 27.

75 In *LHJ*: XXXVI (May, 1919), 33, 146; XXXVI (August, 1919), 37; XXXVI (September, 1919), 1; XXXVI (September, 1919), 33; XXXV (November, 1918), 114.

76 *LHJ*, XXXVI (September, 1919), 35, 36; *LHJ*, XXXVI (October, 1919), 53, 173.

77 *LHJ*, XXXVI (October, 1919), 164.

78 Bok, *Twice Thirty*, 382–83.

79 Interview with Esther Everett Lape, May 11, 1966. Bok endowed the Philadelphia Award to Citizens, 1921; the Citizen's Award, 1922; the Philadelphia Forum, 1921, for lecturers in arts and sciences; the Philadelphia Commission (with others) in 1926. See also Selig Adler, *The Isolationist Impulse: Its Twentieth Century Reaction* (New York: Collier, 1961), 115, 184–86.

80 Other members of the policy committee were John W. Davis, Nathan L. Miller,

Mrs. Ogden Reid, Melville E. Stone, Mrs. Frank Vanderlip; on the Jury of Award, James Guthrie Harbord and Ellen F. Pendleton.

81 Interview with Esther Everett Lape, May 11, 1966; New York *Times,* November 16, 1923, p. 1, col. 4.

82 Wilson to Bok, November 2, 1922, in Correspondence of Edward William Bok, Wilson Papers.

83 Esther Everett Lape, ed., *Ways to Peace* (New York: Charles Scribner's Sons, 1924); New York *Times,* January 17, 1924, p. 15, col. 5; New York *Times,* March 30, 1924, Sec. 2, p. 7, col. 5; Adler, *Isolationist Impulse,* 202.

CONCLUSION

1 Interview with Esther Everett Lape, May 11, 1966. See also Orcutt, *Celebrities Off Parade,* 234; "News-Week in Fourth Estate; Curtis: Leader in Newspaper and Magazine Field Dead," *News-Week,* I (June 17, 1933), 27.

2 Cyrus Curtis to C. H. Ludington, August 14, 1919, in Cyrus H. K. Curtis Collection, Historical Society of Pennsylvania, Philadelphia.

3 Curtis to George H. Lorimer, August 18, 1919, *ibid.* The "thirty-year old rut" undoubtedly referred to Bok's thirty-year career as editor of the *Journal.*

4 "Why Is a Trust a Bad Thing?" *LHJ,* XXIX (March, 1912), 61.

5 "What, Really, Is Socialism?" *LHJ,* XXIX (February, 1912), 68.

6 Edward Bok, "Our Schools and Our Teachers," *LHJ,* XII (September, 1895), 12. See also, "Coming: A Springtime Christmas," *LHJ,* XXVII (April, 1910), 5.

7 "Men Who Save," *LHJ,* XXXVI (December, 1919), 1.

8 Charles Stelzle, "What I Saw in 69 Small Cities," *LHJ,* XXXVI (June, 1919), 43, 76.

9 "The Greatest Thing in the World," *LHJ,* XXXVI (August, 1919), 1.

10 Imogen B. Oakley, "Turning Garbage and Ashes into Use," *LHJ,* XXXVI (November, 1919), 185.

11 "Now Our Own: An Editorial," *LHJ,* XXXV (October, 1919), 1.

Bibliography

There are a number of sources for any study of Edward Bok, the *Ladies' Home Journal*, and the Curtis Publishing Company. Letterbooks of Cyrus Curtis and Edward Bok, dating from 1889 to 1908, with gaps, were available at the Curtis Publishing Company during my research and have since been acquired by the Historical Society of Pennsylvania in Philadelphia. The society also houses important letters in its Cyrus H. K. Curtis and George H. Lorimer-*Post* collections, as well as other Bok items, most notably in the Dreer and Simon Gratz collections.

In 1965, Curtis Publishing Company gave the Rare Books Division of the University of Pennsylvania Library, located in Philadelphia, an important group of materials. The library named these papers after Charles Coolidge Parlin, sometimes called the founder of marketing research in the United States. This collection includes some texts of Parlin's speeches, memoranda, pamphlets, and other Curtis materials such as the company news periodical *Trade Bulletins*, scrapbook tallies of readers' requests for booklets in the years 1912 to 1918, interoffice memoranda, and most important, some William V. Alexander Letterbooks from 1908 to 1911. (Alexander was Bok's managing editor in this period.) Other Parlin collection materials include circulation studies, a 1916 survey of merchant attitudes toward the *Journal* and *Saturday Evening Post* as advertising media, consumer-purchasing surveys, and typescripts of several advertising conferences in 1910, 1913, and 1915, with verbatim texts of all participants.

Several sources in the Library of Congress, Washington, D.C., contain Bok letters. The Manuscripts Division holds Bok items in a number of collections, such as the Harvey Wiley, Albert J. Beveridge, William J. Bryan, and Frank Law Olmstead papers. Especially important for the student of Bok and the *Journal* is information in the Benjamin Harrison and Woodrow Wilson papers. The Carpenter Kipling Papers in the Rare Books Division also include some items. In addition, the Harvey Wiley Letterbooks in the National Archives, Washington, D.C., contain some relevant letters.

Important data on wartime activities may be found in the extensive National Archives collections of the records of the United States Food Administration, 1917–1920, and the records of the Committee on Public Information. The pertinent divisions for study of mass media are General Executive, Civic and Educational Cooperation, Woman's War Work, News, and Advertising. Unfortunately some material in the Magazine and Feature sections of these divisions has already been destroyed.

Trade magazines of the era are an important source for soundings on comparative advertising and journalism issues. Key magazines in this category are *Printer's Ink,* the Rowell Advertising Agency's "Little Schoolmaster of Advertising," and its chief rival, *Profitable Advertising.*

Other sources include all issues of the *Ladies' Home Journal* from 1883 to 1919. In addition, Bok's copious published writings during and after his editorship provide a useful key to the mind and art of the editor. Some important works are listed below. In addition, the Library of Congress recently acquired from the Bok family a collection of memorabilia that includes the manuscripts of some of Bok's books and his autograph collections.

PUBLIC DOCUMENTS

U.S. Federal Trade Commission. *Before F.T.C.–Docket #15 F.T.C. v. The Curtis Publishing Co., Respondent.* Washington, D.C.: Government Printing Office, 1918.

BOOKS AND PAMPHLETS

Adams, Samuel Hopkins. *The Great American Fraud: A Series of Articles on the Patent Medicine Evil, Reprinted from Collier's Weekly. Also—The Patent Medicine Conspiracy Against the Freedom of the Press.* Chicago: Press of the American Medical Association, 1906.

Adler, Selig. *The Isolationist Impulse: Its Twentieth Century Reaction.* New York: Collier, 1961.

Agnew, Hugh E., and Warren B. Dygert. *Advertising Media.* New York: McGraw-Hill, 1938.

The American Foundation. *Edward W. Bok: October 9, 1863–January 9, 1930.* Philadelphia: n.p., n.d.

American Medical Association. *Nostrums and Quackery: Articles on the Nostrum Evil and Quackery Reprinted, with Additions and Modifications from the Journal of the American Medical Association.* Chicago: Press of the American Medical Association, 1912.

———. Council on Pharmacy and Chemistry. *The Propaganda for Reform in Proprietary Medicines.* Reprinted from the *Journal of the American Medical Association.* 7th ed., n.d.

Anderson, Oscar E., Jr. *The Health of a Nation: Harvey Wiley and the Fight for Pure Food.* Chicago: University of Chicago Press, 1958.

Appel, Joseph H. *Growing Up with Advertising.* New York: Business Bourse, 1940.

Asher, Louis, and Edith Heal. *Send no Money.* Chicago: Argus, 1942.

Baker, Ray Stannard. *American Chronicle: The Autobiography of Ray Stannard Baker*. New York: Charles Scribner's Sons, 1945.

Bleyer, Willard Grosvener. *Main Currents in the History of American Journalism*. Boston: Houghton Mifflin, 1927.

Bok, Edward W. *America, Give Me a Chance*. New York: Charles Scribner's Sons, 1926.

————. *The Americanization of Edward Bok*. New York: Pocket Books, 1965 (first published by Charles Scribner's Sons, New York, 1920).

————. *America's Taj Mahal: The Singing Tower of Florida*. Tate, Georgia: Georgia Marble Co., 1929.

————, comp. and ed. *Beecher Memorial: Contemporaneous Tributes to the Memory of Henry Ward Beecher*. Brooklyn, N.Y.: privately printed, 1887.

————. *The Boy Who Followed Ben Franklin: Adapted from a Man From Maine*. Edited, with an introduction by John Louis Haney. New York: Charles Scribner's Sons, 1924.

————. *Dollars Only*. New York: Charles Scribner's Sons, 1926.

————. *Explaining the Editor*. Privately printed, January 19, 1901.

————. *How the Y.M.C.A. Made Good: The Actual Facts Stated*. Reprinted from the Philadelphia *Public Ledger*, n.d.

————. *The Humorous Side of an Editor's Life*. N.p., n.d.

————. *The Keys to Success*. Philadelphia: John D. Morris, 1900.

————. *A Man From Maine*. New York: Charles Scribner's Sons, 1923.

————. *A National Crime at the Feet of American Parents*. Richmond, Va.: B. F. Johnson, 1900.

————. *Perhaps I Am*. New York: Charles Scribner's Sons, 1928.

————. *Real Opponents to the Suffrage Movement Says Mr. Bok are the Women Themselves Whose Peculiar Field of Work Lies Outside of Politics*. Reprinted from the New York *Times*, April 18, 1909, and issued by the New York State Association Opposed to Woman Suffrage, n.p., n.d.

————. *Successward*. New York: F. H. Revell Co., 1895.

————. *Tom: The Letter That His Father Slipped Him When He Left His Mother for 'Somewhere in France.'* Reprinted from *The Ladies' Home Journal* by the National War Work Council of the Y.M.C.A., [1918].

———. *Twice Thirty: Some Short and Simple Annals of the Road*. New York: Charles Scribner's Sons, 1925.

———. *Two Persons: An Incident and an Epilogue*. New York: Charles Scribner's Sons, 1925.

———. *Why I Believe in Poverty as the Richest Experience That Can Come to a Boy*. Boston: Houghton Mifflin, 1915. Originally published in *The Ladies' Home Journal*, April, 1915.

———. *You: A Personal Message*. Boston and New York: Medici Society of America, 1926.

———. *The Young Man and the Church*. Philadelphia: Henry Altemus, 1896.

———. *The Young Man in Business*. Boston: L. C. Page, 1900.

Bok, Edward W., and Mary Bok. *Mary's Son: A Christmas Brochure: Carrying to their Friends the Happy Holiday Greetings of Edward and Mary Bok*. Merion, Pa.: Swastika, 1927.

Borden, Neil H. *The Economic Effects of Advertising*. Chicago: Richard D. Irwin, 1942.

Boyenton, William H. *Audit Bureau of Circulations*. Chicago: Audit Bureau of Circulations, 1948.

Britt, George. *Forty Years—Forty Millions: The Career of Frank A. Munsey*. New York: Farrar & Rinehart, 1935.

Burt, Frank A. *American Advertising Agencies: An Inquiry into Their Origin, Growth, Functions and Future*. New York: Harper & Bros., 1940.

Burt, Nathaniel. *The Perennial Philadelphians: The Anatomy of an American Aristocracy*. Boston: Little Brown, 1963.

Calkins, Earnest Elmo. *The Business of Advertising*. New York: D. Appleton, 1915.

———. *The Advertising Man*. New York: Charles Scribner's Sons, 1922.

———. *And hearing not . . . Annals of an Adman*. New York: Charles Scribner's Sons, 1946.

———. *Louder. Please! The Autobiography of a Deaf Man*. Boston: Atlantic Monthly Press, 1924.

Chamberlain, John. *Farewell to Reform. Being a History of the Rise, Life and Decay of the Progressive Mind in America*. New York: Liveright, 1932.

Collins, Alan C. *Something About the Ladies' Home Journal*.

Philadelphia: Curtis, ca. 1927.

Curtis Publishing Co. *The Curtis Advertising Code.* Philadelphia: Curtis, 1912.

———. *The Curtis Advertising Code with Digest of Rulings (For Use of Representatives Only).* Philadelphia: Curtis, 1914.

———. *The Farm Market.* Philadelphia: Curtis, 1918.

———. *National Advertising: The Modern Selling-Force.* Philadelphia: Curtis, n.d.

———. *100 Thrift Recipes: That Use Little Wheat, Meat, Fat and Sugar.* Philadelphia: Curtis, 1918.

———. Sales Division, Circulation Dept. *Intensive Methods for Sales Promotion by Curtis District Agents.* Philadelphia: Curtis, 1911.

———. *Salesmanship: A Vocation for Boys.* Philadelphia: Curtis, 1915.

———. *Selling Forces.* Philadelphia: Curtis, 1913.

———. *Two Color Advertising: Its Advantages and Uses, with Some Examples of Effective Arrangement, Combination and Treatment.* Philadelphia: Curtis, 1917.

———. *Two Pages Facing: Some Suggestions for Advertising Display.* Philadelphia: Curtis, 1916.

Davenport, Walter, and James Derieux. *Ladies, Gentlemen and Editors.* Garden City, N.Y.: Doubleday, 1960.

Dennis, Charles H. *Eugene Field's Creative Years.* New York: Doubleday, 1924.

Drewry, John E. *Some Magazines and Magazine Makers.* Boston: Stratford, 1924.

Emery, Edwin. *The Press and America: An Interpretive History of Journalism.* Englewood Cliffs, N.J.: Prentice-Hall, 1962.

Filler, Louis. *Crusaders for American Liberalism.* New York: Harcourt Brace, 1939.

Geller, Max A. *Advertising at the Crossroads: Federal Regulation vs. Voluntary Controls.* New York: Ronald Press, 1952.

Goulden, Joseph C. *The Curtis Caper.* New York: G. P. Putnam's Sons, 1965.

Haynes, Merritt Way. *The Student's History of Printing.* New York: McGraw-Hill, 1930.

Hart, James D. *The Popular Book: A History of America's Literary Taste.* New York: Oxford University Press, 1950.

Hays, Samuel P. *Conservation and The Gospel of Efficiency: The Progressive Conservation Movement, 1890–1920*. Cambridge, Mass.: Harvard University Press, 1959.

Hess, Herbert W. *Advertising: Its Economics, Philosophy and Technique*. Philadelphia: J. B. Lippincott, 1931.

Higham, John. *Strangers in the Land*. New York: Atheneum, 1963.

Holbrook, Stewart H. *The Golden Age of Quackery*. New York: Macmillan Co., 1959.

Hotchkiss, George Burton. *Milestones of Marketing: A Brief History of the Evolution of Market Distribution*. New York: Macmillan, 1938.

————. *An Outline of Advertising*. New York: Macmillan, 1933.

Hower, Ralph M. *The History of an Advertising Agency: N. W. Ayer & Sons at Work, 1869–1929*. Cambridge, Mass.: Harvard University Press, 1939.

Hughes, J. R. T. "Eight Tycoons: The Entrepreneur and American History," in Ralph Andreano, ed., *New Views on American Economic Development*. Cambridge, Mass.: Schenckman, 1965.

Kirkland, Edward C. *Industry Comes of Age: Business, Labor and Public Policy, 1860–1897*. Chicago: Quadrangle Paperbacks, 1967.

Klapper, Joseph T. *The Effects of Mass Media*. New York: Columbia University Bureau of Applied Social Research, 1949.

Kobre, Sidney. *The Yellow Press and Gilded Age Journalism*. Tallahassee: Florida State University Press, 1964.

Kolko, Gabriel. *The Triumph of Conservatism: A Reinterpretation of American History, 1900–1916*. New York: Free Press of Glencoe, 1963.

Kraditor, Aileen S. *The Ideas of the Woman Suffrage Movement, 1890–1920*. New York: Columbia University Press, 1965.

Ladies' Home Journal. *Girls Who Have Push*. Philadelphia: Curtis, [1890s]

Lape, Esther Everett. *Americanization in Delaware: A State Policy Initiated by the Delaware State Council of Defense*. N.p., [1919].

Lape, Esther Everett, ed. *Ways to Peace*. New York: Charles Scribner's Sons, 1924.

Lasch, Christopher. *The New Radicalism in America, 1889–1963*.

New York: Alfred A. Knopf, 1965.

Levine, Daniel. *Varieties of Reform Thought*. Madison: State Historical Society of Wisconsin, 1964.

Lochner, Louis P., *America's Don Quixote: Henry Ford's Attempt to Save Europe*. London: Kegan Paul, Trench, Trubner, 1924.

Lord & Thomas. *America's Magazines and their Relation to the Advertiser*. Chicago: Lord & Thomas, 1895.

Lyon, Peter. *Success Story: The Life and Times of S. S. McClure*. New York: Charles Scribner's Sons, 1963.

McClure, S. S. *My Autobiography*. New York: Frederick A. Stokes, 1914.

Mayer, Martin. *Madison Avenue, U.S.A.* New York: Harper & Row, 1958.

Mock, James R., and Cedric Larson. *Words That Won the War: The Story of the Committee on Public Information, 1917-1919*. Princeton, N.J.: Princeton University Press, 1939.

Mott, Frank Luther. *A History of American Magazines*. Vol. IV: *1885-1905*. Vol. V: *1905-1930*. Cambridge, Mass.: Belknap Press of Harvard University Press, 1957, 1968.

_____. *Golden Multitudes: The Story of Best Sellers in the United States*. New York: Macmillan, 1947.

Mowry, George B. *The Era of Theodore Roosevelt: 1900-1912*. New York: Harper & Bros., 1958.

Orcutt, William Dana. *Celebrities Off Parade*. Chicago: Willett, Clark, 1935.

Parlin, Charles C. *Business in 1918*. Philadelphia: Curtis, 1918.

Pease, Otis. *The Responsibilities of American Advertising: Private Control and Public Influence, 1920-1940*. New Haven, Conn.: Yale University Press, 1958.

Peterson, Theodore. *Magazines in the Twentieth Century*. Urbana: University of Illinois Press, 1964.

Pollard, James F. *The Presidents and the Press*. New York: Macmillan, 1947.

Presbrey, Frank. *The History and Development of Advertising*. Garden City, N.Y.: Doubleday, Doran, 1929.

Printers' Ink. *Advertising: Today, Yesterday, Tomorrow*. New York: McGraw-Hill, 1963.

Regier, C. C. *The Era of the Muckrakers*. Chapel Hill: University of North Carolina Press, 1932.

Ross, Ishbel. *Ladies of the Press*. New York: Harper & Bros., 1936.

Rowell, George P. *Forty Years an Advertising Agent, 1865–1905*. New York: Printers' Ink, 1906.

Sedgwick, Ellery. *The Happy Profession*. Boston: Little, Brown, 1946.

Sinclair, Upton. *The Brass Check: A Study of American Journalism*. Pasadena, Calif.: published by the author, 1920.

Stern, J. David. *Memoirs of a Maverick Publisher*. New York: Simon & Schuster, 1962.

Stewart, Kenneth and John Tebbel. *Makers of Modern Journalism*. New York: Prentice-Hall, 1952.

Sullivan, Mark. *The Education of an American*. New York: Doubleday, Doran, 1928.

———. *Our Times*. Vol. IV. New York: Charles Scribner's Sons, 1932.

Tebbel, John. *George Horace Lorimer and The Saturday Evening Post*. Garden City, N.Y.: Doubleday, 1948.

Thayer, John Adams. *Astir: A Publisher's Life Story*. Boston: Small, Maynard, 1910.

———. *Out of the Rut*. New York: John Adams Thayer, 1912.

Turner, E. S. *The Shocking History of Advertising*. New York: E. P. Dutton, 1953.

Wolseley, Roland E. *The Magazine World: An Introduction to Magazine Journalism*. New York: Prentice-Hall, 1951.

Wood, James Playsted. *Magazines in the United States: Their Social and Economic Influence*. New York: Ronald Press, 1949.

Woodward, Helen. *It's an Art*. New York: Harcourt, Brace, 1938.

———. *The Lady Persuaders*. New York: Ivan Obolensky, 1960.

———. *Through Many Windows*. New York: Harper & Bros., 1932.

Young, James Harvey. *The Toadstool Millionaires*. Princeton, N.J.: Princeton University Press, 1961.

Young, James W. *Advertising Agency Compensation in Relation to the Total Cost of Advertising*. Chicago: University of Chicago Press, 1933.

PERIODICALS

Bok, Edward W. "The Day of the Advertisement." *The Atlantic Monthly*, CXXXII (October, 1923), 533–36.

———. "Is the College Making Good? What the Letters of 500 College Seniors Tell." *Outlook*, CIV (August 16, 1913), 851–57.

———. "Modern Literary King." *Forum*, XX (November, 1895), 334–43.

———. "President." *Scribner's Magazine*, LXXVII (January, 1925), 93–95.

———. "What Else Did Father Do?" *Scribner's Magazine*, LXXII (December, 1922), 660–64.

———. "Where I Think Glenn Frank is Wrong." *Century*, CVI (July, 1923), 449–54.

———. "Why People Disbelieve the Newspapers." *World's Work*, VII (March, 1904), 4567–70.

Bullitt, William C. "Dispatches to the Philadelphia *Public Ledger* from the Ford Peace Ship." Reprinted by the New York *Times* January 31, 1916, and February 1, 1916.

Clothier, Robert C. "The Employment Work of Curtis Publishing Company." *Annals of the American Academy of Political and Social Science*, LXV (May, 1916), 94–111.

Curtis Publishing Co. *Counselor*. January, 1916–October, 1919.

Ferree, Marvin. "Mr. Bok." *Independent*, LXXXIII (July 5, 1915), 18–20.

Fogg-Meade, Emily. "The Place of Advertising in Modern Business." *Journal of Political Economy*, IX (March, 1901), 218–42.

Frank, Glenn. "Why Edward Bok Should Not Have Retired." *Century*, CV (April, 1923), 957–60.

French, George. "Masters of the Magazine." *Twentieth Century Magazine*, V (April, 1912), 9–16.

"Great Enterprise: The Ladies' Home Journal of Philadelphia." *The Fourth Estate: A Newspaper for the Makers of Newspapers*, II (January 17, 1895), 10–11.

Grenier, Judson A. "Muckraking and the Muckrakers: An Historical Definition." *Journalism Quarterly*, XXXVII (August, 1960), 552–58.

Holly, Flora Mai. "Notes on Some American Magazine Editors." *Bookman*, XII (December, 1900), 357–68.

McCray, Florine Thayer. "Mrs. Louisa Knapp." *Journalist*, VIII (January 26, 1889), 1–2.

"Magazines, Their Scope and Influence." *Independent*, LXV (October 1, 1908), 796–97.

Pratt, Richard. "Friend of the Family." *Quill*, XXIV (July, 1936), 6–7, 15–16.

"Printers' Ink, Fifty Years: 1888 to 1938." *Printers' Ink*, CXXXVIII (August 28, 1938), sec. 2.

Sandage, C. H. "The Role of Advertising in Modern Society." *Journalism Quarterly*, XXVIII (Winter, 1951), 31–38.

Sherman, Sidney A. "Advertising in the United States." *Publications of the American Statistical Association*, VII (December, 1900), 1–42.

"Simple Faith." *New Republic*, V (December 4, 1915), 110–11.

Stote, Amos. "Case History: The Ladies' Home Journal." *Magazine World*, II (July 1, 1946), 6–8, 16–17.

"Strangling the Magazines." *Nation*, XCIV (May 2, 1912), 431–32.

REPORTS

Curtis Publishing Co. Advertising Dept. *Advertising Charts, 1915–1922, Showing Advertising Expenditures in Leading National and Farm Publications*. Philadelphia: Curtis Publishing Co., 1923.

"Ladies' Home Journal" Annual Trend of Columns and Lineage by Offices from 1892 to Date and Annual Trend of Revenues by Offices from 1892 to Date. An unpublished Curtis Company report.

Seventh Annual Convention of the Associated Advertising Clubs of America. Held in Boston, August 1–4, 1911. Boston: Pilgrim Publicity Association, 1912.

UNPUBLISHED MATERIAL

Caldwell, Dorothy Johnson. "Education, Citizenship and Vocations in the *Ladies' Home Journal*." M.A. thesis, University of Missouri, 1954.

Gaw, Walter A. "Some Important Trends in the Development of Magazines in the United States as an Advertising Medium." Ph.D. dissertation, New York University, 1942.

Giffen, Daniel Harris. "The Contributions of Edward Bok and the *Ladies' Home Journal* to American Domestic Architecture." M.A. thesis, University of Pennsylvania, 1962.

INTERVIEWS

Lape, Esther Everett, May, 1966.
Bok, Mrs. Curtis, September, 1964, June, 1966.

Index

Abbott, Lyman, 109
Addams, Jane, 69, 86, 109, 115, 138, 164n58
Advertisers' Protective Association, 105
Advertising in periodicals: growth of, xii, 20; influence of, xiii; and trusts, 21, 29–30. *See also* Balmer, Thomas; Bok, Edward W., *Journal* editorship; Curtis, Cyrus H. K.; Curtis Publishing Company; *Ladies' Home Journal*; Lord & Thomas; Thompson, J. Walter
Alexander, William V., 21, 45, 57, 110
American Civic Association, 91
American Foundation, 142
American Medical Association, 104, 171n16
American News Company, 11
American Red Cross, 117, 126, 133
Audit Bureau of Circulation, 13
Ayer, F. Wayland, 9
Ayer, N. W., 8, 9, 27, 156n64

Balmer, Thomas, 27
Baruch, Bernard M., 132
Beecher, Henry Ward, 37
Bellamy, Edward, 41
Bok, Edward W.
—early life: employment of, 2, 32, 36–37; family of, 34, 35, 36, 75 158n3, 161n7; education of, 36; marriage of, 37

—*Journal* editorship: views on editing, xiv, xv, 50–54; and advertising, xiv 60–63, 65; relationship with readers, 22, 34, 50, 52; and feature articles, 44, 53–55, 58, 160n43; and taboo subjects, 47–48, 54, 161n9; goals of, 50, 52, 76, 111–12, 177n58; relationship with staff, 51, 54, 55, 56, 57, 58, 161n12, 171n11; fights plagiarism, 58–59; as company vice-president, 60; retires, 140, 143, 144, 178n3
—post-*Journal* years: autobiographies, 36, 40, 121; philanthropy, 63, 141–42, 177n79
—reforms: and critics, xiv–xv, 76–77; and public education, xv, 85, 86–87, 97, 168n34; and cultural uplift, xv; and sex education, xv, 42, 76, 107–12, 172n32, 173n37; and health, xv, 89; and means to reform, xvii–xviii, 42, 43, 96–97, 100, 126, 145; and temperance, 43, 87–89, 100–101, 168n41; and middle-class reforms, 44, 77–79, 96–97; and women's clubs, 67–68, 71, 109; and suffrage, 65, 67, 68–70, 71, 72–73, 164n58; and patent medicines, 76, 97–106; and the Church, 79–81, 96, 109, 147; and the farm, 81–82, 96; and the environment, 90–97
—views: on success, 38–39, 41, 159n11; on religion, 39–41, 145; on business,

41-42, 145-47; on women, 44, 52,
65, 66-67, 70-71, 72, 101-102,
106-107, 113-14, 130, 133-35, 144,
164n49; political affiliation of, 48,
148; on social class, 77-79, 95, 97,
120, 145, 147. *See also* Alexander,
William V.; Harriman, Karl; *Ladies'
Home Journal;* World War I
Bok, Mary Louise Curtis, 37
Bok, William, 36, 37
Bryan, William Jennings, 115, 121
Burleson, Albert S., 128-29

Clayton Act, 11
Clemens, Samuel, 53
Committee on Public Information, 119,
120, 127
Country Gentleman, 83, 128
Conwell, Russell H., 118
Creel, George, 119, 127
Curtis, Cyrus H. K.: as administrator, 1,
2, 16-17, 19, 143; early career of, 1,
32; advertising and circulation
strategies, 3-10, 11-14, 15, 21, 22,
23, 25-28, 29, 155n55, 156n64,
157n73; and marketing research, 7, 8,
20-21, 155n52. See also *Saturday
Evening Post*
Curtis, Louisa Knapp, 2, 76
Curtis Publishing Company: reorganization, xiv; incorporation and capitali-
zation, 15, 16; by-products, 17-18;
advertising code, 24-25; Marketing
Research Division, 30-31; advertising
offices, 157n77

Dunne, Finley Peter, 58, 65, 163n48

Federal Council of Churches, 147
Federal Trade Commission, 11
Food Administration, 124, 125, 126,
175n29, 176n41. *See also* World
War I
Fowler, Nathaniel C., 9

Hamill, Samuel McClintock, 42
Hapgood, Norman, 105
Harmon, Dudley, 116, 118

Harriman, Karl, 55, 57, 70, 121
Harrison, Benjamin, 48, 58, 62n, 67, 84
Heyburn, Weldon Brinton, 104, 105
Hoover, Herbert, 124, 125
Howells, William Dean, 54
Hughes, J. R. T., 65

Keller, Helen, 109
Kipling, Rudyard, 53, 163n9
Kirkland, Edward, xii
Kraditor, Aileen, 69

Ladies' Home Journal: influence of advertising volume, xi; circulation of, xi,
12-14; reform objectives, xiii, xv;
readers of, xv-xvii, 4, 7, 19, 56,
83-84, 98-102, 167n25; as a service
model, xvi, 52, 76; and political advertising, 2; early history of, 2-3;
color printing in, 17, 19; effect of reforms on circulation of, 20, 99, 100,
111; separation of advertising and
editorial matter in, 22-23; advertising
rates, 25; art bureau of, 28, 157n79;
view of, toward minorities, 45-47, 49,
137-39; criticizes advertising, 64-65.
See also Bok, Edward W.; Curtis,
Cyrus H. K.; World War I
*Ladies' Home Journal and Practical House-
keeper,* 2
Lane, Franklin K., 138
Lape, Esther Everett, 48, 57, 138-39,
141, 142
Latshaw, Stanley R., 30
Link, Arthur S., 116
Lord & Thomas, 27
Lorimer, George Horace, 51, 143-44.
See also *Saturday Evening Post*
Ludington, C. H., 143

McClure, S. S., 37, 51
McClure's Magazine, xiii
McFarland, J. Horace, 90-94
Marketing research. *See* Curtis, Cyrus
H. K.; Curtis Publishing Company;
Parlin, Charles Coolidge
Mass magazines, xi-xiii; 19
Muckraking magazines, xiii, 63-64, 94,

102, 111

Niles, W. S., 23, 156n64

Parkhurst, Charles, 41, 159n20
Parlin, Charles Coolidge, 29, 30, 31, 179
Patent medicines. *See* Bok, Edward W., and patent medicines; Curtis, Cyrus H. K., and marketing research
Peterson, Theodore, xiii
Pierce, V. Mott, 102–103
Pinchot, Gifford, 86, 91
Printers' Ink, 5, 83, 92, 103, 107, 180
Profitable Advertising, 24, 51, 92, 99, 103, 180
Prohibition. *See* Bok, Edward W., and temperance; World War I

Rankin, Jeannette, 131
Roosevelt, Theodore, 42, 48, 85, 90, 117, 121, 122, 137
Root, Elihu, 141, 142
Royal Baking Powder Company, 26

Saturday Evening Post, 6, 18, 51, 83, 128, 152n14. *See also* Lorimer, George Horace
Sears, Roebuck, and Company, 28, 158n81
Sedgwick, Ellery, 6, 66
Sex education. *See* Bok, Edward W.; *Ladies' Home Journal*
Shaw, Anna Howard, 123, 135, 175n29
Shaw, Bernard, 52
Sheldon, Charles, 41, 80
Sherman Act, 71
Sinclair, Upton, 64

Sullivan, Mark, xiv, 75, 102, 105

Taft, William H., 89, 175n27
Thayer, John Adams, 28, 155n53, 152n17
Thompson, J. Walter, 5, 27
Trademarks, xiii–xiv, 28

War Industries Board, 126, 132
Webster, Jean, 54
Wiley, Harvey, 105
Wilson, Woodrow: and Bok, 48, 121, 124, 128–29, 135, 136, 139, 174n24; and *Ladies' Home Journal,* 70, 116, 122, 127; and preparedness, 116, and American Peace Award, 142. *See also* World War I
Women's magazines. *See* Mass magazines
Women's suffrage. *See* Bok, Edward W., and suffrage
World War I: and efficiency, 113, 129, 130, 131, 132; effects of, on United States, 114, 115, 118; and war relief, 115–16; and preparedness, 116, 117; and clubwomen, 118–19; and class consciousness, 120; food programs, 123, 125, 126; and pragmatism, 126; Liberty bonds, 126–27; and the community church, 132–33; and workers, 133, 134–35; and suffrage, 134, 135; and child welfare, 135–36; and immigration, 136–37; and Americanization, 137–39; and immigration, 138. *See also* American Red Cross; Baruch, Bernard M,; Committee on Public Information; Creel, George; Lane, Frederick K.; Lape, Esther Everett; Rankin, Jeannette; Roosevelt, Theodore; Shaw, Anna Howard; War Industries Board; Wilson, Woodrow